0(

Other books by Jack P. Jones

Creating Space without Adding On
Small Space/Big Bucks: Converting Home Space into Profits

House Framing

Jack P. Jones

AN AUTHORS GUILD BACKINPRINT.COM EDITION

House Framing
All Rights Reserved © 1995, 2001 by Jack P. Jones

AN AUTHORS GUILD BACKINPRINT.COM EDITION

Published by iUniverse.com, Inc.

For information address:
iUniverse.com, Inc.
5220 S 16th, Ste. 200
Lincoln, NE 68512
www.iuniverse.com

Originally published by McGraw Hill

ISBN: 0-595-18034-5

Printed in the United States of America

For John, Kathy, and Rosemary

Contents

9 Wall framing   155

Acknowledgments

My thanks to the following companies and organizations for providing material used in the preparation of this book:

The American Plywood Association
P.O. Box 11700
Tacoma, WA 98411-0700

American Forest & Paper Association
1250 Connecticut Ave., NW
Second Floor
Washington, DC 20036

Simpson Strong-Tie Co., Inc.
P.O. Box 1568
San Leandro, CA 94577

Carl Hickman Construction
Eastman, GA 31023

TECO
P.O. Box 203
Colliers, WV 26035

Alpine Engineered Products, Inc.
P.O. Box 2225
Pompano Beach, FL 33061

Council of American Building
Officials
5203 Leesburg Pike
Falls Church, VA 22041

Introduction

If medicine is the second oldest profession, then house framing has to be the third. Many professional framers consider themselves tradesmen of the highest order, and I'm inclined to agree with them. After over a quarter of a century building and remodeling houses, framing work is the part I enjoy most.

Framers have a system—a procedure ensuring the chronological unfolding of events that gets the framing up with the least amount of lost motion.

Experienced framers will tell you that the job site takes on a rhythm when carpenters lift hammer and saw. The aroma of fresh lumber, the whine of power saws, and the pounding of hammers is a symphony of sorts.

This book is written for the beginner as well as experienced framer. Whether you're considering a weekend how-to project or planning to build a house, these pages contain the help you'll need: detailed, step-by-step instructions from the footing to dry-in. Perhaps you're looking for information explaining the best way to stake out a footing or which type girder to use. Well, here it is.

This book covers all areas of house framing, such as squaring with batter boards, sizing the footing, and building the foundation. Details of floor, wall, ceiling, and roof framing are fully explained and accompanied by photos and drawings. You'll also find a full explanation of the building materials commonly used in house framing, including all-wood foundation and basement systems.

The cost of building materials is of prime concern to everyone involved in home construction. Framing on a modular system can greatly reduce costs; this book contains complete how-to instructions on this important subject.

Not all framing is the same. There's a specific type common to your type of building. This book will help you find out what it is and how to successfully build it.

How familiar are you with framing lumber? Are some species better than others? What size and strength should you use for a given joist span to comply with building codes? This book will give you the answers.

House framing is a lot more than just sawing lumber and driving nails. Most houses require girders. How do you determine the girder size to support a 20-foot span? Calculating girder loads and determining girder size and strength are fully explained in chapter 6.

Are you building in an earthquake- or hurricane-prone area? There are steel framing anchors that greatly reduce the possibility of the framing coming apart in such occurrences. Find out where and how to attach the anchors.

This book will teach you the right and wrong way to lay out floor, wall, and roof sheathing panels in order to save materials and labor. You'll also learn what size and type nails are recommended for sheathing installation.

For the framer, time is money—in or out of the pocket. You need to know how many labor hours it takes, for example, to install 75 16-foot-long 2 × 10 floor joists. Can you come up with a reasonable estimate? You'll have to if you're going to turn your time into money. You'll find out how to estimate not only the labor hours for major tasks, but also the materials for the job.

So turn the pages and learn about smart framing, professional short cuts, and doing the job right.

1
Start at the beginning

House framing can be referred to as *rough carpentry*. The frame is the skeleton of the structure. The term *finish carpentry* generally includes interior drywall, ceiling, and floor applications. It also includes exterior siding and paneling. All interior and exterior trim work is finish work.

The rough carpenter, or *framer*, will *dry-in* a house, that is, carry the framing work to the stage where the structure is rain-proof. This includes installing floor, wall, and roof sheathing and covering the roof with roofing felt (building paper). The windows and exterior doors are, of course, installed to complete the dry-in. Figure 1-1 is a house near dry-in completion.

House framing requires precision work and as much dedication to detail as finish carpentry. The only difference between rough carpentry and finish carpentry is that the nailer is permitted to leave hammer marks on the wood—provided he doesn't leave too many in one spot.

1-1 The dry-in nears completion.

Over many years of building houses, I've seen the best and worst of house framers. While most competent framers have their own ways and methods of building, they all adhere to a basic procedure that ensures a strong and well-built structure with fitted joints, and strong ties and bracing. A house can also be built in strict accordance with the building code and still be as weak as a ladder built with 1 × 3s. The code doesn't always mean quality construction.

There are a few who have expanded the science of framing to near art. Such people enjoy the sound of saws and hammers and nearly flip out over the smell of new wood. Nothing pleases them more than the organized rhythm of a construction site. These are the professionals who take a great amount of pride in their work, and their reputations keep them booked months ahead. How did these "artists" get their start? How did they begin?

They began at the beginning. That's about the best way to learn anything, and that's what we're going to do here. We're going to start at the beginning and work through to the dry-in. You're the framer. I'm going to tag along for the ride and maybe answer a few of your questions, the ones no one else seems to want to bother with. I've been in the construction business—in one form or another—for 40 years. Most of it I learned through trial and error and, while I certainly have a lot more to learn, I can build a house that'll make the owner boast about its quality 30 years later. A quality house begins with the foundation.

STAKING OUT THE FOUNDATION

You must start right to end right. The most aggravating thing a framer can face is an unsquare and unlevel foundation. Nothing from the sill plate to the rafters will fit as it should. This is why many framers prefer to lay out and build the foundation themselves.

Now everyone has heard the story about the person who built a house with part of it extending over the property line. Make sure this doesn't happen to you. When in doubt, verify property lines and check the code for set-back requirements. A typical code requires a house to be set back a minimum of 25 feet from the street and 10 feet from adjoining property lines. Check the code!

Figure 1-2 shows a simple method for establishing outside foundation lines. Locate each corner of the house and drive small stakes into the ground. Drive a nail into the top of each stake to pinpoint the outside line of the foundation wall. The footing will extend two to five inches beyond the line. More on this later.

SQUARING THE FOUNDATION

You check the squareness of a foundation by measuring diagonally from corner to corner. If the foundation layout is square, each diagonal measurement will be the same.

There's another way to determine the squareness of any corner. Measure down one side of the wall line a distance of six feet and mark the spot. Now measure down the other wall line a distance of eight feet and mark this spot. The diagonal line from spot to spot should measure exactly 10 feet. If it doesn't, the corner isn't square. Figure 1-3 explains this method, called the 6-8-10 method. A 3-4-5 measurement will also work, as will any multiples of these numbers.

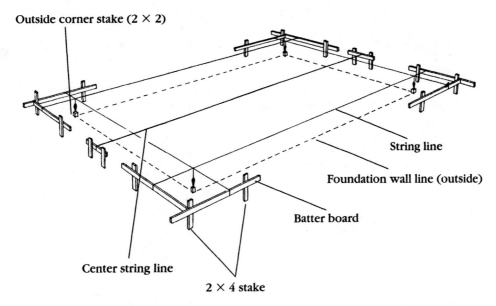

Outside corner stake (2 × 2)

String line

Foundation wall line (outside)

Batter board

Center string line

2 × 4 stake

1-2 Laying out the foundation. American Plywood Assoc

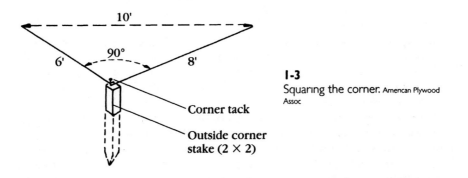

10'

90°

6'

8'

Corner tack

Outside corner
stake (2 × 2)

1-3
Squaring the corner. American Plywood
Assoc

When you start a layout, you line up the front of the house with the street or drive or whatever, and drive stakes representing the front corners of the house to reflect the alignment. If the layout isn't square, you then have to relocate a stake or two to correct the problem. You can't relocate either of the two front stakes, however, without changing the alignment of the layout. Correct the problem by changing the two rear stakes. Figure 1-4 shows how to square a T-shape foundation.

ERECTING BATTER BOARDS

With the layout square, you're ready to erect the batter boards. Batter boards hold the strings that mark the exterior wall line. Once this line is in place, footing lines, chimney lines, and inside wall lines can be accurately established.

At each corner, drive three 1 × 4 (or 2 × 4) stakes, as illustrated in Fig. 1-2. Place these stakes three to four feet outside the actual foundation line. Nail 1 × 4 (or 1 × 6) batter boards horizontally so the top edges are all level and at the same grade. Use a

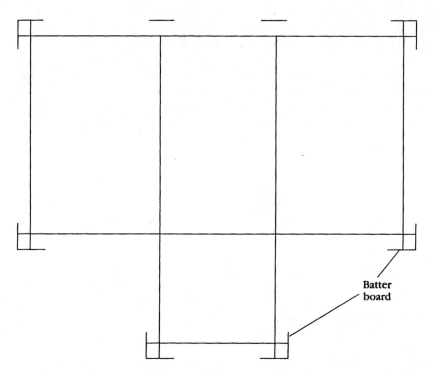

1-4 Squaring a T-shaped foundation.

transit to obtain an accurate grade reading. The top of the foundation must be level around the entire perimeter of the house.

Pull a taut nylon string across the tops of opposite batter boards and position a plumb bob directly over the nails in the corner stakes. Cut saw kerfs ¼-inch deep in the batter boards so the string lines can be accurately replaced if disturbed or broken. Make certain all saw kerfs are the same depth since the line provides a reference line to ensure uniform depth of footing excavation in addition to defining the outside edge of the foundation wall.

The outside foundation lines are accurately fixed when the saw kerfs in the eight batter boards are cut, and the four lines are securely attached in position (see Fig. 1-2).

The lengthwise girder is a common requirement in most framed floors over crawlspaces and basements. It's usually on the centerline of the structure. The house plan will show its exact location. Some plans require that the girder be set off centerline to support an interior bearing wall. To find the line, measure the correct distance from the corners and install batter boards and string line as you did for the exterior wall. Where the plan calls for a second lengthwise girder, follow the same procedure for installing batter boards for that girder.

ENSURING FOUNDATION LEVELNESS

When the house length is 48 feet or less, a taut line and string level can give a fairly adequate reading concerning the levelness of the foundation wall and footing excavation. In many houses in this category, I use a string level when the foundation wall is concrete block laid on a poured concrete footing.

An excellent method of ensuring that batter boards and string lines are level is the straightedge (see Fig. 1-5). Use a straight, 10-foot-long 2 × 4 and a two-foot or longer level. Drive temporary stakes about nine feet apart around the foundation perimeter. You want to drive each stake the same height, checking each with the level and straightedge as you work around the perimeter. The final check on the overall levelness is when you level the last stake with the batter board where you began. If the straightedge is level at this point, then the foundation line is level.

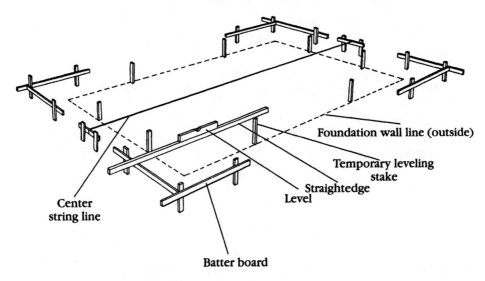

Foundation wall line (outside)

Temporary leveling stake

Straightedge

Level

Center string line

Batter board

1-5 Using the straightedge method. American Plywood Assoc

Make sure the batter boards are secure because now you're going to remove the corner stakes and temporary leveling stakes to dig the footing. The batter boards and string lines will be what establish the corners and foundation levelness from here out.

The foundation layout discussed in this section works for concrete-block foundations, poured concrete foundations, and permanent wood foundations (PWFs). PWFs are covered in detail in chapter 2.

EXCAVATING THE FOOTING

For crawlspace and on-slab construction, footing excavation means trench digging. If you don't use a backhoe to dig the trench, you'll have to dig it by hand.

You want the footing 12 inches below the frost line unless the code specifies otherwise. The footing should be a minimum of six inches into undisturbed soil. If you're digging in Maine, go down 48 inches. In Florida, a six-inch footing will suffice. In Montana, 36 inches is okay. In most areas, an eight-inch-thick concrete footing with a five-inch projection on each side of the foundation wall is sufficient for a two-story house with a basement and either a masonry or masonry veneer wall.

To allow adequate working space, excavate about two feet beyond the outside of the wall. Don't overdig and, if you do, don't refill with dirt. Refill with concrete. Figure 1-6 shows how to locate foundation-wall corners at the footing depth with a plumb line.

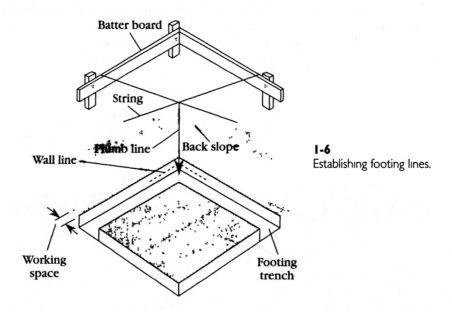

1-6
Establishing footing lines.

Table 1-1 gives the footing sizes commonly required for a conventionally loaded wall on soil of average bearing value, which is approximately 2,000 psf (pounds per square foot) or better. Dig the footing at the same depth around the wall perimeter, using the batter-board string line as the measuring point.

Where it's necessary to use form boards for the footing, install forms of $^{15}\!/_{32}$-inch APA plywood or 2 × 8s supported by 2 × 4 stakes driven into the ground

Table 1-1 Footing sizes

	Frame		Masonry or masonry veneer	
# of stories	Minimum thickness (inches)	Projection each side of wall (inches)	Minimum thickness (inches)	Footing projection each side of foundation wall (inches)
One story				
No basement	6	2	6	3
Basement	6	3	6	4
Two stories				
No basement	6	3	6	4
Basement	6	4	8	5

about two feet apart, as shown in Fig. 1-7. A four-inch projection on each side of the wall is provided.

Stepped footing

Stepped footings are required whenever the ground slopes more than a foot or two. The height of the vertical step should not exceed ¾ of the horizontal distance between the steps. The horizontal distance between steps should be at least two feet. Make the vertical connection the same width as the footing and at least six inches thick, as explained in Fig. 1-8. For a concrete-block foundation wall, make the vertical step eight inches high to accommodate the height of the block.

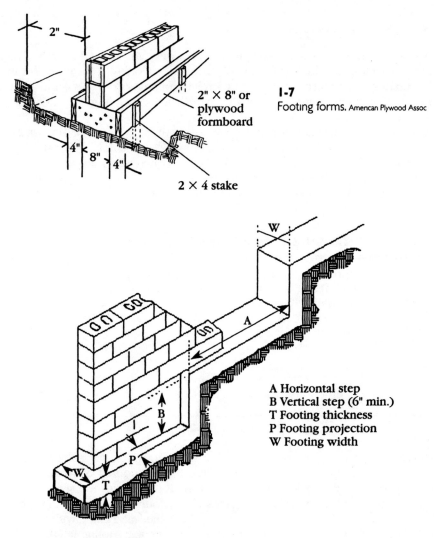

1-7
Footing forms. American Plywood Assoc

A Horizontal step
B Vertical step (6" min.)
T Footing thickness
P Footing projection
W Footing width

1-8 Stepped footing.

Locating pillar footings

You can locate the footings for the girder pillars by using the lengthwise girder string. When the girder is in the center of the house, the centerline string is your guide. In multigirder situations, you'll of course have erected batter boards and strings for each girder.

The pillar or post spacing, as well as the footing size, should be specified on the house plans. Pillars should generally be spaced no more than eight feet on center. Pillar footings are commonly 20 inches square. Check your code since soil conditions dictate the footing size. Other specifications might also apply. Make the bottom of the footing the same level as the perimeter footing. The height of the pillar should be at least eight inches above ground level in a crawlspace house.

POURING THE FOOTING

For most footings, you'll use five-bag ready-mix concrete. This mix has five bags of cement per cubic yard of concrete. The American Concrete Institute specifies that the mixture must work readily into corners and angles of forms, and around reinforcement without segregation of the materials or puddling of water on the surface.

The concrete should have a compressive strength, at 28 days, of at least 2,000 psi. Generally, the more water used in a mix, the weaker the concrete is when set.

In isolated areas, you might prefer to mix the concrete on the job site. Table 1-2 gives some acceptable mixes. Don't overwet the mix. The proportions are for aggregates measured by volume and in a damp and loose condition.

Table 1-2 Proportions for field mixing

Max. size course aggregate	Approx. cement (sacks per cubic yard)	Approx. water (gallons per sack)	Approx. Proportions (by volume) per sack of cement		
			Cement	Fine aggregate	Coarse aggregate
¾"	6 0	5	1	2½	2¾
1"	5.8	5	1	2½	3
1½"	5 4	5	1	2½	3½
2"*	5.2	5	1	2½	4

* Not recommended for slabs or other thin sections

Concrete will dry rapidly in extremely hot weather, which stops the hardening process too soon. Keep it moist for several days. Freshly poured concrete must be protected against freezing. You want the top of the footing level and smooth to ensure a neat and well-built wall. Drive stakes about four feet apart in the footing trench before pouring the concrete. You can establish the stake grade with the string or a four-foot level. When using forms, set the form height at footing height, and either pour the concrete to the top of the stakes or form and smooth.

BUILDING THE FOUNDATION WALL

Begin the concrete-block wall construction at a corner. With the foundation-wall string lines in place (see Fig. 1-2), drop a plumb bob from the string line, pinpoint the outside wall corners on the footing, and mark them with chalk. If you're inexperienced at block laying, you can lay the first course of blocks without mortar all around the perimeter to determine joint spacing and whether you have to cut any blocks. Space blocks ⅜ to ½ inch apart, then mark each joint on the footing. Go back to the house plan and check requirements for openings, vents, drains, etc. Your corners should look like the ones in Fig. 1-9.

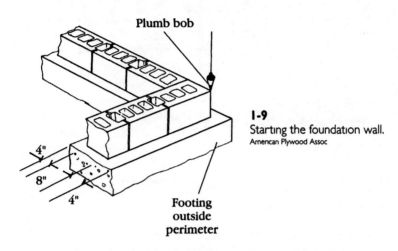

1-9
Starting the foundation wall.
American Plywood Assoc

Of course, if you have some experience building concrete-block foundation walls, dispense with laying unmortared blocks. You can calculate from the house plans the number of blocks required for a course. Plumb bob the corners, snap a chalk line and start laying the blocks.

Foundation drains

Generally, a house with a basement or habitable space below grade must have a sump and drain below the level to be protected, which is at the footing level. The drain should discharge into a drainage ditch or storm drainage system. Additionally, the wall must be waterproofed. Figure 1-10 illustrates the concept.

Mixing mortar

Masonry units are set on a mortar bed, which creates a bond with adjoining units and permits plumbing and leveling of each unit. Each block must be placed correctly so the mortar will create a strong, weathertight wall. Mortar for reinforced masonry structures should be either type M or type S with a minimum compressive strength of 2,500 or 1,800 psi, respectively.

The cement used in mortars can be either portland or masonry cement. With portland cement, you'll generally use type I or type II. Type III is used when high early strength is required. Mix two parts cement with four to six parts of damp mortar sand. Add only enough water to make a plastic mortar that clings to the trowel

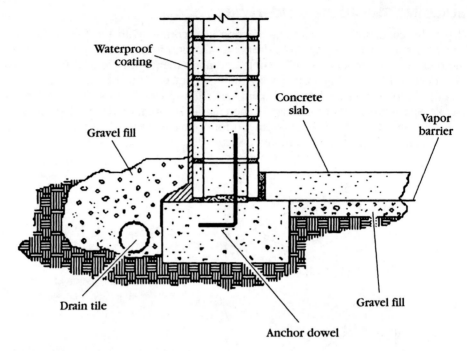

Waterproof coating

Concrete slab

Vapor barrier

Gravel fill

Drain tile

Gravel fill

Anchor dowel

1-10 Basement wall construction.

and block but isn't so pliable that it squeezes down too much under a block. Place the mix on a wet mortar board after mixing.

Figure 1-11 provides a quick overview of the wall work. The finished height of the foundation wall should be at least 12 inches above the finish grade. The ground level within the crawlspace should generally be above the outside finish grade unless drainage is provided or if water won't collect because of soil conditions.

Plan on at least 18 inches of clearance from the ground level to the bottom of floor joists, and 12 inches to the bottom of the wood girder. A minimum of two feet is required between the ground and floor joists where mechanical equipment such as ductwork runs through the crawlspace.

Hollow concrete block is the most common material used for foundation walls and piers of crawlspace construction in many parts of the country, and the 8 × 8 × 16-inch block is a favored size. The height of the wall or pillar should not exceed four times its thickness unless properly reinforced as prescribed by local code. All blocks must conform to ASTM C-90.

A hollow load-bearing concrete block of 8 × 8 × 16 inches in nominal size will weigh from 40 to 60 pounds if made from a heavyweight aggregate such as sand, gravel, crushed stone, or air-cooled slag. The same block made with a lightweight aggregate (expanded shale, clay, slag, or natural lightweight materials such as volcanic cinders or pumice) will weigh from 25 to 35 pounds.

Both heavyweight and lightweight units are used for all types of masonry construction. The choice of unit depends on what's available at a reasonable price and the requirements of the structure being built. Lightweight units usually cost more to buy but less to install.

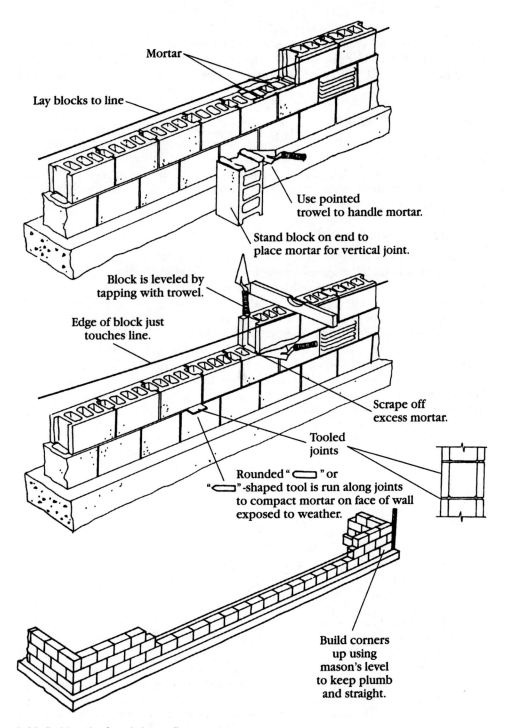

Mortar

Lay blocks to line

Use pointed
trowel to handle mortar.

Stand block on end to
place mortar for vertical joint.

Block is leveled by
tapping with trowel.

Edge of block just
touches line.

Scrape off
excess mortar.

Tooled
joints

Rounded "⊂⊃" or
"⊂⊃"-shaped tool is run along joints
to compact mortar on face of wall
exposed to weather.

Build corners
up using
mason's level
to keep plumb
and straight.

I-II Building the foundation wall. American Plywood Assoc

Concrete blocks are manufactured in grades N and S. Grade N is used in exterior walls below and above grade that might be exposed to moisture penetration or weather, and for interior and backup walls. Grade-S block is limited to use above grade in exterior walls with weather-protected coatings and in walls not exposed to the weather.

LAYING THE CORNERS

Use corner blocks, laying the flat (smooth) end to the outside corner. Build the corners up to full height, using a level to keep the blocks plumb and level. Lay the first course in a full mortar bed the width and length of the block. For succeeding courses, apply mortar on the face shell of horizontal and vertical joints. A ⅜- or ½-inch joint makes a good bond.

SETTING ANCHOR BOLTS

Look at Fig. 1-12. Before you lay the last two courses, locate and position ½-inch-diameter anchor bolts, as specified on the house foundation plan or as shown here if not indicated on the plan. Completely fill with concrete the cells of the top two courses in which the bolt is placed. Provide at least two bolts for each individual sill plate (or mudsill). Fill all cells in the top course, cover with four-inch solid masonry block, or use a wood-sill plate wide enough to bear on both the inner and outer shells of the block. A 2 × 8 generally qualifies as covering the full width of an eight-inch-wide block, even though a dry (cured) 2 × 8 is actually only 7¼ inches wide.

Figure 1-13 shows the use of a strap anchor in lieu of a ½-inch-diameter anchor bolt. Position the strap into the concrete-filled cells. After the concrete has set, drill a ¾-inch hole in the center of the sill plate, place the plate in position, and wrap the

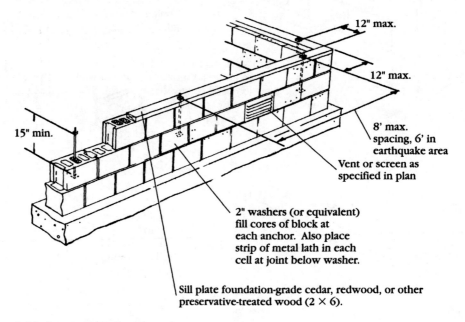

12" max.

12" max.

15" min.

8' max. spacing, 6' in earthquake area

Vent or screen as specified in plan

2" washers (or equivalent) fill cores of block at each anchor. Also place strip of metal lath in each cell at joint below washer.

Sill plate foundation-grade cedar, redwood, or other preservative-treated wood (2 × 6).

1-12 Setting sill-plate anchor bolts. American Plywood Assoc

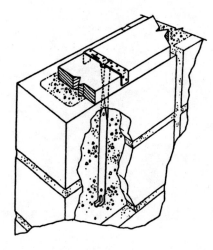

1-13
Strapping the sill down. Simpson Strong-Tie Co

strap over the plate, as shown. Secure with six 1½-inch nails. The maximum spacing of the strap is 42 inches on center (oc) when used as a replacement for six-foot, oc, ½-inch-diameter anchor bolts.

Sill sealer

Install fiberglass sill sealer between the block foundation wall and the wood-sill plate. Place a metal termite shield between the masonry and wood sill in areas where termite infestation is likely. Check your code. Wait at least seven days before placing backfill against the wall. On basement walls, don't backfill until the floor sheathing is installed.

With the foundation wall complete and the pillars in place (see Fig. 1-14), you're ready to begin framing. Don't waste labor by not having framing material on hand, close to the building site and stacked according to size. Look at Fig. 1-15. Not much effort will be wasted here carrying boards and searching for the right size board.

1-14 The framing can now begin.

1-15 Stack framing lumber close by and sort by size.

ESTIMATING MATERIALS

To estimate ready-mix concrete for the footing (or slab) I use the following rule of thumb: Multiply the length of the footing (or slab) in feet times the width in feet times the thickness in inches, then divide by 314. Thus, a footing 144 feet long by 1.5 feet wide by six inches thick would be:

$$
\begin{array}{r}
144' \text{ (length)} \\
\times \ \underline{1.5'} \text{ (width)} \\
216 \\
\times \ \underline{\hspace{0.5cm} 6''} \text{ (thick)} \\
1{,}296 \div 314 = 4.13
\end{array}
$$

So the number of cubic yards of concrete required for the footing is 4.13 yards.

Concrete block

An $8 \times 8 \times 16$-inch concrete block is actually $7\frac{5}{8}'' \times 7\frac{5}{8}'' \times 15\frac{5}{8}''$. A $\frac{3}{8}$-inch mortar joint will give the block a full 16-inch length and 8-inch height.

The standard $8 \times 8 \times 16$-inch block is commonly used in foundation walls. It takes 110 of these blocks per 100 square feet of wall and, allowing for waste, 3.25 cubic feet of mortar when using $\frac{3}{8}$-inch joints.

Here are the steps in estimating the number of standard blocks required for a wall:
1. Multiply the height of the wall in feet by $1\frac{1}{2}$, which equals the number of courses (H).
2. Multiply the length of the wall in feet by $\frac{3}{4}$, which equals the number of blocks in each course (L).
3. Multiply H by L, which equals the number of blocks required.

Let's do an example. As shown in Fig. 1-16, the foundation wall plan gives a total wall length of 120 feet and height of three feet, so:

$$
\begin{array}{l}
3 \ \times 1.5 \ = 4.5 \text{ (H)} \\
120 \times 0.75 = 90 \text{ (L)}
\end{array}
$$

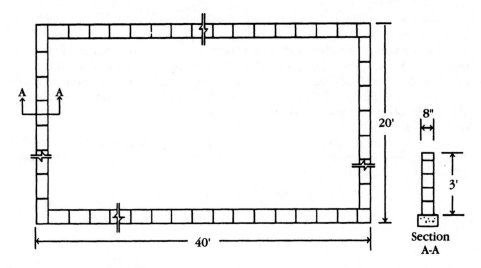

1-16 Foundation wall plan.

There are 90 blocks in each course. Since there are 4.5 courses, you know that the top course must be a four-inch cap block. Therefore:

$$4 \text{ (H)} \times 90 \text{ (L)} = 360 \quad (8 \times 8 \times 16 \text{ block})$$
$$1 \text{ (H)} \times 90 \text{ (L)} = 90 \quad (4 \times 8 \times 16 \text{ cap})$$

This method counts the corners twice, so deduct for *two* corners:

$$2 \times 4 \text{ (H)} = 8 \quad (8 \times 8 \times 16 \text{ block})$$
$$2 \times 1 \text{ (H)} = 2 \quad (4 \times 8 \times 16 \text{ cap})$$

for the $8 \times 8 \times 16$ block:

$$\begin{array}{r} 360 \\ -\ \underline{8} \\ 352 \end{array}$$

and the $4 \times 8 \times 16$ cap:

$$\begin{array}{r} 90 \\ -\ \underline{2} \\ 88 \end{array}$$

To lay 100 standard blocks, a 70-pound bag of masonry mix and three cubic feet of sand will be required.

ESTIMATING LABOR

Generally, a carpenter and helper can stake out a foundation for an average-sized, rectangle-shaped house in four hours. This includes erecting batter boards and pulling strings.

Footing excavating

House footings can be hand or machine dug. For most houses, the footing is a trench. Deep trenches are best handled by a backhoe. Hand digging is common where the trench is two to three feet deep. It will take anywhere from 1 to 2½ hours per cubic yard to hand-dig a trench two feet deep, depending on the soil type.

A footing trench 16 inches wide and 2 feet deep has 9.9 cubic yards (cy) per 100 linear feet (lf). A 12-inch-wide footing that's 12 inches deep has 3.7 cy per 100 lf. (To find the volume, multiply the length by the width by the height. To convert cubic inches into cubic feet, divide the cubic inches by 1,728. To convert cubic feet into cubic yards, divide the cubic feet by 27. To convert cubic inches into cubic yards, divide the cubic inches by 46,656.)

Here's an example using a plan of a 48' × 24' house requiring a footing trench 18 inches wide and 6 inches thick, which is sufficient for a two-story, brick-veneer structure (see Table 1-1):

$$48 + 48 + 24 + 24 = 144 \text{ lf}$$

You want the footing at least 12 inches below the frost line (which, let's say, is 12 inches). The trench depth must therefore be 30 inches (2'6") deep. A trench 18 inches wide, 30 inches deep, and 1,728 inches (144 feet) has:

$$18 \times 30 \times 1{,}728 = 933{,}120" \div 46{,}656 = 20 \text{ cy}$$

It takes 1½ labor hours to dig 1 cy in a trench two to six feet deep where the soil type is medium clay (see Table 1-3). The labor is then:

$$1.5 \text{ hours} \times 20 \text{ cy} = 30 \text{ hours}$$

Table 1-3 Trench excavation labor

Work element	Unit	Manhours per unit
0 to 2 feet deep		
Average-density soil	cy	1 to 1.2
Sandy loam	cy	1 to 1.4
Medium clay	cy	1.2 to 1.5
Heavy clay	cy	1.5 to 2
2 to 6 feet deep		
Average-density soil	cy	1.2 to 2
Sandy loam	cy	1.4 to 2.5
Medium clay	cy	1 5 to 3
Heavy clay	cy	2 to 3.5

Block laying

A mason and one helper, working with 8 × 8 × 16 blocks in a foundation wall, can lay 30 blocks an hour. In the previous foundation example (Fig. 1-16), where 352 standard block and 88 cap blocks are required, the mason and helper could do the job in 14.66 hours. (It takes about the same amount of time to lay cap blocks as it does standard blocks.)

2
The wood foundation system

Wood knows no limits. The early Romans sank wood piers in the water, and found out that if the poles were thoroughly scorched with a hot fire to an almost charcoal-like stage the piers would last much longer. Natural-wood piers quickly decay above the water line. Ships, of course, were first built of wood. A few of them are still around.

Today's technology makes it possible to use pressure-treated wood for house footings, foundations, and basement walls.

PERMANENT WOOD FOUNDATIONS

The system is called permanent wood foundation, or PWF. It's a load-bearing, wood-frame wall system designed for below-grade use as a foundation for light-frame construction, such as one- and two-story houses. It combines proven construction techniques with the latest technology in below-grade moisture control.

While essentially similar to traditional wood-frame construction, the PWF system offers three significant additions to conventional above-grade methods, which, when combined with traditional technology, provide a strong, durable, and dry wood foundation.

First, the stress-grade framing lumber and plywood sheathing are engineered to support lateral soil pressures as well as live, dead, and climatic loadings. Vertical loads are distributed to the supporting soil by a composite footing consisting of a wood footing plate and a structural gravel layer.

Second, all lumber and plywood in contact with or close to the ground is protected against decay and insects by being pressure-treated with highly effective wood preservatives.

Finally, moisture-control measures ensure a dry and comfortable living space below grade. A porous gravel envelope surrounds the lower part of the basement, which diverts ground water to a positively drained sump, thus preventing hydrostatic pressure on the basement walls or floor. Similarly, moisture reaching the upper part of the basement foundation wall is deflected downward to the gravel drainage system by polyethylene sheeting or by the treated plywood wall itself.

Wood-foundation sections of lumber framing and plywood sheathing can be fabricated at the factory or constructed at the job site.

Wood replaces masonry

For those of us in the construction business who think in the "old-school" mode, doing away with masonry footings and foundation walls takes some getting used to. In some areas, the deep south in particular, termites make short work of a piece of untreated wood touching the ground. But, as you'll see in figures later in the chapter, only the basement floor need be concrete—and even that can be done away with, using wood instead. In crawlspace construction, you can also eliminate the masonry and forget about termites and moisture. While PWF has been around for better than a quarter of a century, it's still considered experimental in many areas.

THE MATERIALS

The framing lumber and plywood used in PWF construction must meet certain specifications. Here's a quick look at what is required:

Lumber

The lumber must be of a species and grade for which allowable unit stresses are specified in the current edition of the National Design Specification for Wood Construction, by the National Forest Products Association. The lumber must bear a certain grade mark or have a certificate of inspection issued by a lumber grading or inspection bureau or agency recognized as being competent.

Plywood

Plywood must be all-veneer panels bonded with exterior glue (exposure 1) and graded to indicate conformance with the current edition of U.S. Department of Commerce product standard PS 1, Construction and Industrial Plywood. The plywood must bear the grade mark of an approved plywood inspection station, Federal Housing Administration, and Farmers Home Administration.

Fasteners

Fasteners of silicon bronze, copper, or stainless steel types 304 or 316 can be used in pressure-treated wood above or below ground. Also, certain hot-dipped zinc-coated (galvanized) steel nails can be used under polyethylene sheeting.

Hot-dipped galvanized sheet-metal anchors can be used in PWF construction provided they have the following minimum properties:

Allowable stress in tension	18,000 psi
Yield point	33,000 psi
Ultimate strength	45,000 psi
Elongation in two inches	20 percent

Gravel, sand, and stone

Gravel, sand, and crushed stone used in the PWF system must meet certain requirements. Gravel must be washed and well graded, and the maximum-sized stone cannot exceed ¾ inch. The gravel must be free from clayey, silty, or organic soils.

The sand must be coarse, not smaller than 1/16-inch grains, and be free from clayey, silty, or organic soils. Crushed stones should have a maximum size of 1/2 inch.

Sheeting and sealants

Construction-grade polyethylene (ASTM D4397) is required. The bonding agent for attaching the plastic sheeting to the plywood must be capable of producing a good bond to the wood. The adhesive used to bond the seams of the plastic must ensure a watertight seal. The caulking used on the wall plywood joints must be capable of providing a permanent moisture seal.

PRESERVATIVE TREATMENT

With the exception of the top plate, all lumber and plywood used in exterior foundation walls; all interior, bearing wall framing and sheathing, posts, or other wood supports used in crawlspaces; all sleepers, joists, blocking, and plywood subflooring used in basements and floors; and all other plates, framing, and sheathing in the ground or in direct contact with concrete must be treated with a preservative as prescribed by the American Wood Preservers Bureau standard AWPB-FDN.

You must treat lumber or plywood cut or drilled on the job with an approved preservative by brushing and dipping it.

SOIL CHARACTERISTICS

Generally, soils suited for conventional concrete footings are also suited for the PWF system. Soils are categorized into four broad groups by the Unified Soil Classification system. Group I is excellent, group II is fair to good, group III is rated poor, and group IV is unsatisfactory. Peat and other highly organic soils fall into group IV. You wouldn't want to build a wood foundation on group IV soil without a specific engineered design for the site.

Soil types are rated by their ability to bear weight. Well-graded gravel and gravel-sand mixtures, group I types, have an allowable bearing of 8,000 psf. Peat and other highly organic soils have zero bearing.

GENERAL REQUIREMENTS

For a dry, comfortable, and energy-efficient below-grade living space (above the water table), you want a good seal. (For space below the water table, additional moisture-control measures must be taken, as prescribed by an engineer or local authority.) For a good seal, follow these guidelines:
- Slope the adjacent ground surface away from the foundation at least 1/2 inch per foot, for a distance of six feet or more to a positive fall.
- Place a porous layer (gravel, crushed stone, or sand) at least four inches thick under basement concrete floor slabs or wood basement floors and all wall footings. In group III soils, make the porous layer at least six inches thick. Group III soils are: inorganic clays of high plasticity, fat clays, inorganic silts, micaceous or diatomaceous fine, sandy, or silty soils, and elastic silts that have a bearing of 2,000 pounds per square foot.

- Provide a sump in basement space below grade to drain the porous layer unless the foundation is built in group I soil. Extend the sump at least 24 inches below the bottom of the base floor slab. The sump must be capable of positive gravity or mechanical drainage to remove accumulated water.
- Apply a six-millimeter-thick polyethylene moisture barrier over the porous layer. Pour the concrete floor slab over the plastic or, where a wood floor is used, lay wood sleepers directly on the porous layer, apply the plastic sheeting on top of the sleepers, and install the floor joists on top of the plastic moisture barrier. Do not extend the plastic sheeting beneath the wood footing plate.
- In basement construction, seal the joints of plywood panels with a quality, long-lasting caulk. Caulk any unblocked panel joints when panels are fastened to the framing.
- Install six-mil. polyethylene sheeting over the below-grade portion of exterior basement walls before backfilling. Lap the joints in the plastic sheeting at least six inches and bond with an approved adhesive. Bond the top edge of the sheeting to the plywood sheathing. Attach a treated wood or plywood strip to cover the top edge of the plastic sheeting. Extend the wood strip several inches above and below the finish grade level to protect the plastic from exposure to light and damage. Caulk the joint between the strip and wall. Extend the plastic sheeting down to the bottom of the wood footing plate, but do not overlap or extend into the gravel footing. (See Fig. 2-1.)
- Backfill the space between the side of a basement excavation and the exterior of a basement wall half the height of the excavation, with the same material used for footings. (In well-drained sites in group I soils, it's necessary to backfill only one foot above the footing.) Cover the top of the granular fill outside the basement foundation walls and footings with strips of six-mil. polyethylene or 30-pound asphalt paper. Lap the strips to provide for water seepage while preventing excessive infiltration of fine soils.
- Insulate wood foundation walls enclosing habitable space between the studs. Where a vented air space is not provided between the insulation and plywood foundation wall, install the insulation and vapor barrier from the upper plate down to about one foot below the outside grade. Close off this insulated portion of the stud cavity from the space below by folding an extension of the vapor barrier into the cavity and attaching it to the plywood foundation wall with an adhesive to prevent air seepage. Additional insulation *without* a vapor barrier can be installed below the level, as explained in Fig. 2-2.
- Extend the vapor barrier down to the bottom plate if a vented air space is provided between the plywood foundation wall and insulation. In all cases where insulation is installed between the studs in the below-grade portion of the foundation wall, leave a space at least two inches between the end of the insulation and the bottom plate.

DESIGN LOADS

All parts of the PWF system must be designed and constructed to ensure safe support for all anticipated loads. In any event, design loads should not be less than those specified in the building code having jurisdiction.

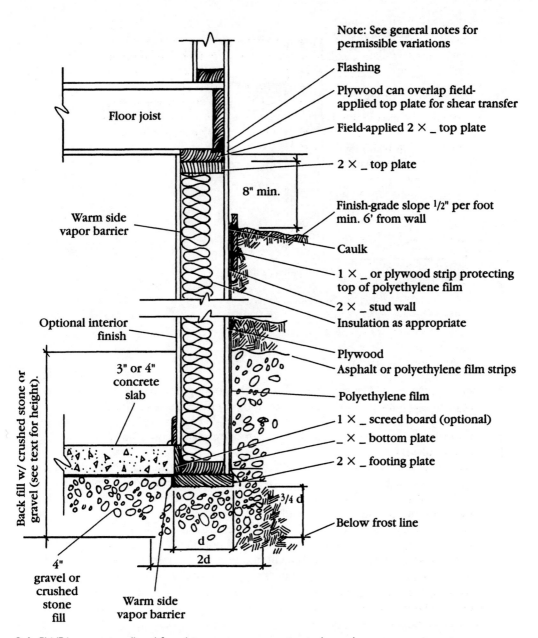

Note: See general notes for permissible variations

Floor joist

Flashing

Plywood can overlap field-applied top plate for shear transfer

Field-applied 2 × _ top plate

2 × _ top plate

8" min.

Warm side vapor barrier

Finish-grade slope 1/2" per foot min. 6' from wall

Caulk

1 × _ or plywood strip protecting top of polyethylene film

2 × _ stud wall

Insulation as appropriate

Optional interior finish

Plywood

Asphalt or polyethylene film strips

Back fill w/ crushed stone or gravel (see text for height).

3" or 4" concrete slab

Polyethylene film

1 × _ screed board (optional)

_ × _ bottom plate

2 × _ footing plate

3/4 d

Below frost line

d

2d

4" gravel or crushed stone fill

Warm side vapor barrier

2-1 PWF basement wall and foundation, using pressure-treated wood. American Forest & Paper Assoc

Design loads should include downward forces on the wall from dead loads and roof and floor live loads, plus the inward pressure from soil. Where required, the foundation should also be designed to resist wind, earthquakes, and other static or dynamic forces. The foundation system should be designed for the worst scenario—the most severe distribution, concentration, or combination of design loads acting on the structure simultaneously.

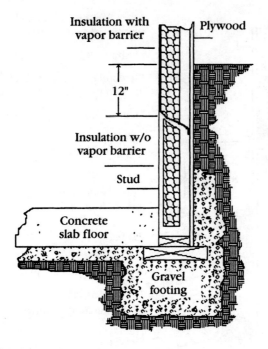

Insulation with vapor barrier

Plywood

12"

Insulation w/o vapor barrier

Stud

Concrete slab floor

Gravel footing

2-2
Insulating the foundation wall.

Footing

The stability of the PWF system depends on the footing, a composite of the wood footing plate and a layer of gravel, coarse sand, or crushed stone. The wood footing plate distributes the axial design load from the framed wall to the gravel layer, which in turn distributes it to the ground. The 2-by footing plate should be wider than the bottom wall plate.

The thickness and width of the granular footing is determined by the allowable bearing pressure of the supporting soil. The granular footing should have a width not less than twice the width and a thickness not less than three-quarters the width of the wood footing plate, and it should be confined laterally by backfill, granular fill, undisturbed soil, the foundation wall, or other equivalent means.

The bottom of the wood footing plate should not be above the frost line unless the granular footing extends to the maximum depth of frost penetration and is either connected to gravity or mechanical drainage at or below the frost line.

Foundation wall

Where there's little backfill (48 inches or less), walls can be constructed of 2 × 4s spaced 16 inches on center. Deeper backfill might require 2 × 6s or larger studs spaced 12 or 16 inches. The lumber species and grade can determine what size stud and spacing is required. PWF walls can be built for a two-story house with a basement. Figure 2-3 shows a PWF for crawlspace construction.

Knee walls under brick veneer

Knee walls can be used to support brick veneer on a wood-foundation footing plate. For brick up to 18 feet in height, frame the knee wall with 2 × 4s spaced 16 inches

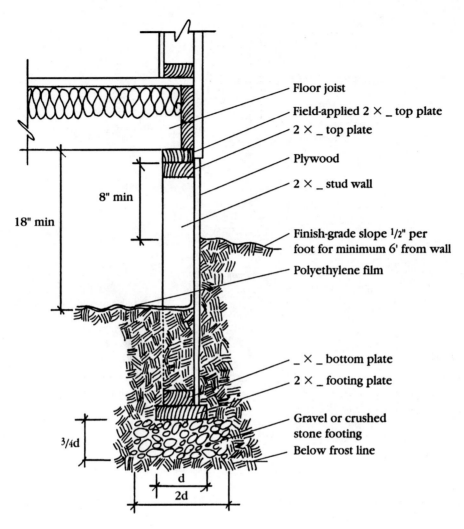

Floor joist

Field-applied 2 × _ top plate

2 × _ top plate

Plywood

2 × _ stud wall

Finish-grade slope ¹/₂" per foot for minimum 6' from wall

Polyethylene film

8" min

18" min

_ × _ bottom plate

2 × _ footing plate

Gravel or crushed stone footing

Below frost line

³/4d

d

2d

2-3 PWF crawlspace construction. American Forest & Paper Assoc

on center, a 1 × 4 bottom plate, and a 2 × 6 top plate. Use a double top plate when the brick is more than 16'8" high.

Position the edge of the 2 × 6 top plate directly against the foundation wall (see Fig. 2-4). The opposite edge should overhang the knee wall studs. Install double studs under the butt joints of the top plate so each end of the plate is fully supported on a stud. Figure 2-4 shows a basement wall with brick veneer on a knee wall. The crawlspace knee wall for a brick veneer is illustrated in Fig. 2-5.

PLYWOOD GRADE AND THICKNESS

Plywood can be installed with the face grain across the foundation wall studs (horizontal application) or the face grain parallel to the studs (vertical application). In other words, a horizontal application is when the long edge of the panel is perpen-

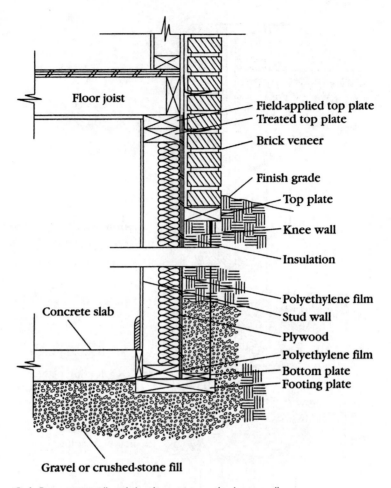

Floor joist

Field-applied top plate
Treated top plate
Brick veneer

Finish grade

Top plate

Knee wall

Insulation

Polyethylene film

Concrete slab

Stud wall

Plywood

Polyethylene film
Bottom plate
Footing plate

Gravel or crushed-stone fill

2-4 Basement wall with brick veneer on the knee wall. American Forest & Paper Assoc

dicular to the studs. Install a two-inch minimum blocking between studs at all horizontal panel joints more than four feet below adjacent ground level.

Plywood should not be less than the following minimum grades, conforming to U.S. product standard PSI:

• Structural I C-D

• C-D bonded with exterior glue (exposure 1)

When a major portion of the wall in exposed above ground and you want a better appearance than this kind of plywood offers, use the following U.S. standard PS 1 exterior grades:

• Structural I A-C, Structural I B-C, or Structural I C-C (plugged)

• A-C exterior I, B-C exterior I, C-C (plugged) exterior I, or MDO exterior I

The required plywood thickness varies from $\frac{15}{32}$ to $\frac{23}{32}$ inch, depending on:

• Height of fill

• Direction of face grain

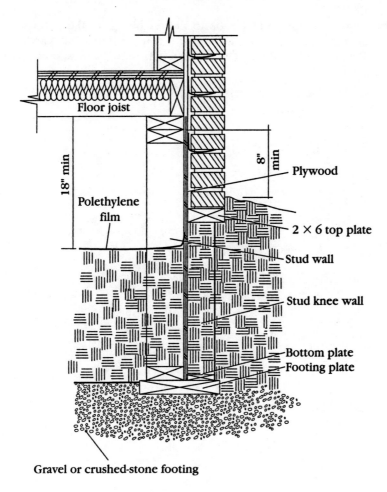

2-5 Crawlspace wall with brick veneer on the knee wall. American Forest & Paper Assoc

- Stud spacing
- Plywood grade

A wall having studs spaced 16 inches on center with face grain across the studs requires a minimum ¹⁹⁄₃₂-inch-thick panel, grade B, for a 48-inch fill and a ²³⁄₃₂-inch-thick panel, grade B, for a 86-inch fill.

COMPARATIVE COST STUDY

A comparative cost study of a PWF and concrete-block foundation revealed, several years ago, about a 10% savings using PWF. The constant price swing in the materials could, however, result in a PWF foundation costing more than a block foundation. I think it would be safe to say that you should have advantages in mind other than the cost. There are advantages and disadvantages to both systems, depending on area, climate, site, and availability of materials.

It's beyond the scope of this book to thoroughly cover the permanent wood foundation system. Complete specifications and construction details can be found in the manual Permanent Wood Foundation System: Design, Fabrication & Installation, available from:

American Forest & Paper Association
1250 Connecticut Ave., NW
Second Floor
Washington, DC 20036

3
Lumber

The framer doesn't have to be an expert on lumber, but it helps to know a little something about the material you work with every day. Lumber is a treasured resource, making it possible for you and I to build quality homes at a reasonable cost. It makes possible an unlimited variety of plans and designs. Only lumber offers the versatility and strength to build toward the sky (see Fig. 3-1) with the inexpensive nail.

There's a lumber size, grade, and species for each framing task. Construction lumber comes from two classes of trees: hardwood and softwood. Hardwood trees include maple, poplar, and oak. These trees have broad leaves that are shed each fall. Softwood trees include fir, spruce, and pine. These are the needle-leaf conifers that keep their leaves all year. Framing lumber is cut from softwood.

3-1 Building toward the sky with wood and nails.

The trunk of a tree is made up of parts. The *pith* is the soft, cream-colored core in the center of the trunk. Around the pith, wood grows in concentric rings called *annual rings* because a new one is added every growing season. Each annual ring is made up of one band of light *springwood* and one band of dark *summerwood*. You can determine the age of a tree by counting the number of annual rings.

The outer rings of the tree make up the *sapwood*. Sapwood carries water and nutrients from the roots of the tree to the leaves. The inner rings are called the *heartwood*. Heartwood is darker and more durable than sapwood and is preferred for construction uses.

LUMBER SPECIES

There are 17 species of wood most commonly used for construction lumber. There are, however, more than 100 types of wood available, but it's not likely you'll find them all in one locality. About 60 native woods are of major commercial importance, and about 30 woods are imported. Most of the imported woods are hardwoods, except those imported from Canada.

Major resources of softwood species are spread across the United States, except for the great plains, where only small areas are forested. Species are loosely grouped in three general growing areas:

- Southern softwoods
  ~ Southern pine
  ~ Bald cypress
  ~ Eastern red cedar
  ~ Atlantic white cedar
- Northern softwoods
  ~ Eastern white pine
  ~ Jack pine
  ~ Red pine
  ~ Eastern hemlock
  ~ Eastern spruces
  ~ Eastern red cedar
  ~ Northern white cedar
  ~ Balsam fir
  ~ Tamarack
- Western softwoods
  ~ Douglas fir
  ~ True firs
  ~ Ponderosa pine
  ~ Idaho white pine
  ~ Sugar pine
  ~ Lodgepole pine
  ~ Western hemlock
  ~ Western red cedar
  ~ Redwood
  ~ Engelmann spruce
  ~ Sitka spruce
  ~ Western larch

~ Port-Orford cedar
~ Incense cedar
~ Alaska cedar

Southern pine

The important southern pines (also known as southern yellow pines) include long-leaf pine, shortleaf pine, loblolly pine, and slash pine. Longleaf pine grows from eastern North Carolina southward into Florida and westward into eastern Texas. Shortleaf pine grows from southeastern New York and New Jersey southward to northern Florida and westward into Texas and Oklahoma. Loblolly pine grows from Maryland southward through the Atlantic coastal plain and Piedmont plateau into Florida and westward into eastern Texas. Slash pine grows in Florida and the southern parts of Georgia, South Carolina, Alabama, Mississippi, and Louisiana.

Southern pine lumber comes mainly from the southern and southern Atlantic states. Georgia, North Carolina, Alabama, Arkansas, and Louisiana are the leaders in the production of southern pine.

Lumber from any one or a mixture of two or more of these species is classified as southern pine by the grading standards of the industry. Lumber, according to these standards, that's produced from trees of the longleaf and slash pine species is classified as longleaf pine if it conforms to the growth-ring and latewood requirements of such standards. Lumber that's classified as longleaf in the domestic trade is known also as pitch pine in the export trade.

The wood of the various southern pines is similar in appearance. The sapwood is yellowish white and the heartwood is reddish brown. Heartwood begins to form when the tree is about 20 years old. In old, slow-growth trees, the sapwood might be only one to two inches thick.

Longleaf and slash pine are classified as heavy, hard, stiff, strong, and high in shock resistance. Shortleaf and loblolly pine are lighter in weight than longleaf. All the southern pines have moderately large shrinkage, but they're stable woods when properly seasoned.

Dense southern pine is used extensively in construction of bridges, trestles, docks, factories, warehouses, etc. Southern pine lumber having a lower density and strength are used for sheathing, subflooring, studs, joists, etc.

Bald cypress

Bald cypress is commonly referred to as just cypress. It's also called southern cypress, white cypress, yellow cypress, and red cypress. The following commercial terms are also used to describe bald cypress:

- Coastal cypress (red)
- Inland cypress (yellow)
- Tidewater red cypress
- Gulf cypress

Most cypress lumber comes from the southern states, and some comes from the southern Atlantic states. There is no longer an abundance of cypress.

The sapwood of bald cypress is narrow and nearly white, while the color of the heartwood varies widely, ranging from light yellowish brown to red, brown, or chocolate. The wood is on the heavy side, fairly strong, and moderately hard. The heartwood of old-growth timber is both decay- and termite-resistant due to the natural oils in the wood.

Cypress is used in construction where resistance to decay is required. It's well suited for siding and other exterior uses. It can also be used for vats in breweries, corn refineries, and wineries because it doesn't add any color, taste, or odor to food products it comes in contact with.

Douglas fir

Douglas fir is also known locally as red fir, yellow fir, and Douglas spruce. The tree grows from the Rocky Mountains to the Pacific coast and from Mexico to central British Columbia. Douglas fir production comes from the coastal states of Oregon, Washington, and California, as well as from the Rocky Mountain states.

The sapwood of the Douglas fir is narrow in old-growth trees but could be up to three inches wide in second-growth trees of commercial size. Fairly young trees of moderate to rapid growth have reddish heartwood and are called red fir. The narrow-ringed wood of old trees might be yellowish brown and is marketed as yellow fir.

Douglas fir wood varies widely in weight and strength. The wood is used mostly for building and construction purposes in the form of lumber, timbers, piling, and plywood.

Douglas fir probably has more uses than any other kind of wood. It doesn't warp or twist, and the large amount of heartwood makes the wood as decay-resistant as the white oak and longleaf pine. You can use the species for framing, sheathing, floors, doors, siding, etc.

Ponderosa pine

Ponderosa pine is also known as pondosa pine, California white pine, western pine, western soft pine, bull pine, and black pine. Jeffrey pine, which grows in close association with ponderosa pine in Oregon and California, is marketed with ponderosa pine and sold under that name.

The major producing areas for this type of lumber are in Washington, Oregon, and California. Idaho and Montana also produce large quantities of the lumber. Lesser amounts come from the Black Hills and Wyoming.

While a considerable proportion of the wood is similar to the white pine in appearance and properties, ponderosa pine belongs to the yellow pine group. The heartwood is light reddish brown, and the wide sapwood is nearly white to pale yellow.

The wood of the outer portions of ponderosa pine of saw timber size is generally light in weight, low in strength, fairly soft, moderately stiff, and low in shock resistance. It generally has a straight grain and small amount of shrinkage, and is uniform in texture with little tendency to warp and twist. Much of the intermediate or lower grades go into sheathing, subflooring, and roof boards.

Western white pine

Western white pine, also known as Idaho white pine or white pine, comes from Northern Idaho, Washington, and Montana. The major portion comes from Idaho.

The heartwood of western white pine is cream colored to light reddish brown, and darkens on exposure. The sapwood is yellowish white and varies from one to three inches wide. The wood is straight-grained, easy to work, easily kiln-dried, and stable after seasoning. The pine is moderate in weight, strength, softness, stiffness, and shock resistance. It has moderately large shrinkage.

Practically all Western white pine is sawed into lumber and used for building construction, matches, boxes, and millwork. It has practically the same uses as Eastern white pine and sugar pine.

Sugar pine

Sugar pine is the largest of all the pines. It can grow to a diameter of 12 feet and a height of 250 feet. These trees are so tall, it might be 75 feet from the ground to the first limb. Many trees are six to seven feet in diameter when cut. Sugar pine is sometimes called California sugar pine. Most of the lumber is produced in the Sierra Nevada region of California and parts of southern Oregon.

Sugar pine heartwood is buff or light brown, sometimes tinged with red, and the sapwood is creamy white. The wood is straight-grained, uniform in texture, and easy to work. The shrinkage is minimal and the wood is readily seasoned without warping or checking. The species is moderately light in weight and moderately low in strength, softness, shock resistance, and stiffness.

Sugar pine, like Eastern white pine, is suitable for use in nearly every part of the house because of the ease with which it can be worked. The wood is mostly used in finish carpentry. It's also used for piano keys, organ pipes, foundry patterns, and millwork.

Lodgepole pine

Lodgepole pine, also known as knotty pine, black pine, spruce pine, and jack pine, grows in the Rocky Mountains and Pacific Coast regions as far north as Alaska.

The heartwood varies from light yellow to light yellow-brown. The sapwood is yellow or nearly white. The wood is mostly straight-grained with narrow growth rings and moderately light in weight with moderately large shrinkage, and has low strength, softness, stiffness, and shock resistance.

Lodgepole pine is being used in increasing amounts for framing, siding, finish carpentry, and flooring.

Western hemlock

Western hemlock is also known as hemlock spruce, western hemlock spruce, West Coast hemlock, western hemlock fir, Prince Albert fir, silver fir, gray fir, and Alaska pine. It grows along the Pacific Coast region of Oregon and Washington and in the northern Rocky Mountains, north to Canada and Alaska.

The heartwood and sapwood are almost white with a purplish tinge. The wood is moderate in weight, hardness, stiffness, and shock resistance. The shrinkage is moderately large.

Western hemlock is good for general construction because of its stiffness and strength-to-weight ratio, which works well for house framing components such as joists, studs, and rafters.

Sitka spruce

Sitka spruce is the largest of the spruces and grows along the northwestern coast from California to Alaska. It's also known locally as yellow spruce, tideland spruce, western spruce, West Coast spruce, and silver spruce.

The heartwood is a light pinkish brown, and the sapwood is creamy white, three to six inches wide or more in young trees. The wood is lightweight and moderately hard. Its long fibers give it a high strength-to-weight ratio. Scaffolding and ladders are commonly made from Sitka spruce.

The key quality of the sitka spruce is resilience. It can absorb shock, bend, and recover after carrying a load. Sitka spruce is used principally for lumber, pulpwood, and cooperage. It makes good finish materials for houses.

DRYING LUMBER

The drying process begins after the tree is cut, delivered to the mill, and sawed into lumber. The moisture must be removed before the lumber can be used in construction. A board is *green* before it's cured or dried. If you nail a green board up, it will dry, shrink, and likely twist and warp. Air seasoning and kiln drying are the two ways lumber is dried.

Air seasoning

Lumber going through the air-seasoning process is stacked in piles in a storage yard. Each layer of boards is separated by strips to allow free circulation of air between the layers. In a few months, the lumber will be dry enough to use for framing.

During peak construction periods, lumber might be delivered to a retail outlet before it's sufficiently dry or air seasoned. If a green shipment arrives on your job, you have a problem. It's difficult to do quality work with lumber that's going to shrink a lot.

Kiln drying

While most houses are framed with air-seasoned lumber, lumber used for interior finish work such as sashes, door frames, doors, cabinets, stairs, etc., is kiln dried.

The lumber is placed in a large chamber called a kiln. The air temperature and humidity are controlled so the moisture content of the lumber reaches the desired level after three or four days. The season or weather doesn't affect the process. Kiln drying also kills the insects and organisms that cause decay.

SHRINKAGE AND SWELLING

A house framer has to work with wet lumber as well as dry. The wood might become thoroughly soaked before or after being nailed into place. Moisture can exist in wood as water vapor in cell lumens (cavities) and as water bound chemically within cell walls. Green wood is commonly defined as wood in which the cell walls are completely saturated with water, but they actually contain additional water in the lumens. The moisture content at which cell walls are completely saturated (all bound water) but no water exists in cell cavities is called the *fiber saturation point*. The fiber saturation point of wood averages about 30% moisture content (MC). Individual species and pieces of wood might vary by several percentage points from that value.

The moisture content of wood below the fiber saturation point, or *green condition*, is a function of both relative humidity and temperature of the surrounding air. The moisture content equilibrium is defined as that moisture content at which the wood is neither gaining nor losing moisture.

Air-seasoned lumber commonly considered dry will swell when exposed to moisture just as green lumber shrinks when used in dry weather.

When commercial softwood framing lumber is dried from its fiber saturation point (about 30% MC) to an average of 19% MC, the lumber shrinks 2.35 percent in thickness and 2.8 percent in width.

The American Lumber Standard definition of *dry* is a moisture content of 19 percent or less. Most framing lumber is used in locations where its moisture content will continue to drop until reaching 15 percent.

While wood is dimensionally stable when the MC is above the saturation point, wood changes dimensions as it gains or loses moisture below that point. This shrinking and swelling might result in warping, checking, splitting, or performance problems that require replacement of the member.

GREEN VS. DRY LUMBER

What concerns the framer is the difference in the size of green and dry lumber and the resulting problems when both are used together, as can happen when lumber from different yards, or lots, is delivered to the job.

Green lumber is slightly wider and thicker than the same-sized dry lumber. A piece of green lumber will shrink to approximately the standard dry size as it approaches 15% MC. For example, a nominal 2 × 10 measures 1½ × 9¼ inches when dry and 1⁹⁄₁₆ × 9½ inches when green. See Table 3-1.

MEASURING LUMBER

Lumber is measured and sold by board feet (BF). A board foot is the amount of lumber needed to fill a space 12 inches wide, 12 inches long, and 1 inch thick. Thus, a board 12 inches wide, 12 inches long, and two inches thick has two board feet of lumber. A 2 × 6 that's 10 feet long has 10 board feet. A 2 × 4 has 0.67 board feet per linear foot.

To find the number of board feet in a piece of lumber, multiply the thickness (in inches) by the width (in inches). Divide by 12 and multiply by the length of the lumber (in feet).

Let's do an example. To find the board feet in a 2 × 10 that's 14 feet long, multiply the thickness (2") by the width (10") to get 20. Then divide the total (20) by 12, which gives you a total of 1.6666. Multiply 1.6666 by the length (14') to get a total of 23⅓ BF.

Lumber such as ¾-inch-thick boards are considered to be 1 inch thick when using the board foot method. Always use the nominal (not actual) dimensions of the lumber. Nominal means the named size, like 2 × 10, not the actual dry size, which is closer to 1½ × 9¼.

Table 3-2 shows nominal and actual sizes, and BF measures for most common lumber.

Table 3-1 Size difference between green and dry lumber

Nominal size (inches)	Surfaced green net size (inches)	Surfaced dry net size (inches)
2 × 2	$1\frac{9}{16} \times 1\frac{9}{16}$	$1\frac{1}{2} \times 1\frac{1}{2}$
2 × 4	$1\frac{9}{16} \times 3\frac{9}{16}$	$1\frac{1}{2} \times 3\frac{1}{2}$
2 × 6	$1\frac{9}{16} \times 5\frac{5}{8}$	$1\frac{1}{2} \times 5\frac{1}{2}$
2 × 8	$1\frac{9}{16} \times 7\frac{1}{2}$	$1\frac{1}{2} \times 7\frac{1}{4}$
2 × 10	$1\frac{9}{16} \times 9\frac{1}{2}$	$1\frac{1}{2} \times 9\frac{1}{4}$
2 × 12	$1\frac{9}{12} \times 11\frac{1}{2}$	$1\frac{1}{2} \times 11\frac{1}{4}$
3 × 4	$2\frac{9}{16} \times 3\frac{9}{16}$	$2\frac{1}{2} \times 3\frac{1}{2}$
3 × 6	$2\frac{9}{16} \times 5\frac{5}{8}$	$2\frac{1}{2} \times 5\frac{1}{2}$
3 × 8	$2\frac{9}{16} \times 7\frac{1}{2}$	$2\frac{1}{2} \times 7\frac{1}{4}$
3 × 10	$2\frac{9}{16} \times 9\frac{1}{2}$	$2\frac{1}{2} \times 9\frac{1}{4}$
3 × 12	$2\frac{9}{16} \times 11\frac{1}{2}$	$2\frac{1}{2} \times 11\frac{1}{4}$
4 × 4	$3\frac{9}{16} \times 3\frac{9}{16}$	$3\frac{1}{2} \times 3\frac{1}{2}$
4 × 6	$3\frac{9}{16} \times 5\frac{5}{8}$	$3\frac{1}{2} \times 5\frac{1}{2}$
4 × 8	$3\frac{9}{16} \times 7\frac{1}{2}$	$3\frac{1}{2} \times 7\frac{1}{4}$
4 × 10	$3\frac{9}{16} \times 9\frac{1}{2}$	$3\frac{1}{2} \times 9\frac{1}{4}$
4 × 12	$3\frac{9}{16} \times 11\frac{1}{2}$	$3\frac{1}{2} \times 11\frac{1}{4}$

LUMBER GRADING

Every piece of lumber you receive on the job should have a grade mark, as shown in Fig. 3-2, stamped on it. The stamp ensures that the lumber has been properly inspected and classified. The stamp will show:

- Grade
- Moisture content
- Species group
- Grading agency
- Mill identification number

The American Softwood Lumber standard (PS 20-70) provides a uniform set of rules for grading lumber, covering grade strength ratios and grade descriptions for dimension lumber (see Table 3-3). PS 20-70 separates dimension lumber into width categories. The grading rule deals only with dimension lumber, that is, lumber from two inches up to (but not including) five inches in nominal thickness.

Under PS 20-70, all construction lumber is placed in one of three categories. They are:

- Stress grade
- Nonstress grade
- Appearance grade

Table 3-2 Lumber size and BF

Nominal size (inches)	Board measure per linear foot
2 × 2	.33
2 × 4	.67
2 × 6	1.00
2 × 8	1 33
2 × 10	1.67
2 × 12	2.00
3 × 4	1.00
3 × 6	1 50
3 × 8	2.00
3 × 10	2.50
3 × 12	3 00
4 × 4	1 33
4 × 6	2.00
4 × 8	2.67
4 × 10	3.33
4 × 12	4.00
6 × 6	3
6 × 8	4
6 × 10	5
8 × 8	5 33
8 × 10	6 67
8 × 12	8
10 × 10	8.33

Stress-graded lumber is mostly framing lumber. Nonstress-graded lumber is mostly one-inch boards. Lumber graded for appearance is seldom used in framing work.

Stress-graded lumber

Dimension lumber is the principal stress-graded lumber item available in your retail yard. It's used primarily for studs, joists, and rafters. Strength, stiffness, and uniformity of size are essential requirements. Dimension lumber is stocked in all yards, frequently in only one or two of the general-purpose construction woods such as pine, fir, spruce, or hemlock. The dimensions 2 × 6, 2 × 8, and 2 × 10 are found in grades of select structural, no. 1, no. 2, and no. 3. These are often in combinations of no. 2&BTR or possibly no. 3&BTR. (BTR means *better.*)

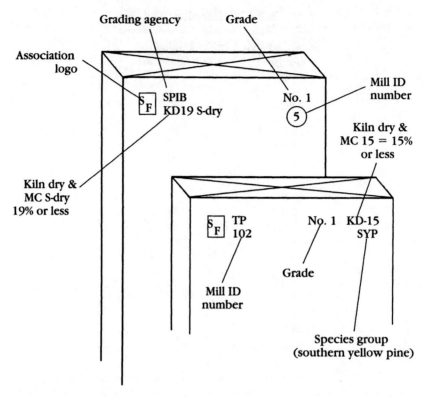

Grading agency   Grade

Association
logo

SPIB
KD19 S-dry

No. 1

Mill ID
number

Kiln dry &
MC 15 = 15%
or less

Kiln dry &
MC S-dry
19% or less

TP
102

No. 1   KD-15
SYP

Grade

Mill ID
number

Species group
(southern yellow pine)

3-2 Typical grade stamp.

In the 2 × 4 size, the grades available would normally be construction and standard, sold as standard and better (STD&BTR), utility and better (UTIL&BTR), or stud, in lengths of 10 feet and shorter.

Dimension lumber is often found in nominal 6-, 8-, 10-, or 12-inch widths and 8- to 18-foot lengths in multiples of two feet. Longer lengths are sometimes available as special-order items.

Other types of stress-graded lumber often available are posts and timbers, with some beams and stringers possibly in stock. Typical stress grades in these products are select structural and no. 1 structural in Douglas fir, and no. 1SR (stress rated) and no. 2SR in southern pine.

Stud grade can be 2 × 2 or 4 × 4, up to 10 feet long. The 2 × 4 is the most common stud dimension. Stud grade is usually identified as PET, which means it has been precision end trimmed to save end-cutting waste. Precut studs 7'8⅝" in length are available for platform framing, which gives a framed ceiling height of 8'1½" from the subfloor to the top of the top plate. More about this in a later chapter.

Nonstress-graded lumber

Boards are the most common nonstress-graded general-purpose construction lumber in your retail yard. Boards are stocked in one or more species, usually in one-inch thickness (¾-inch-thick boards are also available in many yards).

Table 3-3 Grade classifications for framing lumber

Grade	Description
	Structural light framing (2" to 4" thick, 2" to 4" wide)
Select structural and No. 1	Intended primarily for use where high strength, stiffness, and good appearance are desired
No. 2	Popular for most general construction uses
No. 3	For use in general construction where appearance is not a factor
	Light framing (2" to 4" thick, 2" to 4" wide)
Construction and standard	Widely used for general framing purposes. Pieces are of good appearance but graded primarily for strength and serviceability
Utility	Widely used where a combination of good strength and economical construction is desired for studding, plates, bracing, rafters, etc.
	Studs (2" to 4" thick, 2" to 6" wide, 10' and shorter)
Stud	Special-purpose grade intended for all stud uses including load-bearing walls
	Structural joists and planks (2" to 4" thick, 5" and wider)
Select structural and No 1	Intended primarily for use where high strength, stiffness, and good appearance is required
No. 2	Popular for most general uses
No 3	For use in general construction where appearance is not a factor
	Appearance framing (2" to 4" thick, 2" and wider)
Appearance	For use in general housing light construction where lumber knots are allowed but high strength and fine appearance is desired

Standard nominal widths are 2, 3, 4, 6, 8, 10, and 12 inches. Grades most generally available are no. 1, no. 2, and no. 3 (or construction, standard, and utility).

Boards are also sold as square edge, dressed and matched (tongue and groove), or with shiplapped joints.

STRENGTH OF LUMBER GRADES

Table 3-4 gives the bending strength ratio of five grades of visually graded dimension lumber. The ratio is the percentage of strength compared to the average for a clear, straight-grained piece of the same species. Notice that stud grade has less bending strength than construction grade under the light framing category, but more than standard or utility. The two structural classes have similar bending strength ratios.

PS 20-70 has established these classes, grade names, and the minimum bending strength ratios. This strength ratio provides an index of relative quality. The actual strength for any grade depends on the type of tree from which the lumber was cut. For example, a construction-grade Douglas fir will have a higher bending strength than redwood of the same grade. But the strength ratio of both will be the same because grades compare the average of clear wood of the same species.

Table 3-4 Strength ratio table

Lumber classification	Bending strength ratio
Light framing *(2" to 4" thick, 4" wide)*	
Construction	34
Standard	19
Utility	9
Structural light framing *(2" to 4" thick, 2" to 4" wide)*	
Select structural	67
No. 1	55
No. 2	45
No. 3	26
Studs (2" to 4" thick, *2" to 4" wide)*	
Stud	26
Structural joists and planks *(2" to 4" thick, 2" to 4" or wider)*	
Select structural	65
No. 1	55
No. 2	45
No. 3	26
Appearance framing *(2" to 4" thick, 2" to 3" wide)*	
Appearance	55

Descriptions of what visually graded lumber classes look like are in the grading rulebooks published by the grading associations. Grades of lumber have about the same appearance regardless of species. Stud-grade southern pine will have about the same number of knots, checks, and other imperfections as stud-grade fir, but the strength will be different because fir and pine have different bending strengths.

Visual sorting criteria

Visual grading is the oldest stress-grading method. It's based on the premise that the mechanical properties of lumber differ and that these properties can be seen and judged by the eye. The visual characteristics are then used to sort the lumber into stress grades. The following are major visual sorting criteria:

Density

Strength is related to the weight or density of clear wood. Properties assigned to lumber are sometimes modified by using the rate of growth and the percentage of latewood as measures of density. The selection for rate or growth requires that the number of annual rings per inch be within a specified range. It's possible to eliminate some very low-strength pieces from a grade by excluding those that are exceptionally light in weight. You, too, will gain a knack for visual grading after working with framing lumber for a while. Experienced framers often discard light lumber and other poor pieces that have somehow been erroneously graded and arrived on the job site.

Decay

Decay in most forms should be severely restricted or prohibited in stress grades because its extent is almost impossible to determine and its effect on strength can be greater than visual inspection would indicate.

Heartwood and sapwood

Heartwood and sapwood of the same species have equal mechanical properties, and no heartwood requirement need be made in stress grading. Since the heartwood of some species is more resistant to decay than sapwood, heartwood might be required if the untreated wood is to be exposed to a decay hazard. Sapwood, on the other hand, absorbs preservative treatment more readily and should not be limited in lumber that's to be treated.

Slope of grain

In zones of cross grain, the direction of the wood fibers is not parallel to the edges of the lumber. Cross grain reduces the mechanical properties of lumber. Severely cross-grained pieces are also undesirable because of a tendency to warp with changes in moisture content. Also, stresses caused by shrinkage during drying are greater in structural lumber than in small, clear pieces and are increased in zones of sloping or distorted grains.

Knots

Knots interrupt the direction of grain and cause localized cross grain with steep slopes. Intergrown or live knots resist some kinds of stress, but encased knots or knotholes usually don't. On the other hand, distortion of grain is greater around an intergrown knot than around an encased or dead knot. As a result, overall strength effects are more or less equalized, and often no distinction is made in stress grading between live knots and dead knots, and knotholes.

A knot in a piece of lumber modifies some of the clear wood strength properties more than it affects the overall stiffness. The effect of a knot on strength depends approximately on the proportion of the cross section of the piece of lumber occupied by the knot upon the knot location and the distribution of stress in the piece. Limits on knot sizes are therefore made in relation to the width of and location on the face in which the knot appears.

Shake

Shake in members subjected to bending reduces the resistance to shear and therefore is limited most closely in those parts of a bending member where shear stresses are highest. In members subjected only to tension or compression, shake doesn't greatly affect strength. Shake might also be limited because of appearance and because it permits entrance of moisture. Figure 3-3 shows several types of shake.

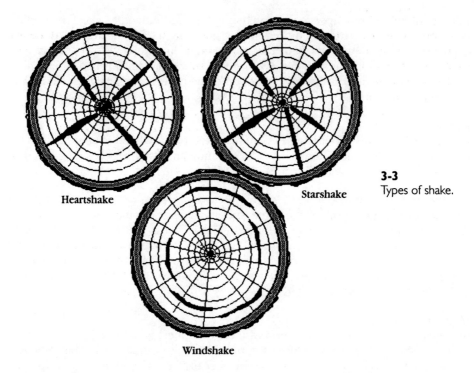

Heartshake   Starshake

3-3
Types of shake.

Windshake

  Heartshake Heartshake has a small cavity at the heart of the tree, and is caused by decay and cracks that extend from the heart out toward the bark. This type of defect is often found in hemlock timber.

  Starshake Starshake is similar to heartshake except there's no sign of decay at the center of the tree.

  Windshake Windshake has a separation of the annual rings, and the separation forms cracks in the body of the tree. Windshakes are caused when high winds wrench the tree. This shake is common in pine lumber.

Checks and splits

While shake indicates a weakness of fiber bond that's presumed to extend lengthwise without limit, checks and splits are rated only by the area of actual opening. An end split is considered equal to an end check that runs through the full thickness of the piece. The effects of checks and splits upon strength and the principles of their limitation are the same as for shake.

Wane

Wane is bark or tapering on the edge or corner of lumber. The need for ample bearing or nailing surfaces generally impose stricter limitations on wane than does strength. Wane is thus limited in structural lumber on that basis.

Pitch pockets

Pitch pockets ordinarily have so little effect on structural lumber that they can be disregarded in stress grading if small and limited in number. A large number of pitch pockets might indicate shake or weakness if found between annual rings.

ALLOWABLE SPANS

Lumber used in construction must be of a dimension and strength to support the intended loads over a specified span. The span is the length of the member between inner faces of supports. The load consists of the dead load and live load.

The *dead load* is the actual weight of all materials making up the construction, including floors, walls, roofs, ceilings, partitions, stairways, and fixed equipment.

The *live load* consists of the weight of all moving and variable loads that can be placed in the building, on floors, roofs, and ceilings—including wind, snow, and earthquake loads, which might act on the structure either singly or in conjunction with other dead and live loads. Table 3-5 shows the minimum live load requirements for floors and Table 3-6 shows the minimum live load requirements for roofs. Your local code might specify greater requirements.

Table 3-5 Floor loads

Location	Live load (psf)[1]
Dwelling rooms (other than bedrooms)	40
Dwelling rooms (bedrooms only)	30
Attics w/permanent or disappearing stairs	30
Attics w/limited storage roof slope over 3/12	20
Attics w/o storage roof slope 3/12 or less	15[2]
Stairs	60
Public stairs and corridors (2-family units)	60
Garages and carports (passenger cars)	100[3]

1 Design live load on any member supporting 150 square feet or more can be reduced at the rate of 0 08% per square foot of area supported by the member

2 Minimum combined live plus average dead load

3 Concentrated wheel loads on floor must be considered

Table 3-6 Roof loads

Roof slope	Live load (per square foot)[1]
Slope 3 in 12 or less:	
Minimum load[2]	20
Roof used as deck	40
Slope over 3 in 12:	
Minimum load[2]	15

1 Actual area measured along slope of roof.

2 Where unusual snow or wind conditions occur, higher design loads might be required to prevent overstressing members.

Span tables

Span tables are available for all the dimension lumber species. Not all species of lumber are available in all parts of the country, but there's no reason to haul lumber thousands of miles when other species with similar characteristics are available locally. For that reason, the lumber species you use will probably depend on the area of the country where you build. For instance, southern pine is probably in limited stock in the Pacific northwest, but there's plenty of locally available Douglas fir in Oregon and Washington.

The span limitations for medium-grain southern (yellow) pine is given in Table 3-7. The span limitation for western white pine is shown in Table 3-8.

CANADIAN LUMBER

Builders in states close to Canadian mills will find their lumber yards stocked with a good selection of Canadian lumber, selling at competitive prices. Canadian dimension lumber grades are identical to American grades and meet all the requirements of the American Softwood Lumber standard PS 20-70. Species combinations, assigned stress values and spans, all conform to standards used by U.S. mills.

SPECIES COMBINATION

Certain species of Canadian lumber are combined and marketed together. The 15 Canadian commercial species combinations are as follows:

Douglas fir-larch (north)
Includes Douglas fir and western larch. The two woods have similar strength and weight, are hard and decay resistant, and have good nailing qualities. Colors range from red-brown to yellow-white.

Hem-fir (north)
Includes western hemlock and amabilis fir. These are light woods with moderate strength, are easy to work, and hold nails well. Colors range from pale yellow-brown to white.

Eastern hemlock-tamarack (north)
Includes eastern hemlock and tamarack. Both woods are moderately strong and are good for general construction. The wood is fairly hard and durable. Color range from yellow-brown to white.

Spruce-pine fir
This is the broadest class of combination species, and includes white spruce, red spruce, black spruce, Engelmann spruce, jack pine, lodgepole pine, alpine fir, and balsam fir. These are moderate-strength woods, are easy to work, and have good nail-holding qualities. Colors range from white to pale yellow.

Western hemlock (north)
Includes only western hemlock, which is a moderately light, hard, strong wood. Colors range from white to pale brown, with little difference between the appearance of the sapwood and heartwood.

Table 3-7 Span limitations for southern yellow pine

Values are given as Ft–In. The six grade columns (No. 1 K.D., No. 2 K.D., No. 3 M.G.-K.D., No. 1, No. 2, No. 3 M.G.) are repeated for two loading conditions. For **Floor joists** rows the left group = *30 lb. live load* and the right group = *40 lb. live load*. For **Ceiling joists** rows the left group = *No attic storage* and the right group = *Limited attic storage*.

Nominal size (inches)	Spacing (inches oc)	No. 1 K.D. 2" dim. 1700f	No. 2 K.D. 2" dim. 1500f	No. 3 M.G.-K.D. 2" dim. —	No. 1 2" dim. 1450f	No. 2 2" dim. 1200f	No. 3 M.G. 2" dim. —	No. 1 K.D. 2" dim. 1700f	No. 2 K.D. 2" dim. 1500f	No. 3 M.G.-K.D. 2" dim. —	No. 1 2" dim. 1450f	No. 2 2" dim. 1200f	No. 3 M.G. 2" dim. —
Floor joists		*30 lb. live load*						*40 lb. live load*					
2 × 6¹	12	11-4	11-4	10-8	11-4	11-4	9-6	10-6	10-6	9-8	10-6	10-6	8-6
	16	10-4	10-4	9-4	10-4	10-4	8-4	9-8	9-8	8-4	9-8	9-8	7-4
	24	9-0	9-0	7-6	9-0	9-0	6-10	8-4	8-4	6-10	8-4	8-2	6-0
2 × 8	12	15-4	15-4	14-8	15-4	15-4	13-0	14-4	14-4	13-0	14-4	14-4	11-8
	16	14-0	14-0	12-8	14-0	14-0	11-4	13-0	13-0	11-4	13-0	13-0	10-2
	24	12-4	12-4	10-4	12-4	12-4	9-2	11-6	11-6	9-2	11-6	11-0	8-2
2 × 10	12	18-4	18-4	18-4	18-4	18-4	16-6	17-4	17-4	16-6	17-4	17-4	14-10
	16	17-0	17-0	16-0	17-0	17-0	14-4	16-2	16-2	14-4	16-2	16-2	12-10
	24	15-6	15-6	13-2	15-6	15-6	11-8	14-6	14-6	11-8	14-6	14-0	10-6
2 × 12	12	21-2	21-2	21-2	21-2	21-2	20-0	20-0	20-0	20-0	20-0	20-0	17-10
	16	19-8	19-8	19-4	19-8	19-8	17-4	18-8	18-8	17-4	18-8	18-8	15-6
	24	17-10	17-10	15-10	17-10	17-10	14-2	16-10	16-10	14-2	16-10	16-10	12-8
Ceiling joists		*No attic storage*						*Limited attic storage*					
2 × 4	12	11-10	11-10	11-6	11-10	11-10	10-10	9-6	9-6	8-2	9-6	9-6	7-4
	16	10-10	10-10	10-0	10-10	10-10	8-10	8-6	8-6	7-0	8-6	8-8	6-4
	24	9-6	9-6	8-2	9-6	9-6	7-4	7-6	7-6	5-10	7-6	6-10	5-2
2 × 6¹	12	17-2	17-2	17-2	17-2	17-2	15-8	14-4	14-4	12-4	14-4	14-0	11-4
	16	16-0	16-0	15-2	16-0	16-0	13-6	13-0	13-0	10-8	13-0	12-10	9-6
	24	14-4	14-4	12-4	14-4	14-4	11-0	11-4	11-4	8-8	11-4	10-6	7-10

Table 3-7 Continued

Ceiling joists

Nominal size (inches)	Spacing (inches oc)	No attic storage						Limited attic storage					
		No. 1 K.D. 2" dim. 1700f	No. 2 K.D. 2" dim. 1500f	No. 3 M.G.-K.D. 2" dim. —	No. 1 2" dim. 1450f	No. 2 2" dim. 1200f	No. 3 M.G. 2" dim. —	No. 1 K.D. 2" dim. 1700f	No. 2 K.D. 2" dim. 1500f	No. 3 M.G.-K.D. 2" dim. —	No. 1 2" dim. 1450f	No. 2 2" dim. 1200f	No. 3 M.G. 2" dim. —
		Ft. In.	Ft. In.	Ft. In.	Ft. In.	Ft. In.	Ft. In.	Ft. In.	Ft. In.	Ft. In.	Ft. In.	Ft. In.	Ft. In.
2 × 8	12	21 8	21 8	21 8	21 8	21 8	21 4	18 4	18 4	16 10	18 4	18 4	15 0
	16	20 2	20 2	20 2	20 2	20 2	18 6	17 0	17 0	14 8	17 0	17 0	13 0
	24	18 4	18 4	16 10	18 4	18 4	15 0	15 4	15 4	12 0	15 4	14 4	10 8
2 × 10	12	24 0	24 0	24 0	24 0	24 0	24 0	21 10	21 10	21 4	21 10	21 0	19 0
	16	24 0	24 0	24 0	24 0	24 0	23 4	20 4	20 4	18 6	20 4	20 4	16 6
	24	21 10	21 10	21 4	21 10	21 10	19 0	18 4	18 4	15 2	18 4	18 0	13 6

Low slope roof joists (Roof slope 3 in 12 or less)

Nominal size (inches)	Spacing (inches oc)	Not supporting finished ceiling						Supporting finished ceiling					
		No. 1 K.D. 2" dim. 1700f	No. 2 K.D. 2" dim. 1500f	No. 3 M.G.-K.D. 2" dim. —	No. 1 2" dim. 1450f	No. 2 2" dim. 1200f	No. 3 M.G. 2" dim. —	No. 1 K.D. 2" dim. 1700f	No. 2 K.D. 2" dim. 1500f	No. 3 M.G.-K.D. 2" dim. —	No. 1 2" dim. 1450f	No. 2 2" dim. 1200f	No. 3 M.G. 2" dim. —
		Ft. In.	Ft. In.	Ft. In.	Ft. In.	Ft. In.	Ft. In.	Ft. In.	Ft. In.	Ft. In.	Ft. In.	Ft. In.	Ft. In.
2 × 6[1]	12	14 4	14 4	12 4	14 4	14 4	11 0	13 8	13 8	11 6	13 8	13 8	10 2
	16	13 0	13 0	10 8	13 0	12 10	9 6	12 4	12 4	9 10	12 4	11 10	8 10
	24	11 4	11 4	8 8	11 4	10 6	7 10	10 10	10 10	8 2	10 8	9 8	7 2
2 × 8	12	18 4	18 4	16 10	18 4	18 4	15 0	17 8	17 8	15 8	17 8	17 8	14 0
	16	17 0	17 0	14 8	17 0	17 0	13 0	16 4	16 4	13 6	16 4	16 2	12 0
	24	15 4	15 4	12 0	15 4	14 4	10 8	14 8	14 8	11 0	14 6	13 2	9 10
2 × 10	12	21 10	21 10	21 4	21 10	21 10	19 0	21 0	21 0	19 10	21 0	21 0	17 8
	16	20 4	20 4	18 6	20 4	20 4	16 6	19 6	19 6	17 2	19 6	19 6	15 4
	24	18 4	18 4	15 2	18 4	18 0	13 6	17 8	17 8	14 0	17 8	16 8	12 6

Rafters
(Roof slope over 3 in 12)

Size	Spacing	Light roofing										Heavy roofing									
		Ft.	In.	Ft.	In.	Ft.	In.	Ft.	In.	Ft.	In.	Ft.	In.	Ft.	In.	Ft.	In.	Ft.	In.	Ft.	In.
2 × 12	12	24	0	24	0	24	0	24	0	24	2	24	0	24	0	24	0	24	0	21	4
	16	23	6	23	6	22	6	22	6	22	0	22	6	22	6	22	8	22	6	18	6
	24	21	2	21	2	20	4	20	4	20	4	20	4	20	4	20	0	20	4	15	2
2 × 4	12	11	6	11	6	9	6	9	0	8	2	10	4	8	0	9	8	9	4	7	4
	16	10	6	10	6	9	2	8	6	7	0	9	6	7	0	8	6	8	6	6	4
	24	9	2	9	0	8	0	6	8	6	0	7	10	5	10	6	10	6	10	5	2
2 × 6¹	12	16	10	16	10	16	6	16	0	15	10	15	6	12	4	14	0	14	10	11	0
	16	15	8	15	8	15	8	15	0	14	2	14	4	10	8	12	0	12	10	9	6
	24	13	10	13	8	13	2	12	4	11	2	11	4	8	8	10	6	11	0	7	10
2 × 8	12	21	2	21	2	21	8	21	6	19	6	19	8	16	10	18	8	19	8	15	0
	16	19	10	19	10	19	0	19	0	18	4	18	4	14	8	17	6	18	8	13	0
	24	17	10	17	10	16	0	16	8	15	6	15	0	12	0	14	8	15	8	10	8
2 × 10	12	24	0	24	0	24	0	24	0	23	6	23	6	21	4	23	6	23	6	19	0
	16	23	8	23	8	23	8	23	8	21	8	21	10	18	6	21	10	21	10	16	6
	24	21	4	21	4	21	4	21	0	19	8	19	8	15	2	19	8	18	0	13	6

¹ Spans for 2" × 6" lumber having actual dressed size of 1⅝" × 5⅝" can be increased by 2½ percent

Notes: Spans can be increased 5 percent from those shown for rough lumber or lumber surfaced two edges (S2E).

Spans can be decreased 5 percent from those shown for lumber more than 2 percent but not more than 5 percent scant from American Lumber Standards sizes measured at a moisture content of 19 percent or less Lumber scant more than 5 percent will not be acceptable.

Courtesy: U.S. Dept. HUD, FHA

Table 3-8 Span limitations for western white pine

Nominal size (inches)	Spacing (inches oc)	No. 1 dimension (¹)		No. 2 dimension (¹)		No. 1 dimension (¹)		No. 2 dimension (¹)	
		Floor joists							
		30 lb. live load				*40 lb. live load*			
		Ft.	In.	Ft.	In.	Ft.	In.	Ft.	In
2 × 6	12	9	6	7	4	8	6	6	8
	16	8	2	6	4	7	4	5	8
	24	6	8	5	2	6	0	4	8
2 × 8	12	13	4	10	0	12	0	9	0
	16	11	6	8	8	10	4	7	10
	24	9	6	7	2	8	6	6	4
2 × 10	12	16	4	14	4	15	6	12	10
	16	15	2	12	4	14	0	11	0
	24	12	10	10	2	11	6	9	0
2 × 12	12	18	10	18	2	17	10	16	2
	16	17	6	15	8	16	6	14	0
	24	15	10	12	10	14	2	11	6
		Ceiling joists							
		No attic storage				*Limited attic storage*			
2 × 4	12	8	10	6	10	6	4	4	10
	16	7	8	6	0	5	6	4	2
	24	6	4	4	10	4	6	3	6
2 × 6	12	15	4	12	0	10	10	8	6
	16	13	4	10	6	9	6	7	4
	24	10	10	8	6	7	8	6	0
2 × 8	12	19	4	16	6	15	4	11	8
	16	18	0	14	4	13	4	10	0
	24	15	4	11	8	10	10	8	2
2 × 10	12	23	0	23	0	19	4	16	6
	16	21	6	20	2	18	0	14	4
	24	19	4	16	6	14	8	11	8
		Low slope roof joists *(Roof slope 3 in 12 or less)*							
		Not supporting finished ceiling				*Supporting finished ceiling*			
2 × 6	12	10	10	8	6	10	0	7	10
	16	9	6	7	4	8	8	6	10
	24	7	8	6	0	7	2	5	8
2 × 8	12	15	4	11	8	14	4	10	10
	16	13	4	10	0	12	4	9	4
	24	10	10	8	2	10	0	7	8

Table 3-8 Continued

Nominal size (inches)	Spacing (inches oc)	No. 1 dimension (¹)		No. 2 dimension (¹)		No. 1 dimension (¹)		No. 2 dimension (¹)	
2 × 10	12	19	4	16	6	18	8	15	4
	16	18	0	14	4	16	8	13	2
	24	14	8	11	8	13	8	10	10
2 × 12	12	22	4	21	0	21	6	19	4
	16	20	10	18	2	20	0	16	10
	24	18	4	14	10	17	0	13	8

		Rafters (Roof slope over 3 in 12)							
		Light roofing				Heavy roofing			
2 × 4	12	7	4	5	8	6	4	4	10
	16	6	4	5	0	5	6	4	2
	24	5	2	4	0	4	6	3	6
2 × 6	12	12	8	10	0	10	10	8	6
	16	11	0	8	8	9	6	7	4
	24	9	0	7	0	7	8	6	0
2 × 8	12	18	0	13	8	15	4	11	8
	16	15	6	11	10	13	4	10	0
	24	12	8	9	8	10	10	8	2
2 × 10	12	22	6	19	2	20	10	16	6
	16	21	0	16	8	18	0	14	4
	24	17	2	13	8	14	8	11	8

1 Denotes grade is not a stress grade.

Notes: (a) Spans may be increased 5 percent from those shown for rough lumber or lumber surfaced two edges (S2E)

(b) Spans shall be decreased 5 percent from those shown for lumber more than 2 percent but not more than 5 percent scant from American Lumber Standards sizes measured at a moisture content of 19 percent or less Lumber scant more than 5 percent will not be acceptable

Courtesy: U S. Dept. HUD, FHA

Coast sitka spruce

Contains only coast sitka spruce, a light, resilient, moderately strong wood that's easy to work and holds nails well. Colors range from creamy white to light pink, with a large proportion of clear wood.

Ponderosa pine

Contains only ponderosa pine, which is moderately strong and easy to work. The wood seasons readily and holds nails well. The sapwood color is pale yellow and the heartwood ranges in color from deep yellow to red-brown.

Western cedars (north)

This group includes western red cedar and Pacific Coast yellow cedar. The two woods aren't equal in strength, but both are decay resistant, have a nice appearance, and are easy to work. Red cedar has red-brown heartwood and light sapwood. Yellow cedar has a uniform yellow color.

Red pine (north)
Contains only red pine, a fairly strong, easy-to-work wood that holds nails well. Moderately durable, it seasons with little checking or cupping. The sapwood is thick and pale yellow in color. The heartwood color ranges from pale brown to red.

Eastern white pine (north)
Contains only eastern white pine, the softest of the Canadian pines. Eastern white pine isn't as strong as most pines, but it doesn't split or splinter. It holds nails well and shrinks less than any other Canadian species except the cedars. The color of the sapwood is almost white, and the heartwood color ranges from creamy white to light straw-brown.

Western white pine
Contains quaking aspen, bigtooth aspen, and balsam poplar. These are lightweight woods of relatively low strength. Colors range from almost white to gray-white.

Black cottonwood
Includes only black cottonwood, a hardwood. It's similar to northern aspens, but lower in strength and stiffness.

Northern species
Any Canadian softwood species included in NLGA standard grading rules for Canadian lumber can be classed as a northern species.

Coastal species
Includes Douglas fir, western larch, western hemlock, amabilis fir, and coast sitka spruce. The characteristics of these species are listed in previous sections.

Not all of these species combinations are available in all grades and sizes. Regardless of your area, you'll find a choice of quality lumber, U.S. or Canadian, for all your framing needs.

4
Basic frame types

Aside from the exotic or experimental, such as the geodetic and some futuristic designs, most houses are constructed using one of the following four basic framing types:
- Platform (western)
- Modern braced
- Balloon
- Plank and beam

Wood frame construction using one of these methods is the predominant method of building housing in the United States.

The building frame includes support posts, girders, sill plates, floor joists, studs, and rafters. While framing practices will vary from area to area, each of the principal regions of the United States—the Atlantic Coast, the South, the Midwest, the West, and the Pacific Coast—has some unique characteristics. However, the same basic principles of framing and bracing are used throughout all regions.

PLATFORM (OR WESTERN) FRAME

Platform construction (see Fig. 4-1) is the framing method generally used when building a home. Each story of the house is built as a separate unit, and the subfloor is laid before the walls are raised. This provides a safe working platform. Platform framing is similar to modern braced framing (see Fig. 4-2) except that the ends of the joists form a bearing for the side and center-wall studs. This system allows for equal shrinkage at both side and center walls.

Wood, as explained in the previous chapter, shrinks and expands due to moisture content, temperature, and humidity. Additionally, the compression caused by the load on the lumber will cause shrinkage.

Platform is probably the fastest and safest form of good construction. The method permits more short wood to be used for studs, and the studding extends only one story and rests on a sole plate installed on top of the subfloor.

The second-floor joists are supported by a plate installed on top of the first-floor studding. Since the subfloor extends to the outside edge of the framing, no wooden firestops are required. Figure 4-3 shows how this simplifies the framing.

In platform framing, a continuous joist header is used at the first floor. It is the same size as the floor joists. As shown in Fig. 4-3, the bottom edge of the joist header rests on the sill. Its outside face is flush with the outside edge of the sill, to form a *box sill*. On the second floor, a continuous header can be used in the same manner, or the floor joists can extend flush to the outside of the plate, giving a full 3½-inch bearing for the joists. Blocking is nailed between the joists, as shown in Fig. 4-4.

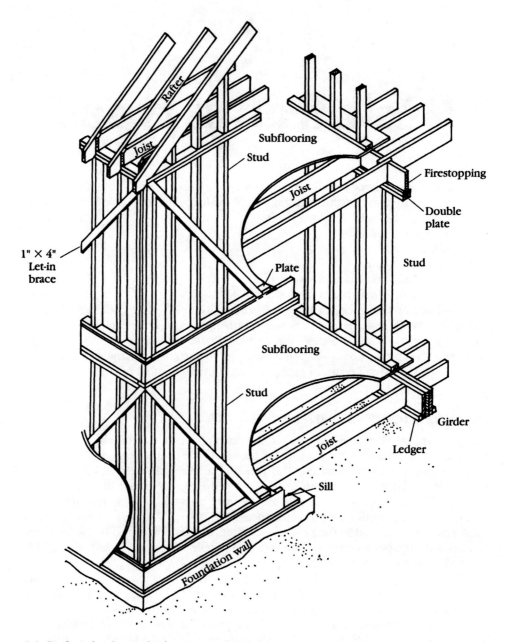

4-1 Platform framing method. Amencan Forest & Paper Assoc

Partitions are built and supported the same as in other framing systems, requiring girders, double-joist support, and sole plates.

Outside wall members are framed the same way as interior partitions—supported by the same thickness of horizontal wood. This makes the shrinkage uniform for both outside walls and partitions. Thus, floors and ceilings should remain level

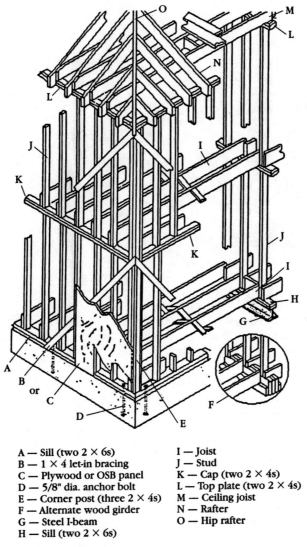

A — Sill (two 2 × 6s)
B — 1 × 4 let-in bracing
C — Plywood or OSB panel
D — 5/8" dia. anchor bolt
E — Corner post (three 2 × 4s)
F — Alternate wood girder
G — Steel I-beam
H — Sill (two 2 × 6s)

I — Joist
J — Stud
K — Cap (two 2 × 4s)
L — Top plate (two 2 × 4s)
M — Ceiling joist
N — Rafter
O — Hip rafter

4-2 Modern braced framing method.

regardless of shrinkage. Where a steel beam is used for the girder, wood of the same cross-section size (thickness) as the sill plate should be used on top of the steel to ensure equal shrinkage. Figure 4-2 illustrates this concept.

Figure 4-5 shows how to construct western framing over a foundation wall. Figure 4-6 shows western framing built over pillars using a sill beam constructed of 2-by lumber.

My choice of framing methods is the western system. I've used it in both one- and two-story houses. After the subflooring is nailed down, you can build the walls horizontally on the floor deck and then raise them into place in a single operation (see Fig. 4-7).

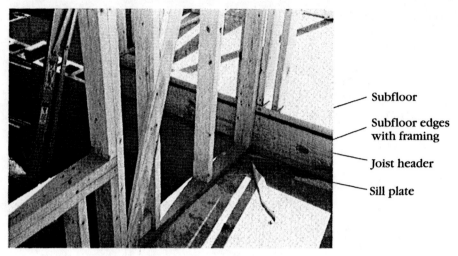

Subfloor

Subfloor edges
with framing

Joist header

Sill plate

4-3 Subfloor extended to the edge of the frame.

MODERN BRACED FRAME

The modern braced frame (Fig. 4-2) has studs of the side walls and center partitions cut to the same length. The side-wall studs are nailed to the sill, and the partition studs are attached to the girder. This permits uniform shrinkage in the outside and inside walls.

To provide rigidity to the walls, diagonal braces are let into the studs at the corners. Other systems of bracing can be used at the corners, depending on the placement of openings in the side or end walls. The joists are lapped and nailed to the side-wall studs. The joists are either continuous between the two opposite side walls, or are side-lapped and nailed at the center partition. Either method forms a strong tie for the two side walls. Where required, the joists are bridged. The joists are supported by the full width of the sill and girder. You want to install wall firestops at the end of all the joists.

BALLOON FRAME

In balloon framing, the exterior-wall studs continue through the first and second stories. First-floor joists and exterior-wall studs both bear on the sill, as illustrated in Fig. 4-8. The second-floor joists are supported by a ribbon let into the studs. Firestops are required between the side-wall and end-wall studs.

Balloon framing replaced old braced framing, but it's now less common than modern braced and western framing in most areas.

In two-story buildings having either a stone or brick veneer exterior finish, balloon framing reduces variations in the settlement of the framing and masonry finish because horizontally laid lumber is kept to a minimum.

The balloon framing method permits for quick erection of the exterior studs because they extend the full two stories, from the sill plate to the rafter plate. The center load-bearing partition can also be built with two-story length studs, but the preferred method is shown in Fig. 4-8. The second-floor joists rest on a 1 × 6 ribbon or ledger board, and are nailed to the stud with three 12d nails. The second-story ceiling joists rest on the double top plate.

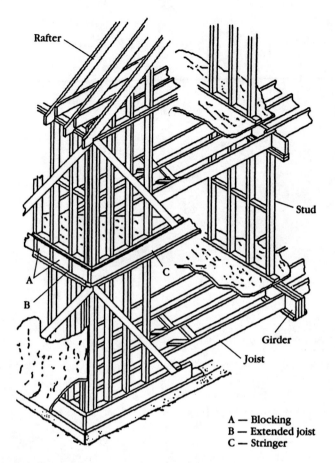

Rafter

Stud

A

B

C

Girder

Joist

A — Blocking
B — Extended joist
C — Stringer

4-4 Second-floor joists extended and blocked.

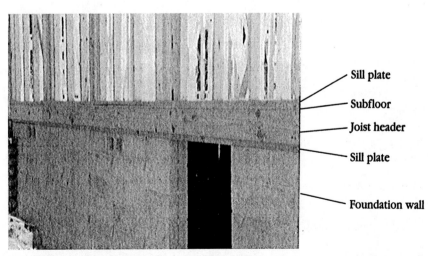

Sill plate

Subfloor

Joist header

Sill plate

Foundation wall

4-5 Western framing supported by foundation wall.

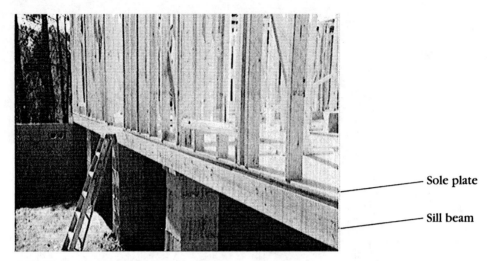

Sole plate

Sill beam

4-6 Western framing supported by pillars.

4-7 Raising assembled walls into place.

The flue effect in openings between the studs is strong, making firestopping members essential. Without firestops, flames from the basement or crawlspace could sweep to the top plate or into the attic. Install blocking at the sill and at the second-floor height, or as required by your code.

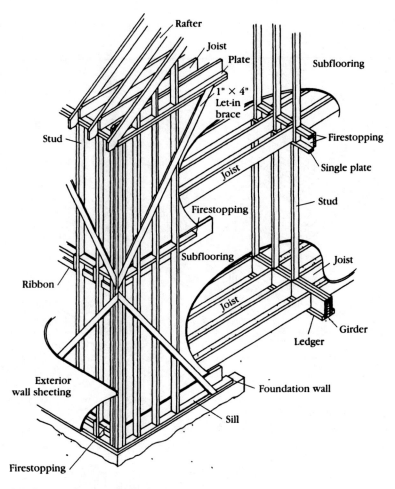

4-8 Balloon framing method. American Forest & Paper Assoc

The balloon frame is not as rigid as braced frames until the wall sheathing has been nailed on. With the sheathing applied, a balloon frame is as strong and stiff as the other types. When plywood or structural-grade sheathing panels are used, 1 × 4 diagonal braces can be omitted

PLANK-AND-BEAM FRAME

Plank-and-beam (P&B) framing, also called post-and-beam framing, is adaptable to modern building styles It works well with one-story structures, large glass areas, open spans, and modular set-ups The system can also make excellent use of glue-laminated beams where large spans are involved

In conventional framing, members (joists, studs, and rafters) are commonly spaced 12 to 24 inches on center. The P&B system uses fewer but larger pieces of lumber spaced farther apart Figure 4-9 offers a comparison of the two systems.

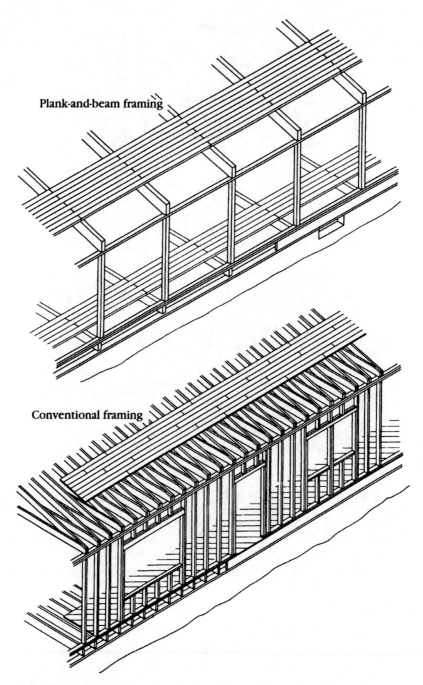

Plank-and-beam framing

Conventional framing

4-9 Comparison of conventional and plank-and-beam systems. American Forest & Paper Assoc

The P&B frame concentrates the structural load on fewer and larger framing members than the conventional method Plank subfloors and roofs, usually of a two-inch nominal thickness, are supported on beams spaced up to six and eight feet apart The ends of beams are supported on posts or piers. Supplementary framing, as required for exterior and interior finishing, is provided in the wall spaces between posts This supplementary framing provides lateral bracing for the structure.

Designing a plank-and-beam house

Plank-and-beam framing was adopted from heavy timber construction. It can, of course, be used for framing floors and roofs in combination with ordinary wood stud or masonry walls, or as the skeleton frame in curtain wall construction.

It's important that a P&B house be designed from the beginning for this type of framing. There must be proper correlation between the structural frame components and the exterior dimensions as well as the location of doors, windows, and interior partitions If not, you're likely to have big problems Plank-and-beam framing isn't something you want to do on a trial-and-error basis.

The house should be laid out on a two-foot module, with every dimension a multiple of two feet, to ensure a minimum of cutting, fitting, and waste. The most efficient use of two-inch plank occurs when it's used over more than one span. If you're using standard lengths of lumber, such as 12, 14, or 16 feet, space beams six, seven, or eight feet apart This naturally dictates the overall dimensions of the house. Where plank end joints are permitted between supports, tongue-and-groove or splined random-length planks can be used, and the beam spacing can then be adjusted to fit the dimension of the house Figure 4-10 shows the P&B framing method for a one-story house.

You can combine conventional framing with the P&B system, as shown in Fig. 4-11

Plank structural flooring (two-inch nominal thickness) is laid on beams spaced six to eight feet apart Where conventional roof framing is used with P&B construction, install a header to carry the load from the rafters to the posts.

The P&B system is commonly designed to take advantage of the exposed plank-and-beam ceiling The roof plank can serve as the finish ceiling Stain, sealer, or paint is all that's required for the finish

The P&B frame can save time, material, and money over conventional methods due to the dual function of materials. There are fewer pieces to handle, and cross-bridging of joists is unnecessary.

The plank floors are designed for moderate, uniform loads Heavy, concentrated loads of bearing partitions, bath tubs, freezers, refrigerators, etc , require additional framing beneath the planks to carry the load to the beams.

Rigid insulation can be installed over roof planking where the underside of the planking is used as the finish ceiling. Use a type of insulation that won't deform or compress under a load.

Construction details

While a P&B frame requires a lot less materials and labor, top-quality workmanship is essential in this type of construction All joints must fit exactly since there are fewer contacts between members

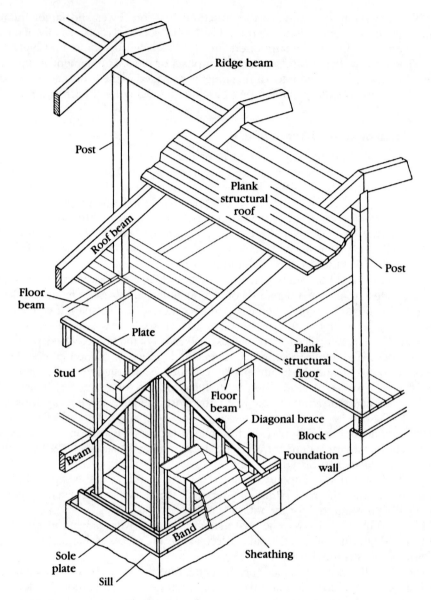

Ridge beam

Post

Plank
structural
roof

Roof beam

Post

Floor
beam

Plate

Plank
structural
floor

Stud

Floor
beam

Diagonal brace

Beam

Block

Foundation
wall

Band

Sole
plate

Sheathing

Sill

4-10 Plank-and-beam framing for a one-story house. American Forest & Paper Assoc

Foundations for P&B framing can be a continuous wall or piers. With posts spaced up to eight feet apart in exterior walls, the system is well suited to pier foundations for houses without a basement.

Install posts that are large enough to carry the load and provide full bearing for beam ends. Posts smaller than 4 × 4 probably shouldn't be used. Posts can be solid or made up using several pieces of two-inch lumber nailed together.

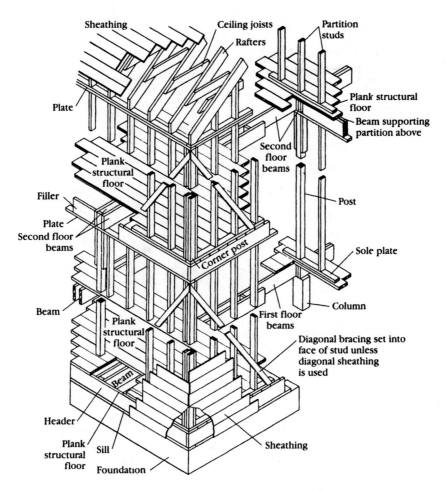

Sheathing
Ceiling joists
Rafters
Partition studs
Plate
Plank structural floor
Beam supporting partition above
Plank structural floor
Second floor beams
Filler
Plate
Second floor beams
Post
Corner post
Sole plate
Beam
Plank structural floor
Column
First floor beams
Diagonal bracing set into face of stud unless diagonal sheathing is used
Header
Plank structural floor
Sill
Sheathing
Foundation

4-11 Plank-and-beam framing combined with conventional framing in a two-story house. American Forest & Paper Assoc

The required beam size depends on the span and spacing. Beams can be built up, spaced, glue-laminated, or solid. Cover built-up and spaced beams with a finish material to improve the appearance (see Fig. 4-12)

You must consider both the appearance and the structural requirements for a two-inch plank floor or roof when the underside serves as the finish ceiling for the floor below. Tongue-and-groove or grooved-for-spline planks are required to properly distribute the load. Figure 4-13 portrays some methods for joining planks.

Use a good grade of well-seasoned plank for the finish ceiling or you'll have wide cracks at the joints, which is unacceptable. Install planks continuously over more than one span, e.g., a 16-foot plank over beams spaced eight feet apart A plank that's continuous over two spans is approximately 2½ times as stiff as a plank that extends over a single span, as would be the case if you used an eight-foot plank over beams spaced eight feet apart. Nail the plank to each beam with two 16d nails.

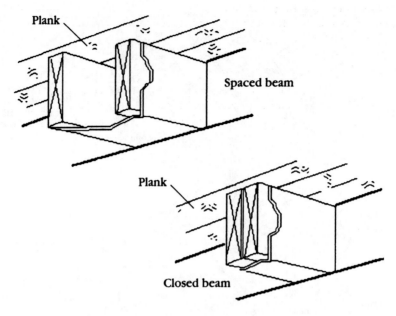

Plank

Spaced beam

Plank

Closed beam

4-12 Covering beams.

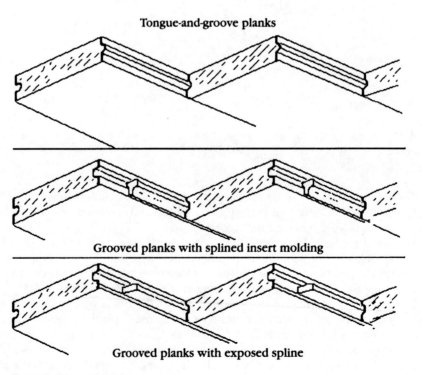

Tongue-and-groove planks

Grooved planks with splined insert molding

Grooved planks with exposed spline

4-13 Joining exposed ceiling planks.

Lay wood-finish flooring at right angles to the plank subfloor in the same manner as laying conventional framing. Use nails that don't penetrate the plank subfloor if the underside is the finish ceiling for the floor below.

Partitions

A P&B frame normally has nonbearing partitions. Where bearing partitions do exist, support must be provided. If the partition wall cannot be placed over a beam, a supplementary beam must be added. Nonbearing partitions at right angles to the planks need no additional support because the load is distributed across a number of planks (see Fig. 4-14).

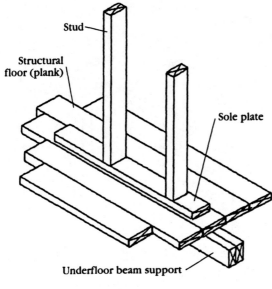

Stud

Structural floor (plank)

Sole plate

Underfloor beam support

4-14
Support for nonbearing partition, parallel to plank.

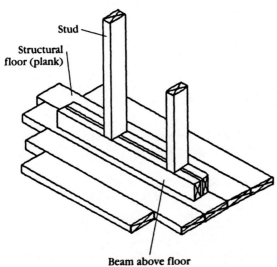

Stud

Structural floor (plank)

Beam above floor

Lateral bracing

The key element in any building is bracing. Without bracing, a structure cannot withstand the elements. Lateral bracing is required in P&B framing as in conventional framing to provide adequate resistance to wind forces. This is provided by installing solid panels at intervals to tie the wall framing and posts together. You can use structural sheathing or diagonal bracing.

Roof horizontal thrust

Where sloped or gable roofs are used, you must install components to absorb the horizontal thrust. Figures 4-15 and 4-16 show how this can be accomplished.

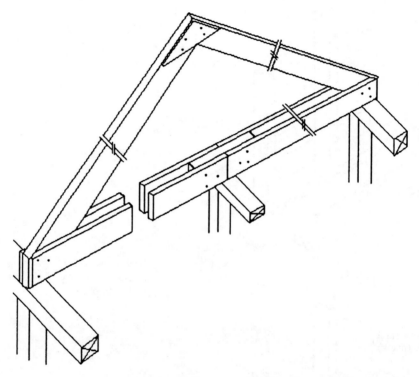

4-15 Absorbing horizontal thrust with roof and floor beams.

Local building codes generally specify design loading requirements for P&B construction. A live load of 40 pounds per square foot is commonly required for floors, and 20 to 40 psi for roofs.

Framing anchors can be used to secure the roof beam to post (Fig. 4-17). Metal ties are also available for securing other components of P&B frames.

THE MODULAR PLAN

The modular plan involves three dimensions: length, width, and height. The modular length and width dimensions form the base; in combination they're the two most im-

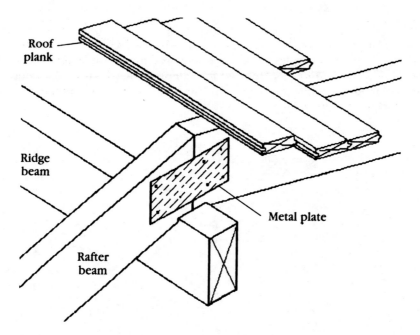

4-16 Absorbing horizontal thrust with rafter beam on ridge beam.

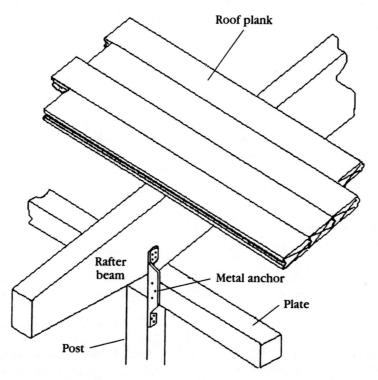

4-17 Securing members with metal anchors.

portant dimensions. The planning grid shown in Fig 4-18 is a horizontal plane divided into units of 4, 16, 24, and 48 inches Overall dimensions are multiples of four inches.

The 16-inch unit provides flexibility in the spacing of windows and doors. Increments of 24 and 48 inches are used for exterior dimensions of the house. The purpose of modular building is to conserve materials and labor, and thereby, hopefully, cut the cost of housing.

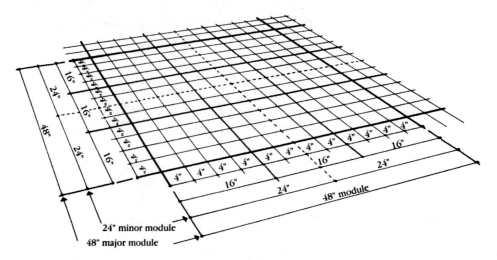

4-18 Modular planning grid American Forest & Paper Assoc

Builder experience with various sizes and spacings of joists, studs, and rafters together with standard 4 × 8 panel dimensions can result in a fast and economical method of house framing

Carpenters who have framed more than a few houses often see a big waste of lumber on some jobs because plan dimensions are poorly coordinated with material dimensions. Modular plans for houses to be built with components of conventional framing are designed to exact size on the grid A grid layout provides a rapid means of accurate planning.

Thickness and tolerance variables

Divide the house into horizontal and vertical elements at regular intervals, as shown in Fig 4-19.

There are many thickness variables for exterior walls and partitions, and, depending on their structural requirements, roof and floor construction can also vary in thickness.

Coordinating a typical floor plan to a planning grid is illustrated in Fig. 4-20 This grid represents the basic four-inch module. Basic modular dimensions are on the outside face of the stud walls, and the outside face of the band joists is flush with the face of the studs. Floor-joist lengths for modular house depths are based on the measurement indicated in Fig 4-20 The joists are shown in-line and are jointed at

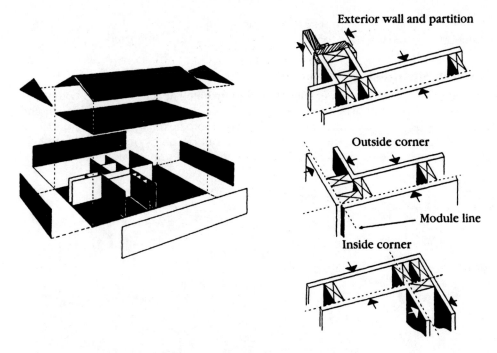

Exterior wall and partition

Outside corner

Module line

Inside corner

4-19 Division of houses into plane sections, with thickness and tolerance variables. American Forest & Paper Assoc

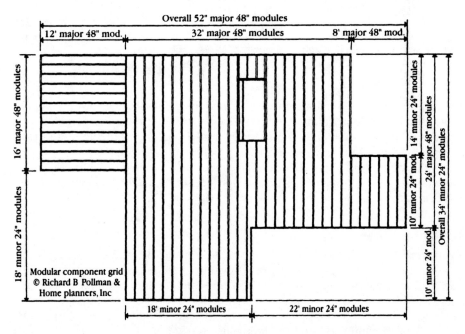

Overall 52" major 48" modules

12' major 48" mod.   32' major 48" modules   8' major 48" mod.

16' major 48" modules

18' minor 24" modules

Modular component grid
© Richard B Pollman &
Home planners, Inc

18' minor 24" modules   22' minor 24" modules

14' minor 24" modules

10' minor 24" mod.

24' major 48" modules

Overall 34' minor 24" modules

10' minor 24" mod.

4-20 Floor plan drawn on a modular grid. American Forest & Paper Assoc

the bearing point by metal plates By using multiples of two to four feet for house exteriors, fractional spaces for floor and roof framing are eliminated

Exterior walls, doors, and windows

With planning, exterior-wall elements can be separated at natural division points, as explained in Fig 4-21. The overall house dimensions are based on the 48-inch and 24-inch modules. The 16-inch module gives you more flexibility in placing door and window openings. Furthermore, if you locate wall openings on a 16-inch module, you'll eliminate the extra studding frequently required in nonmodular framing.

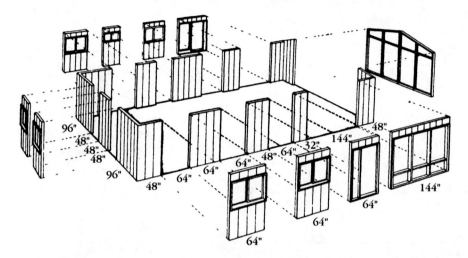

4-21 Separating the exterior wall components American Forest & Paper Assoc

Dimensioning the roof

Increments for house depths are in 24-inch multiples. Six 48-inch module depths and five 24-inch module widths fulfill most roof-span requirements (see Fig. 4-22). Standard roof slopes combined with modular house depths provide all dimensions required for design of rafter, truss, and panel roofs.

The pivotal point in Fig. 4-22 is the fixed point of reference in the module line of the exterior wall. Modular roof design and construction dimensions are determined from this point

FLOOR FRAMING

You can waste as much as 5 to 15 percent of your materials in floor framing if the front-to-back dimension (house depth) isn't evenly divisible by four (see Fig. 4-23).

Space floor joists at 12, 16, or 24 inches on center, depending on the floor load. The joists can be lapped or in-line A 48-inch module for the house depth permits greater use of full 4 × 8-foot-panel subflooring using plywood or oriented strand board (OSB), and eliminates a lot of cutting and waste

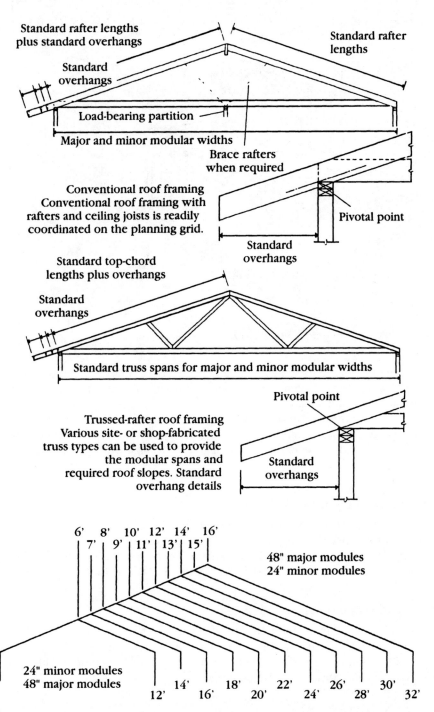

Standard rafter lengths plus standard overhangs

Standard rafter lengths

Standard overhangs

Load-bearing partition

Major and minor modular widths

Brace rafters when required

Pivotal point

Conventional roof framing
Conventional roof framing with rafters and ceiling joists is readily coordinated on the planning grid.

Standard overhangs

Standard top-chord lengths plus overhangs

Standard overhangs

Standard truss spans for major and minor modular widths

Pivotal point

Trussed-rafter roof framing
Various site- or shop-fabricated truss types can be used to provide the modular spans and required roof slopes. Standard overhang details

Standard overhangs

6' 8' 10' 12' 14' 16'
7' 9' 11' 13' 15'

48" major modules
24" minor modules

24" minor modules
48" major modules

12' 14' 16' 18' 20' 22' 24' 26' 28' 30' 32'

4-22 24-inch increments provide a variety of module house depths. American Forest & Paper Assoc

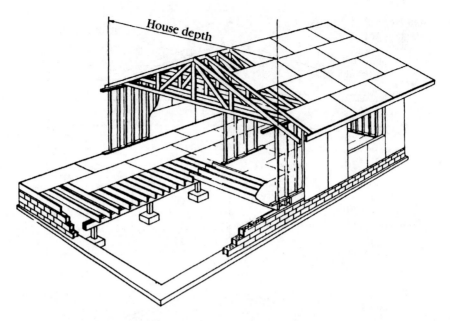

4-23 Use a 4-foot module house depth. American Forest & Paper Assoc

Joist material is sized in two-foot increments, with a tolerance of minus zero and plus three inches. Joists 12 feet and longer are usually an extra half inch or more longer to allow for end squaring.

In normal platform construction with lapped joists bearing on top of a center support, the joist length required is half the house depth. The deduction of 1½ inches (the thickness of the band joist) is taken up by half of the required overlap (1½ inches). Figure 4-24 explains

House depths and lumber lengths

Joist lengths corresponds to standard lumber sizes when the house depth is on the four-foot module of 24, 28, or 32 feet. The same total linear footage of standard joist lengths is required to frame the floor of a 25-foot house depth as it is for a 28-foot house depth The same holds true for a 29-foot and 32-foot house depth. See Table 4-1.

Switching to module depths

If joist spans are increased when changing to the four-foot module, the allowable span for the lumber, species, and grade being used should be rechecked. In many cases, it will be satisfactory. Also, where spans are reduced to comply with a four-foot module, smaller joists might be possible.

Subfloor panel layout

Four-foot-wide panels can be used without ripping for 24, 28, and 32-foot house depths when joists are either lapped or trimmed for in-line installation. A panel lay-

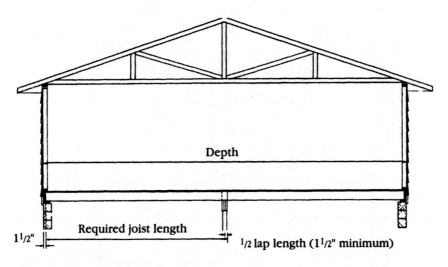

Depth

Required joist length

1½"

½ lap length (1½" minimum)

4-24 Required joist length. American Forest & Paper Assoc

Table 4-1 Required linear footage of joists for various house depths

House depth (ft.)	Joist length Required (ft.)	Joist length Standard (ft.)	Linear feet 16" joist spacing	Linear feet 24" joist spacing	Required footage of joists per 4' of house length based on standard joist length BF per sq. ft. of floor area[1] 16" oc 2 × 8	2 × 10	24" oc 2 × 20	2 × 12
21	10½	12	72	48	1 14	1 43	95	1 14
22	11	12	72	48	1 09	1 36	.91	1 09
23	11½	12	72	48	1 04	1 30	.87	1 04
24	12	12	72	48	1 00	1 25	83	1 00
25	12½	14	84	56	1 12	1 40	93	1 12
26	13	14	84	56	1 08	1 35	89	1 08
27	13½	14	84	56	1 04	1 30	86	1 04
28	14	14	84	56	1.00	1 25	.83	1 00
29	14½	16	96	64	1 10	1 38	92	1 10
30	15	16	96	64	1 07	1 33	89	1 07
31	15½	16	96	64	1 03	1.29	86	1 03
32	16	16	96	64	1 00	1 25	84	1 00

1 Floor area = house depth times 4'

out option for a 28-foot house depth using lapped joists is illustrated in Fig. 4-25. Similar layouts can be used with other lapped-joist designs.

EXTERIOR WALL FRAMING

The cost of exterior wall framing, in both materials and labor, can be cut by up to 25 percent with a module layout. For example, look at Fig. 4-26. The cost savings

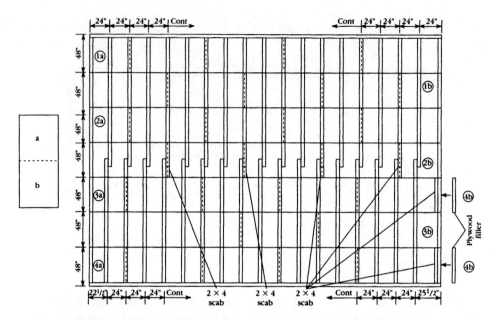

4-25 Subfloor 4' × 8' panel layout. Amencan Forest & Paper Assoc

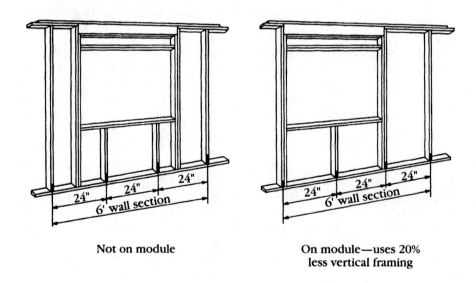

Not on module

On module—uses 20% less vertical framing

4-26 Windows located on a module can save framing. Amencan Forest & Paper Assoc

will be greatest when the overall size of the house plus the size and location of wall openings coincide with standard modular stud spacing.

Your modular plan should show the location of all wall components. Planning the actual location of studs will save on framing lumber and reduce the amount of cutting for sheathing and siding.

Figure 4-27 shows how most people frame walls, spacing studs 16 inches on center and locating openings without regard to module layout. Modular, planned framing is shown in Fig. 4-28. As illustrated, there's much less material in the modular concept. Of course, there has to be a trade-off. The wall in Fig. 4-28 isn't as sturdy as the one in Fig. 4-27, but it's strong enough to do the job.

Stud spacing

Studs can be spaced 24 inches on center in virtually any style of house where exterior and interior facing materials can span 24 inches. Tests and structural analyses show that, for many installations, studs spaced 24 inches can be used even for walls supporting the upper floor of a two-story house.

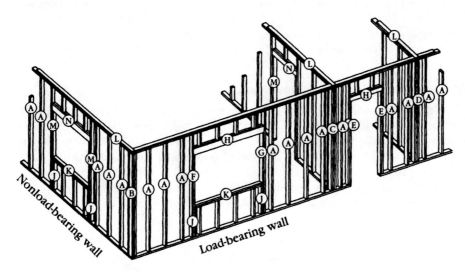

4-27 Conventional wall framing on 16-inch centers. American Forest & Paper Assoc

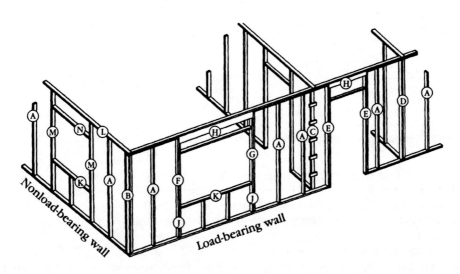

4-28 Modular wall framing on 24-inch centers. American Forest & Paper Assoc

For window and door openings, have one side of the window's or door's rough opening fall on a regular stud position. Details E, F, and M in Fig. 4-28 illustrate this modular principle.

When possible, install windows and doors that have a rough-opening width a multiple of the stud spacing. This allows both sides to be on the stud module, reducing the number of studs required. It also permits the installation of sheathing and siding without a lot of waste. Figure 4-28 shows how this might look. With the cost of lumber constantly rising, module framing on 24-inch centers can help reduce the cost of housing.

Detail D in Fig. 4-28 shows the partition located at a normal wall stud, eliminating the need for a corner nailer on one side of the partition. You can use scrap wood for backup cleats for nailers on the opposite corner. Obviously, no one will locate a partition at a certain point just to save a couple studs. A workable floor plan is the first priority. However, when only a few inches are involved, savings are possible.

Wall corners and intersections

Three studs are normally used to fabricate exterior-wall corner posts and partition intersection tees in traditional framing. Figure 4-29 shows how the studs are arranged to provide nailing surfaces for material. These components are shown in details B, C, and D of Fig. 4-27. The space between the studs can be blocked with short (12" to 16") pieces of 2 × 4s for added stability. The remaining space should be filled with insulation *before* the sheathing is applied, which means that you, the framer, must install the insulation—a task normally left to others.

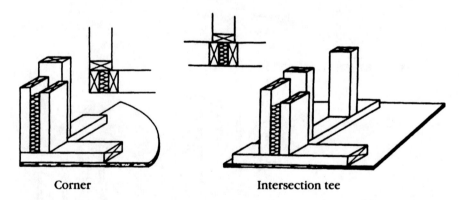

Corner   Intersection tee

4-29 Stud arrangements for corners and intersections. American Forest & Paper Assoc

An alternate method of building corners and tees is illustrated in Fig. 4-30 and details B and D in Fig. 4-28. This stud arrangement eliminates spacer blocks, and provides backup support for wall materials like the traditional method. Insulation can be installed after the sheathing is applied, from the inside of the dried-in house by others.

Another alternative is shown in Fig. 4-28, detail C, and Fig. 4-31. Here you can eliminate the studs that serve only as backup for finish materials on interior corner nailing surfaces by attaching backup cleats to the partition stud. The cleats can be any

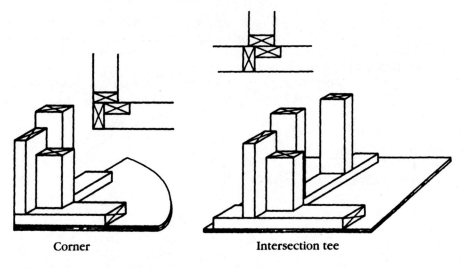

Corner   Intersection tee

4-30 Corner and tee alternatives. American Forest & Paper Assoc

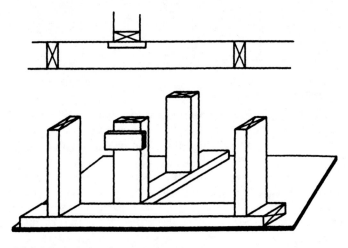

4-31 Using cleat nails. American Forest & Paper Assoc

suitable scrap material, ⅜-inch plywood or OSB, or 1-inch lumber. As the framer, you want to nail these backups securely to prevent them from being knocked off during installation of the finish material. A similar arrangement of cleats can be used to eliminate the backup nailer stud at interior corners, shown in Fig. 4-30.

WINDOW AND DOOR FRAMING

It has long been a suspicion of framers that architects purposely design and place windows and doors where the most lumber will be required. A window a few inches too wide or too narrow, or located a few inches too far left or right usually means you'll need at least one extra stud.

Details J and K in Fig. 4-27 show double sills under windows, plus short support studs (cripples) at each sill end. Figure 4-32 shows that vertical loads at windows are transferred downward by the studs that support the headers. The sill and wall beneath the window are nonbearing Details J and K in Fig. 4-28 and Figs. 4-26 and 4-32 show how to eliminate the second sill member and two sill-support cripples The ends of the sill are secured by end-nailing through the adjacent stud with two 16d nails.

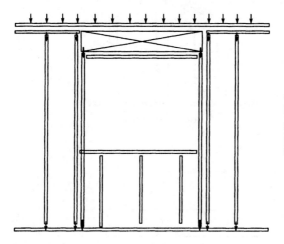

4-32
Load distribution through header and support studs at opening in load-bearing wall. Amencan Forest & Paper Assoc

Framing nonbearing walls

Most houses have two or more nonbearing exterior walls. The walls run parallel to the joists and roof components, such as trusses or rafters, and support only their own weight. These walls can be framed the same way as interior partitions (see details K, L, M, and N of Fig. 4-28).

Frame doors and windows with single members since there are no loads to transfer. A single top plate is enough if you use metal straps or plates to tie them together at the butt joints. The single top-plate system requires studs to be 1½ inches longer than the exterior side walls, which have two-member top plates. You might prefer to cut these longer studs on the job instead of ordering two lengths of precut studs.

Wall blocking

Mid-height wall blocking between wall studs is mostly a thing of the past even though some of us old-timers still adhere to the practice as a strengthening component The top and bottom plates provide adequate firestopping, and ½-inch drywall (gypsum board) applied horizontally doesn't require blocking for support when studs are centered 24 inches or less.

Wall bracing

Strong winds can play havoc with a poorly braced building. Most codes require that exterior walls have minimum "racking" strength for stability under wind loads. Structural-grade sheathing at corners provide sufficient racking strength, and no additional let-in bracing is needed. Where structural-grade sheathing is not used, install 1 × 4 let-in bracing at corners. Use metal anchors and hangers for maximum strength, as shown in Figs. 4-33 and 4-34.

4-33 Steel hangers ensure maximum strength.

4-34
Simpson Strong-Tie model HD5A metal anchor.

5
Sills

A sill is generally the bottom horizontal part of a component. In a framed window opening, it's the lower horizontal member; in balloon framing, it's the piece that the studs and joists rest on that's anchored to the foundation wall or floor slab; in western framing, it's the bottom piece of the box sill. The sill is also called a *mudsill*. In a wood-frame building, the sill plate usually rests directly on the foundation wall. When a termite shield is used, the shield rests directly on the foundation wall and the sill rests on the shield.

Good woods for sills are southern yellow pine, cypress, redwood, and Douglas fir. Any wood placed in direct contact with masonry should be pressure treated with a preservative to protect against moisture and insects. More about this later in the chapter.

Figure 5-1 shows a stud wall resting on a sill that's anchored to a concrete floor slab. In Fig. 5-2, a concrete floor slab (carport floor) joins a box sill on a block foundation wall. As shown, the sill in these instances is laid flush to the outside surface of the wall and slab. When the sheathing is to line up flush with the foundation wall, locate the sill the thickness of the sheathing back from the wall edge.

2 × 4 sill

5-1 The wall sill on a concrete floor slab.

Box sill

Slab sill

5-2 Installing sills.

BOX SILL

The box sill (Fig. 5-3) is associated with platform construction. It provides support and anchorage for the floor joists and joist headers (band), and gives a solid bearing upon which to secure the subfloor. The box sill's horizontally laid wood includes

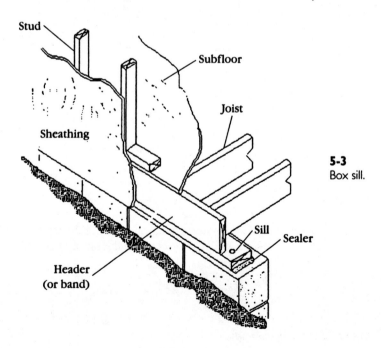

Stud

Subfloor

Joist

Sheathing

5-3
Box sill.

Sill

Sealer

Header
(or band)

the sill, joist, and wall plate, which can cause shrinkage problems in two-story houses having brick or stone exteriors. A sill sealer or termite shield is used between the masonry and sill plate. Lay the subflooring flush with the outside of the joist header on the side walls and with the outside face of the end-wall floor frame. The joists and joist header are toe-nailed to the sill. Some codes require that the joists and joist header be anchored to the sill with metal anchors.

Alternate box sill

The alternate box sill (see Fig. 5-4) places the joist header directly on the foundation wall, which permits face-nailing into the sill. The end-wall joist is notched at the bottom to fit over the sill and at the top to receive the side-wall plate. Each floor joist must be identically notched, but this system of notching the joist weakens the member. The let-in notch for the sill, shown in Fig. 5-5, uses a double sill to provide full-width support for the joist on the sill. Lap the double plate at the corners for a stronger tie-in (Fig. 5-6).

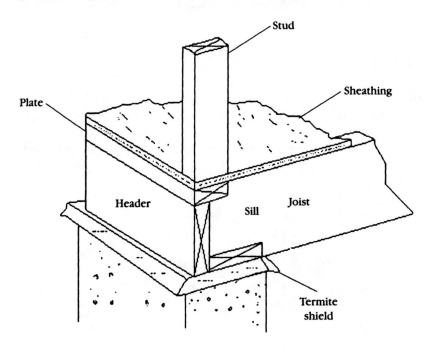

5-4 Alternate box sill.

The alternate box sill requires considerable labor to install due to the cutting required. This system is probably not widely used due to the labor cost and extra material required.

BALLOON-FRAME SILL

Balloon-frame construction also uses a nominal two-inch or thicker wood sill, as explained in Fig. 5-7. The sill rests on the foundation wall. (Be sure to use sill sealer

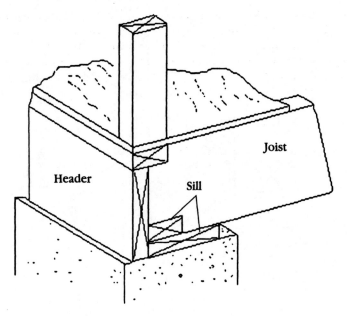

5-5 Double sill plate.

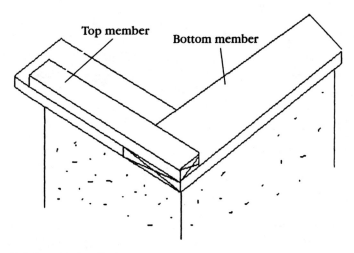

5-6 Lapping the sill plate.

or a termite shield between the sill and foundation wall.) The floor joists bear on top of the sill. The studs also rest on top of the sill and are nailed to both the sill and joists. Subfloor panels are installed at right angles to the joists, and firestops are placed between the studs at the floor line.

The balloon frame has a minimum of horizontally laid wood in the exterior-wall frame, which reduces potential shrinkage. Select straight wood for the sill plate. You want a straight and true surface on which to install the joists and studs.

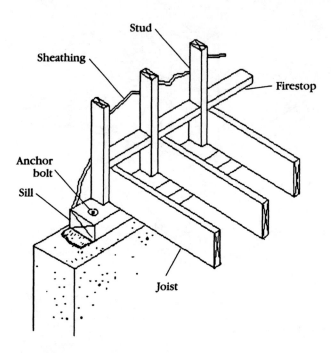

Stud

Sheathing

Firestop

Anchor
bolt

Sill

Joist

5-7 Balloon frame sill.

SOLID BEAM SILL

A beam sill can be solid, built-up, glue-laminated, or one of the other fabricated types. A beam sill is commonly used with exterior pier construction. The floor joists rest directly on the beam, as shown in Fig. 5-8.

SILL ANCHORAGE

One-half-inch-diameter bolts (anchor rods) should be embedded a minimum of 15 inches in solid-filled cores of concrete block and six inches in concrete pillars (piers), and spaced no greater than eight feet apart. Earthquake and hurricane designs require spacing to be six feet or less. There must be at least two bolts in each piece (see Fig. 5-9).

Using straight, 16-foot-long pieces of lumber, place the sill on top of the foundation wall against the anchor bolts, as illustrated in Fig. 5-10. Do not permit butt joints over openings in the foundation wall.

Use a steel square to square the lines from each anchor bolt across the sill plate. Measure, along the line, the distance from the outside edge of the sill to the center of the bolt hole. The outside edge of the sill can be dropped back from the outside edge of the foundation wall by the thickness of the sheathing to allow the sheathing to line up flush with the foundation. Also, if a joist header is used, as shown in Fig. 5-4, locate the sill accordingly.

Mark the center of the bolt hole and drill one-inch-diameter holes to allow for slight adjustment of the sill. A double sill plate can be measured and fitted in the same manner, or you can use the member previously marked as a pattern. Allow for

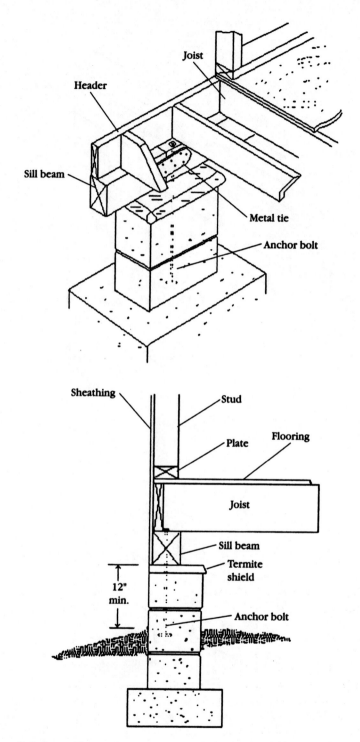

5-8 Beam sill.

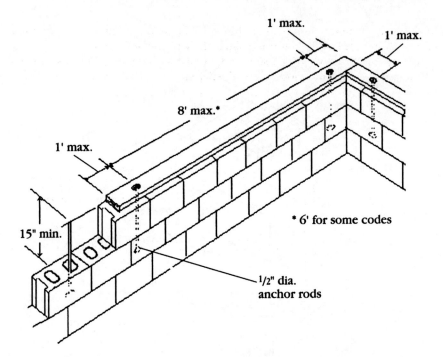

1' max.

1' max.

8' max.*

1' max.

* 6' for some codes

15" min.

½" dia.
anchor rods

5-9 Anchor requirements.

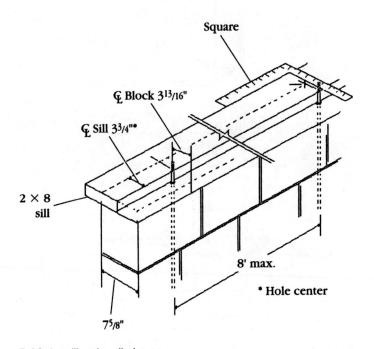

Square

C_L Block 3¹³/₁₆"

C_L Sill 3³/₄"*

2 × 8
sill

8' max.

* Hole center

7⁵/₈"

5-10 Installing the sill plate.

lap joints at corners when using a double sill. Square the end cuts so butt joints and corners fit tightly. Install a termite shield or sealer as required.

Place the sill in position, using wide washers on the anchor bolts. Finger tighten the nuts and check the corners to make sure the plate is square. Make the necessary adjustment and tighten the bolts. Don't overtighten.

TREATED LUMBER

Wood that comes in contact with masonry should be treated with a preservative to protect against moisture and insects. Wood preservatives fall into two classes: oils, such as creosote and petroleum solutions of pentachlorophenol, and water-borne salts that are applied as water solutions.

Most of the chemicals used for house-framing lumber are water-borne preservatives and are odorless and safe to handle. Standard wood preservatives used in a water solution include:
- Acid copper chromate
- Ammoniacal copper arsenite
- Chromated copper arsenate (types I, II, and III)
- Chromated zinc chloride
- Fluor chrome arsenate phenol

These preservatives are often used when cleanliness and paintability of the treated wood are required.

The chromated zinc chloride and fluor chrome arsenate phenol formulations resist leaching less than preservative oils, and are seldom used to protect wood that's in contact with masonry or the ground. Several formulations with a combination of copper, chromium, and arsenic have shown high resistance to leaching and give good performance. The ammoniacal copper arsenite and chromated copper arsenate preservatives are now included in specifications for building foundations, building poles, utility poles, etc. Water-borne preservatives leave the wood surface fairly clean, paintable, and free from unpleasant odors.

Construction methods that assure long service and avoid decay in buildings include:
- Building with dry lumber, free of incipient decay, blue stain, and mold.
- Designs that keep the wood dry and accelerate rain runoff.
- Preservative-treated wood used where decay hazards are caused by moisture.
- Maintaining a minimum of eight inches of clearance between soil and framing, and six inches between soil and siding.

Sill plates and other wood that rests on a concrete slab foundation should be pressure treated, and further protected with a moisture-resistant membrane of heavy asphalt roll roofing or polyethylene installed below the slab. Also, girder and joist openings in masonry walls should be big enough to assure an air space around the ends of each member. If the members are below the outside soil level (finish grade), apply a moisture barrier to the outer face of the wall.

Another framing concern is proper ventilation of the crawlspace. Damp ground can cause condensation during cold weather, which can cause the wood to become wet. This can cause serious problems over a period of time. Openings on opposite sides of the foundation walls for cross ventilation can prevent condensation. There should be a foundation-wall vent near each corner of the building. The total net area should be equal to 1/160 of the ground area when no soil cover is installed, and 1/150 of the ground area when the ground surface is covered with a vapor barrier. (For example, when no soil cover is used on ground area of 1,200 square feet, a total net ventilating area of approximately eight feet is needed. Each of the four vents should have two square feet of net vent area, or use eight one-foot vents. Corrosion-resistant screens of no. 8 mesh work well.)

A minimum 18-inch clearance between the soil and floor joists is required.

SILL/PILLAR RELATION

A pillar (also called a *pier*) has to carry a heavy load. The downward force placed on the pillar by the sill and floor system is concentrated, and the line of thrust is considered to be about the center of the sill beam. To avoid tipping the pillar, the downward thrust should be near the center of the pillar and be spread by a wide sill. Don't use narrow shims between the sill and pillar. See Fig. 5-11.

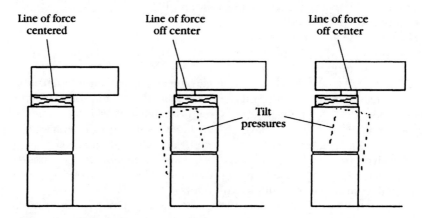

5-11 Sill/pillar relation.

As stated previously, sill beams can be solid, built-up, glue-laminated, or of other fabrications. Most framers prefer built-up sill beams for house construction on pillars. The sill is built on site by nailing together 2-by lumber. Three members are generally required since the pillars are spaced on eight-foot centers. See Fig. 5-12.

It works well to install strap (flat-bar) anchors in pillars at the sheathing thickness plus three inches from the outside face of the pillar to allow for proper placement and anchoring of the beam, as shown in Fig. 5-13.

Place two 2-by sill members together (crowns up) and arrange them so the center member butts over a different pillar than the two outer members (Fig. 5-12). These are the outside and the center members. Spike these together with 12d nails spaced as shown in Fig. 5-12.

Place the two-member component on the pillars and against the strap anchor. Nail the anchor to the sill as shown in Fig. 5-13, with 10d nails. Position the third

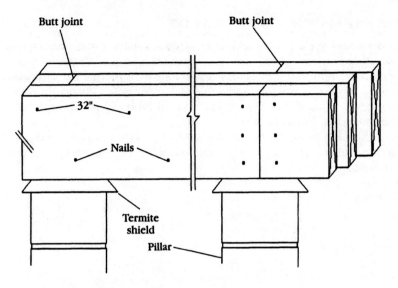

Butt joint   Butt joint

32"

Nails

Termite
shield

Pillar

5-12 Using a built-up sill beam.

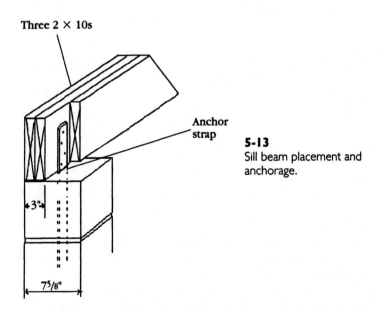

Three 2 × 10s

Anchor
strap

5-13
Sill beam placement and
anchorage.

3"

7⁵/₈"

member, the inside piece, in place, mark the location of the anchor on the member, and notch out to allow the sill members to fit tightly. Nail the third member in place with 12d nails, staggering the nails as in the first member.

Concrete-block pillars should have all cells filled with concrete to ensure a solid anchorage of the framing.

ESTIMATING MATERIALS AND LABOR

In this and remaining chapters, we'll be estimating materials and framing labor. Material estimating is referred to as *taking off* quantities, or just plain *take off*.

When taking off quantities from a plan, follow the sequence of construction: foundation, floor, walls, ceilings, and roof. This reduces the chance of overlooking something, an easy thing to do. In practice, you'll probably group together all lumber of the same description on a separate sheet.

Use a checklist when taking off material quantities since no one can be expected to remember all the items required. The following can serve as a guideline:

- Batter boards
- Beams
- Blocking
- Bracing
- Bridging
- Building paper
- Columns
- Cornice
- Cripples
- Door frames
- Dormers
- Fascia
- Flashing
- Framing clips
- Furring
- Girders
- Headers
- Hip jacks
- Insulation board
- Jack rafters
- Joists, ceiling
- Joists, floor
- Ledgers
- Nails
- Pillar pads
- Plates
- Porches
- Posts
- Rafters
- Ribbons
- Ridges
- Roof edging
- Roof trusses
- Scaffolding
- Sheathing, roof
- Sheathing, wall
- Sills
- Sleepers
- Soffit
- Stairs
- Straps
- Studs
- Subfloor
- Timber connectors
- Trimmers
- Valley flashing
- Valley jacks
- Vents
- Window frames
- Windows

Arrange and list the items in a systematic way so you can find them at any time without having to go through the plan or complete take-off list. You always need to know where each piece of lumber in the stack fits into the framing. Here's what you should include as a minimum on a framing material list:

- The number of pieces of each size
- The thickness of the lumber
- The width of each piece
- The length of each piece
- The grade of lumber
- The wood species
- Nail sizes and quantities

Table 5-1 is a nail chart. You might want to tab this page for quick reference because I'll be referring to the nail sizes used for various framing tasks throughout the book. Table 5-2 gives the nailing schedule for framing and sheathing tasks. It also helps to know approximately how many nails you get in a pound.

Nail size	Number	Nail size	Number
2d	876	16d	49
3d	568	20d	31
4d	316	30d	24
6d	181	40d	18
8d	106	50d	14
10d	69	60d	11
12d	63		

Figure 5-14 is an estimate sheet that lists materials by the construction sequence. You can use this sheet, or one like it, to calculate your material and labor estimates.

Table 5-1 Nail chart

Penny (d) sizes

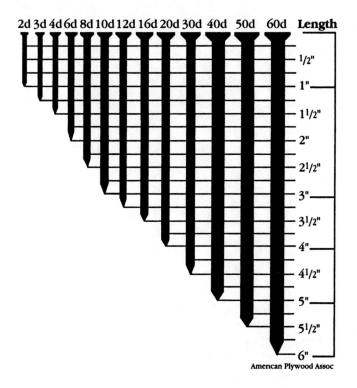

American Plywood Assoc

Table 5-2 Recommended nailing schedule

Joining	Nailing method	Number	Nails (size and placement)
Header to joist	end-nail	3	16d
Joist to sill/girder	toe-nail	2	10d or
		3	8d
Header and stringer joist to sill	toe-nail		10d 16" oc
Bridging to joist	toe-nail each end	2	6d
Ledger to beam	face-nail	3	16d at each joist
Subfloor panels			
at edges	face-nail		8d 6" oc
at intermediate joist	face-nail		8d 8" oc
Subfloor (2 × 6 T&G) to joist/girder	blind-nail (casing) & face-nail	2	16d
Sole plate to stud			
horizontal assembly	end-nail	2	16d at each stud
top plate to stud	end-nail	2	16d at each stud
Stud to sole plate (upright assembly)	toe-nail	4	8d
Sole plate to joist or blocking	face-nail		16d 16" oc
Double studs	face-nail, stagger		10d 16" oc
End stud of tee wall to ext. wall stud	face-nail		16d 16" oc
Upper top plate to lower top plate	face-nail		16d 16" oc
Upper top plate, laps & intersections	face-nail	2	16d
Ceiling joist to top wall plate	toe-nail	3	8d
Ceiling joist laps at partition	face-nail	4	16d
Rafter to top plate	toe-nail	2	8d
Rafter to ceiling joist	face-nail	5	10d
Rafter to valley or hip rafter	toe-nail	3	10d
Ridge board to rafter	end-nail	3	10d
Rafter to ridge board	toe-nail	3	10d or 4 8d
Collar beam to rafter			
2" member	face-nail	2	12d
1" member	face-nail	3	8d
1" diagonal let-in brace			
each stud & sole plate		2	8d
2-member top plate		4	8d
Built-up corner studs			
to blocking	face-nail	2	10d each side
to intersecting wall tee	face-nail		16d 12" oc
Built-up girders/beams, 3 or more members	face-nail		20d 32" oc each side
Wall sheathing, vertically applied plywood or OSB	face-nail		8d 6" edge 12" intermed

Joining	Nailing method	Number	Nails (size and placement)
Wall sheathing, vertically applied plywood or OSB	face-nail		8d 6" edge 12" intermed
Wall sheathing, vertically applied fiberboard	face-nail		1½" roofing nail, 3" edge & 6" intermediate
Roof sheathing panels	face-nail		8d 6" edge & 12" intermed

Task	Material size	Qty.	Unit	BF	Nails size qty.	Price	Labor hrs.
Batter board							
Termite shield							
Sills							
Double plate							
Single plate							
Built-up							
Post							
Wood							
Metal							
Girder							
Built-up							
Steel							
Ledger							
Floor joist							
Header (band)							
Stringer							
Bridging							
Blocking							
Subflooring							
Wall							
Sole plate							
Studs							
Top plate							
Bracing							
Firestop							
Window header							
Stringers							
Cripples							

5-14 Estimate sheet for materials and labor.

Task	Material size	Qty.	Unit	BF	Nails size qty.		Price	Labor hrs.
Door header								
Stringers								
Cripples								
Ceiling joist								
Bridging								
Blocking								
Purlins								
Rafters								
Ridge								
Purlins								
Bracing								
Band								
Roof trusses								
Gable studs								
Vents								
Wall sheathing								
Roof sheathing								
Building paper								

5-14 Continued.

Estimating materials

Start at one corner and measure around the building. List the sizes, lengths, and number of sills on the estimate sheet. The result is the linear feet of sill needed for the job. Thickness and width measurements of the lumber are listed on the house plan or in the specifications. Generally, sill plates are 2 × 6, 2 × 8, or 2 × 10. Sill beams can be 4 × 6, 6 × 6, or larger. Built-up sill beams can be three 2 × 8s, 2 × 10s, or 2 × 12s spiked together, depending on the span and load.

Estimating labor

Allow for three skilled and two unskilled hours to measure, grout with sealer, and bolt in place 100 linear feet of sill plate. Built-up sill beams require 1.25 skilled hours and 0.5 unskilled hours per 100 BF (board feet) to build and install. A 20-foot beam built up with three 2 × 10s requires 100 BF.

6
Girders

The girder is the center support for a structure, and is a major component of house construction (see Fig. 6-1). A centerline girder lets you use shorter and smaller floor joists. The load-bearing interior partition rests on the girder. As illustrated in Fig. 6-2, the girder supports key elements of the house.

Figures 6-1 and 6-2 are for crawlspace construction. In basement construction, wood or steel posts are used to support a wood or steel girder. Concrete block pillars (piers) and treated wood posts are commonly used in crawlspaces.

STEEL-POST GIRDER SUPPORT

In basement construction, four-inch-diameter steel posts work well as girder supports. The house plan will specify post spacing, which is usually eight to ten feet. Use a four-inch, round steel post, with ¼- to ½-inch-thick steel bearing plates at each end. Anchor the top of the post securely to the girder. You can mount the base plate to the footing using the floor slab as an anchor, as illustrated in Fig. 6-3, or use a concrete pedestal as a base and attach the post plate to the top of it.

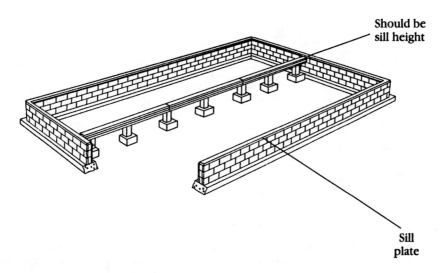

Should be
sill height

Sill
plate

6-1 The centerline girder. Amencan Plywood Assoc

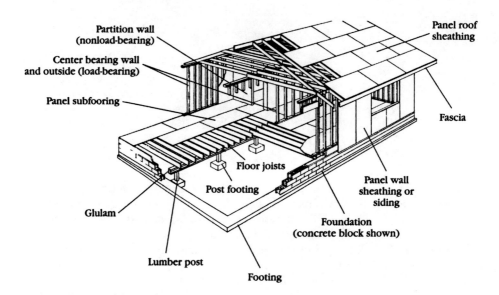

Partition wall
(nonload-bearing)

Center bearing wall
and outside (load-bearing)

Panel subfooring

Glulam

Lumber post

Post footing

Floor joists

Footing

Foundation
(concrete block shown)

Panel wall
sheathing or
siding

Fascia

Panel roof
sheathing

6-2 Girder loads. Amencan Plywood Assoc

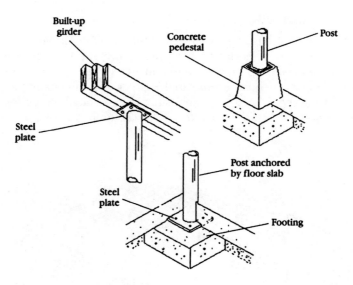

Built-up
girder

Steel
plate

Steel
plate

Concrete
pedestal

Post

Post anchored
by floor slab

Footing

6-3 Steel post installation.

WOOD-POST GIRDER SUPPORT

Wood posts used in a basement to support a girder should be solid and no smaller than 6" × 6". When the post is installed in a 2 × 4 wall frame, you can use a 4 × 6 to match the stud depth. Square the post on both ends.

Attach the wood post securely to the girder, as shown in Fig. 6-4. Support the bottom of the post on a masonry pedestal that extends two to three inches above the finish floor, and pin the post to the pedestal. A preservative-treated post assures a long post life free from termite and moisture. An elevated, steel post base can also be used.

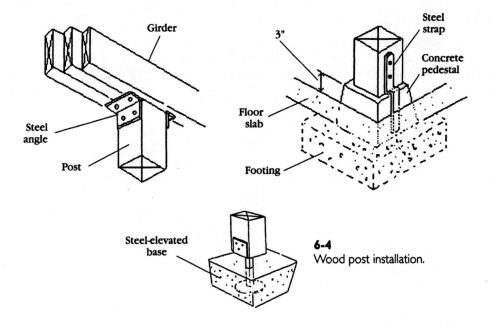

6-4
Wood post installation.

You can also use treated wood posts in crawlspace construction. Determine the length of posts at each location by stretching a taut line from opposite sill plates. Measure down from the line to the post footing, subtract the girder depth from the dimension, and cut the post to length. The post should be anchored to the footing with an anchor rod or bar. Figure 6-5 explains.

You can install a piece of 15-pound asphalt-impregnated building felt between the concrete footing and post as an added precaution in damp areas.

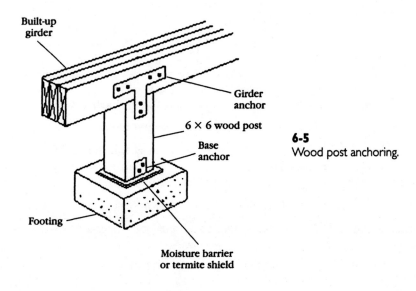

6-5
Wood post anchoring.

POST LOADING

The distribution of loads on a post is illustrated in Fig. 6-6. The girder is joined over the post and supported by the foundation wall at each end. The post supports half the total girder load on each side, making the load on the post half the girder weight plus half the load carried by each length of girder.

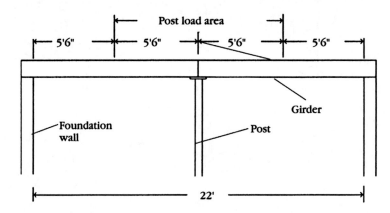

6-6 Post loading.

CALCULATING LOADS

Girder loads can be determined fairly easily. Let's use a two-story house, 24 feet wide and 48 feet long, as an example. The house has a basement and the average total load on floors is 40 psf (pounds per square foot). (More on floor loads later in this chapter.) You can find the total load on the girder by multiplying 12 (half the house width) by 48 feet (the length), which gives you 576 square feet:

$$\begin{array}{r} 576 \text{ sq. ft. (first floor)} \\ + \underline{\,576\,} \text{ sq. ft. (second floor)} \\ 1152 \text{ sq. ft.} \\ \times \underline{\,\,40\,} \text{ psf} \\ 46{,}080 \text{ pounds total girder load} \end{array}$$

Posts are generally spaced 10 feet apart. Thus, in a 48-foot length there would be four posts spaced 10 feet apart, which would give you four girder spans at 10 feet and one girder span at eight feet. First, find the load per linear foot of girder:

$$46{,}080 \text{ lbs} \div 48 \text{ feet} = 960 \text{ pounds per linear foot}$$

As previously stated, a post will carry half the girder weight plus half the load supported by each girder span. Thus, posts spaced 10 feet apart will carry 10 linear feet of the girder load minus five feet to each side:

$$960 \times 10 \text{ linear feet} = 9{,}600 \text{ pounds}$$

In this example, a 48-foot house would have one post spaced eight feet from the foundation wall, which is:

$$5 + \tfrac{1}{2} \text{ of } 8 = 9 \times 960 = 8{,}640$$

Three post loads of 9,600 = 28,800
One post load of 8,640 = 8,640
Floor weight supported at walls = 3,840 + 4,800 = 8,640 pounds
Total floor load = 28,800 + 8,640 + 8,640 = 46,080

Figure 6-7 illustrates these equations.

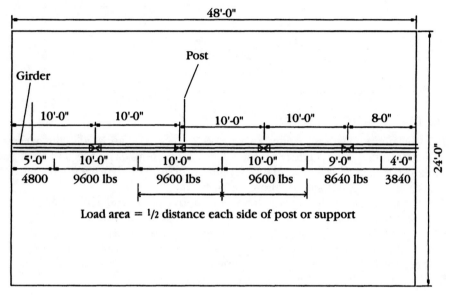

6-7 Girder and post loads.

If you know how much weight a girder and a post must carry, you can determine the post size. The loads imposed on a post are called *compressive* and tend to bend the column unless the cross-section size is a certain proportion to the length. Table 6-1 gives the maximum loads, in pounds, for Douglas fir or no. 1 southern pine for various heights. A seven-foot-long basement post in a 6 × 6 size would be required to support 28,800 pounds. Table 6-2 shows steel-post load capabilities.

Table 6-1 Maximum post loads

Height of post	Size of post				
	4 × 4	4 × 6	6 × 6	6 × 8	8 × 8
4'0"	12,920	19,850	30,250	41,250	56,250
5'0"	12,400	19,200	30,050	41,000	56,250
6'0"	11,600	17,950	29,500	40,260	56,250
6'6"	10,880	16,850	29,300	39,950	56,000
7'0"	10,040	15,550	29,000	39,600	55,600
7'6"	9,300	14,200	28,500	39,000	55,000

Table 6-2 Steel post capacities

Size (inches)	3	3½	4	4½	5	6
Wall thickness (inches)	.216	.226	.237	.247	.258	.280
Length (feet)			Thousand pounds			
5	29.0	34.5	41.2	48.0	55.5	72.5
6	28.5	34.5	41.0	48.0	55.5	72.5
7	26.0	34.0	41 0	48 0	55.5	72.5
8	24.0	31.5	40.0	48.0	55.5	72.5
9	21.7	29 0	37.5	46.0	55.0	72 0
10	19.4	26.5	35.0	43.0	54.0	72.0

BUILT-UP WOOD GIRDERS

While the girders shown in Figs. 6-1 and 6-2 are glue laminated (glulam), most framers fabricate built-up girder on the job site. Solid lumber girders and steel girders are also available. When solid lumber girders are installed, place them so the top is ⅛ inch above the sill plate to allow for shrinkage.

Built-up girders have a proven track record, having been in use for many years. The grains of the individual pieces run differently, giving them a greater stability. A built-up girder is made by spiking together two or more pieces of 2-by lumber, such as a 2 × 10 and 2 × 12. The ends of the pieces should join over a different support. In a three-member built-up girder, the center-member end is staggered to fall over a different support than the two outer members. See Fig. 6-8.

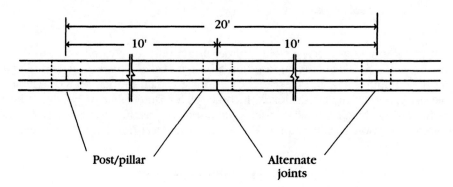

6-8 Built-up wood girder.

Nail a two-member girder from one side with 10d nails, two at the ends and staggered 16 inches apart along the length. A three-member girder is nailed from each side with 20d nails, staggered 32 inches along the length. Drive two 20d nails at each end.

Use straight lumber when building a girder. Don't make the mistake of turning all the crowns up. The girder will seldom depress over the allowable span. If the lumber is crowned, I reverse the crowns of the individual pieces, draw the members in line with a clamp, and then nail.

For posts or pillars spaced 10 feet apart, start the fabrication with one piece cut to span the dimension from the foundation wall to the center of post no. 1. This will be the center member. The two outer members will span the distance from the foundation wall to the center of post no. 2. Insert the next center member between the outside members to extend from the first post to post no. 3. The next two outer members extend from post no. 2 to post no. 4, and so on to the opposite foundation wall (see Fig. 6-8).

You can nail the first outside member to the center member with 10d nails staggered 16 inches apart, and then nail the other outside member in place with 10d nails 16 inches apart. Don't drive the nails directly opposite those on the other side.

Joining glulam and solid wood girders

Glue-laminated and solid wood girders can be notched and lapped, as shown in Fig. 6-9. This is a half-lap crowned joint, which works well. With glulam and solid wood girders, you want to place the crown up. Use a steel plate or strap to tie the beam over a post. Figure 6-10 shows how to secure the girder to a wood post. In lieu of the half-lap joint, you can secure the solid beams together with steel straps. Use straps at least 18 inches long and bolt to each side of the beam. See Fig. 6-11.

FABRICATED BEAMS

There's an assortment of fabricated beams and joist components available to the framer. Laminated veneer lumber (LVL) is structural-grade timber veneers glued to-

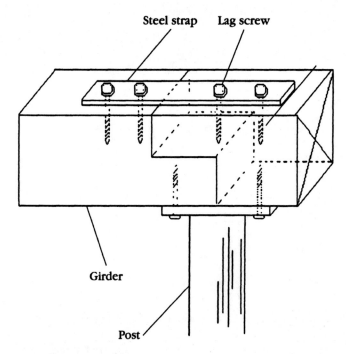

6-9 Installing solid girders.

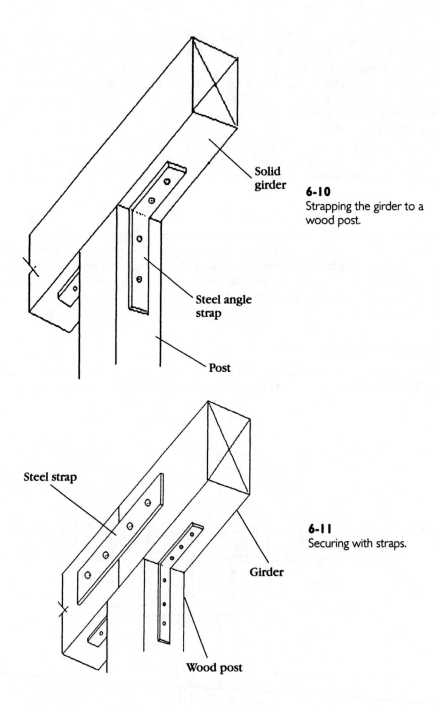

Solid girder

6-10
Strapping the girder to a wood post.

Steel angle strap

Post

Steel strap

6-11
Securing with straps.

Girder

Wood post

gether under pressure to form a dimensional stable and uniform product. LVL won't twist, shrink, or warp like solid lumber.

Wood I beams and joists are available for various spans and loads. Also, truss beams having top and bottom chords of various sizes are built for long spans.

Fabricated framing components are available under various trade names, and they offer the framer a choice when considering materials for projects. Most rough carpenters have at one time or another fabricated a beam by glue-nailing pieces of ¾-inch plywood in a sandwich of various depths. Four pieces of ¾-inch, 16-inch-wide, eight-foot-long pieces glue-nailed in a sandwich and placed between 2 × 4-inch top and bottom flanges makes a beam capable of carrying tremendous loads over a 7'9" span.

GIRDER SPACING

The house plans will indicate whether to a centerline girder or a different configuration calling for two girders. The joist length and depth, and the location of bearing partitions on the floor above determines girder spacing.

Generally, there should not be more than 16 feet between girders. For a 25-foot span, one girder located midway between walls is sufficient. For a 35-foot span, use two girders spaced equally.

Figure 6-12 shows different girder locations. As illustrated, the bearing partitions govern the girder locations. In no. 1, the girder is centerline and there's no bearing partition on the floor above. In no. 2, a bearing partition is midway between the two side walls and the girder is directly under the partition. In no. 3, the bearing partition is 10 feet from one side wall and 16 feet from the other wall. The girder is necessarily under the partition. In no. 4, there are two bearing partitions and each must be supported. In basement construction where a minimum of posts is desired, use a glulam beam for long, uninterrupted spans.

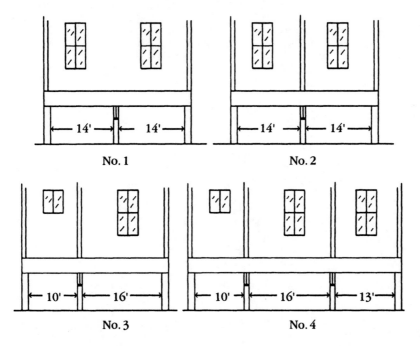

6-12 Girder placement.

The ends of wood girders should bear a minimum of four inches on the masonry wall or pilaster. Where the joists rest on the girder, the top of the girder should be level with the top of the sill plates (see Fig. 6-13).

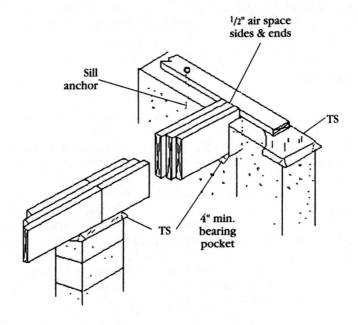

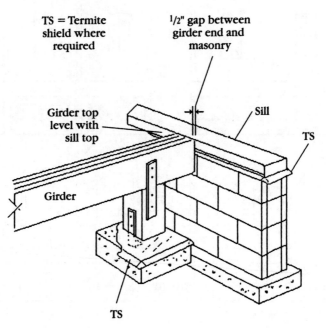

6-13 Girder top aligns with top of sill plate. Amercian Plywood Assoc

When using untreated wood, leave a ½ inch of air space at the ends and sides of the girder. Install a metal termite shield between the wood and masonry in infested areas.

DETERMINING GIRDER SIZE AND STRENGTH

While many framers with years of experience can look at a board and judge whether it qualifies as girder material, you must consider how the length, width, and depth of the girder will affect its strength when deciding what size girder or beam to use. Here's how it works:

Length
A plank that's supported at each end and carries a load evenly distributed along its entire length will bend. A plank twice as long that carries the same load per foot will bend much more and might break. If you double the length, the safe load is reduced to one quarter and not one half as you might suppose. However, if you place a single concentrated load at the center, doubling the length reduces the safe load to only one half.

So the greater the span of the girder, the stronger the girder must be. You can increase girder strength by using a stronger material or a wider or deeper, or both, beam.

Width
Doubling the width of a girder doubles its strength. One double-width girder can carry the same load as two single-width girders placed side by side.

Depth
Doubling a girder's depth permits the girder to carry four times the load. This means that a beam 4½ inches wide and 10 inches deep can support four times the load of a beam 4½ inches wide by 5 inches deep.

STRUCTURAL LOADS

The girder is the main structural support of a house; the building load is carried by the girder and the foundation walls. The ends of the floor joist rest on the girder, which places a greater load on the girder than on the foundation walls. In fact, the girder carries half the weight while the two foundation walls carry the other half, which is split between the two walls if the girder is centered. Girders, of course, aren't always located in the center of the building. What then?

A general rule provides that a girder carries the weight of the floor on each side to the midpoint of joists that rest upon it. Both dead and live loads must be considered in finding the total floor load.

The first category of load to consider consists of all the weight of the building components, called the *dead load*. The dead load per square foot of floor area, which is carried to the girder either directly or indirectly by way of the bearing partitions, will vary due to the method of construction and building height. Building components included in the dead load category are all:
- Floor joists
- Flooring materials
- Bearing partitions
- Attic partitions

- Ceiling joists
- Finish material

Add the dead load allowance per square foot of a frame house to find the total dead load. Allow 10 pounds per square foot for a typical subfloor, finish floor, and joists for the first floor without basement plaster. Allow an additional 10 pounds for plastered basement ceilings, and another 10 pounds per square foot if the attic is floored and used for storage, for a total of 30 psf.

The second category of load is the weight of anything not a part of the structure, such as people and furniture. This is the *live load* and is considered to be 40 psf for a residence. Add to this 20 psf when the attic is floored and used for light storage.

The second floor is generally designed to carry a live load of 30 psf. Roofs are designed for live loads from 12 to 20 psf, depending on area snowfall and roof pitch.

You can determine the load per linear foot on the girder when the total dead and live load per square foot of floor area is known. Figure 6-14 is a structure with a girder located off center, which requires a 16-foot joist length on the left side and a 12-footer on the right. The result is that the girder load span is half the joist span on each side and the foundation walls carry the other half. Half of 16 is 8, plus half of 12, which is 6, so 6 + 8 = 14 feet, the load area we're concerned about.

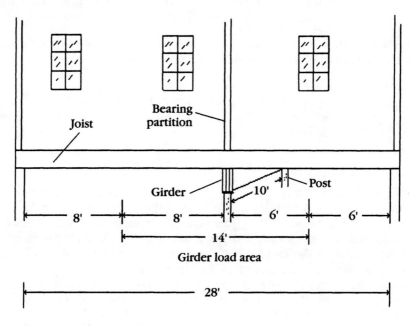

6-14 Computing girder load.

The span of the girder between supports is 10 feet and, assuming the dead plus live load is 60 psf, multiply the length times the load area (10' × 14 = 140 square feet). It looks like this:

$$
\begin{array}{r}
140 \\
\times \underline{\quad 60} \text{ psf load} \\
8,400 \text{ psf total load}
\end{array}
$$

Table 6-3 shows the girder requirements for various configurations, based on FHA recommendations. The values shown are for a structure having a clear-span trussed roof and a load-bearing partition on or within one foot of the center in two-story construction.

Table 6-3 Wood girder spans

Width of bldg.	# of beams and sizes	Maximum clear span			
		1 story		2 stories	
		1000 f*	1500 f*	1000 f*	1500 f*
24'	3 2 × 8s	6'7"	8'1"	——	4'7"
	4 2 × 8s	7'8"	9'4"	5'2"	6'2"
	3 2 × 10s	8'5"	10'4"	4'11"	7'6"
	4 2 × 10s	9'9"	11'11"	5'7"	7'10"
	3 2 × 12s	10'3"	12'7"	6'0"	7'2"
	4 2 × 12s	11'10"	14'6"	8'0"	9'7"
26'	3 2 × 8s	6'4"	7'9"	——	4'3"
	4 2 × 8s	7'4"	9'0"	4'9"	5'8"
	3 2 × 10s	8'1"	9'11"	4'7"	5'6"
	4 2 × 10s	9'4"	11'6"	6'1"	7'3"
	3 2 × 12s	9'10"	12'1"	5'6"	6'8"
	4 2 × 12s	11'5"	13'11"	7'5"	8'10"
28'	3 2 × 8s	6'2"	7'5"	——	——
	4 2 × 8s	7'1"	8'8"	4'5"	5'4"
	3 2 × 10s	7'10"	9'6"	4'3"	5'1"
	4 2 × 10s	9'0"	11'1"	5'8"	6'9"
	3 2 × 12s	9'6"	11'7"	5'2"	6'2"
	4 2 × 12s	11'0"	13'5"	6'10"	8'3"
32'	3 2 × 8s	5'5"	6'6"	——	——
	4 2 × 8s	6'7"	8'1"	——	4'8"
	3 2 × 10s	6'11"	8'4"	——	4'6"
	4 2 × 10s	8'5"	10'4"	5'0"	6'0"
	3 2 × 12s	8'5"	10'2"	4'6"	5'2"
	4 2 × 12s	10'3"	12'7"	6'0"	7'3"

* Allowable bending stress of the lumber

The values shown assume a clear-span trussed roof and load-bearing center partition in a two-story construction Beams and/or load-bearing partitions can be offset from the centerline of the house up to one foot. (Based on data from Manual of Lumber and Plywood Savings, NAHB Research Foundation, Inc.)

Courtesy: U.S Dept. HUD

No. 2 southern pine, no. 1 lodgepole pine, no. 2 Douglas fir-larch, and no. 2 hem-fir are some of the species having an allowable bending stress not less than 1,000 psi. A no. 1 grade of the species has an allowable bending stress of not less than 1,500 psi.

Table 6-4 gives the allowable span between supports for steel and wood girders. Table 6-5 offers a birds-eye view of wood and steel girder sizes, columns and footings under various loading conditions to support roofs, interior bearing partitions, and floors. The placement of "S" girders is shown in Fig. 6-15. The steel designations shown in Tables 6-4 and 6-5, such as S5x10, M10x9, and W6x12, mean:

S
Standard beam (formerly I beam).

M
H or light beam (junior).

W
W beam (formerly wide flange beam).

Table 6-4 Steel girder spans

Size of wood girder[1]	Size of steel girder[3]	Floor live load (in lbs. per sq. ft.)	"S" spacing of girders[2] 4'	6'	8'	10'	16'
4" × 4"	——	——	30	5'6"	4'6"	3'6"	3'0"	2'6"
			40	5'0"	4'0"	3'6"	3'0"	2'6"
4" × 6"	——	——	30	8'0"	6'6"	5'6"	5'0"	4'6"
			40	7'6"	6'0"	5'6"	4'6"	4'0"
4" × 8"	6" × 6"	S3 × 5.7	30	11'0"	9'0"	8'0"	7'0"	5'6"
			40	10'0"	8'6"	7'6"	6'6"	5'0"
4" × 10"	6" × 8"	S4 × 7 7	30	14'0"	11'6"	10'0"	8'6"	6'0"
		M6 × 4.4	40	13'0"	10'6"	9'6"	8'6"	5'6"
4" × 12"	6" × 10"	S5 × 10	30	16'6"	14'0"	12'0"	11'0"	9'0"
		M7 × 5.5	40	16'0"	12'6"	11'0"	10'0"	8'0"

[1] Spans based on no 2 or standard-grade lumber

[2] "S" is the tributary load of the girder It is found by adding unsupported spans of the floor joists on each side, which are supported by the girder, and dividing by 2

[3] Steel members indicated are adequate typical examples; other steel members meeting structural requirements can be used

Courtesy. CABO

Table 6-5 Wood and steel girder sizes

Girder size required Wood[1]	Steel[5]	"S" spacing of girders[3]	Type of loading[2] A	B	C	Size of column[4] Steel Wood	Footing[4] Size
4 × 12	S5 × 10	10'	5'6"	—	—		
or		15'	4'0"	—	—		
6 × 10	M7 × 5.5	20'				4' × 4'	2' × 2'
6 × 12	S5 × 14 75	10'	8'6"	5'0"		3"	
	M10 × 9	15'	6'0"	4'0"	—	steel	
	W6 × 12	20'	4'6"	—	—	pipe	

Table 6-5 Continued

Girder size required Wood[1]	Steel[5]	"S" spacing of girders[2]	Type of loading[3] A	B	C	Size of column[4] Steel	Wood	Footing[4] Size
	S7 × 15 3	10'	12'0"	9'0"	8'0"			
—	M12 × 11.8	15'	10'0"	8'0"	7'0"		6' × 6'	4' × 4'
	W8 × 15	20'	8'0"	7'0"	6'0"			
—	S10 × 25 4	10'	16'0"	12'6"	11'0"			
	W8 × 24	15'	13'6"	10'6"	10'0"			
		20'	12'0"	9'6"	8'0"		8' × 8'	4'3" × 4'3"
—	W14 × 22	10'	20'0"	16'0"	13'6"			
	W10 × 29	15'	17'0"	13'6"	11'6"			
		20'	15'0"	12'0"	10'0"			

[1] Spans for wood girders are based on no 2 or standard-grade lumber.

[2] The "S" spacing is the tributary load to the girder It is found by adding the unsupported spans of the floor joists on each side, which are supported by the girder, and dividing by 2

[3] Figures under type of loading columns are the allowable girder spans.

[4] Required column size is based on girder support from two sides. Size of footing is based on allowable soil pressure of 2000 lbs psf

[5] Steel members listed are typical examples

Courtesy: CABO

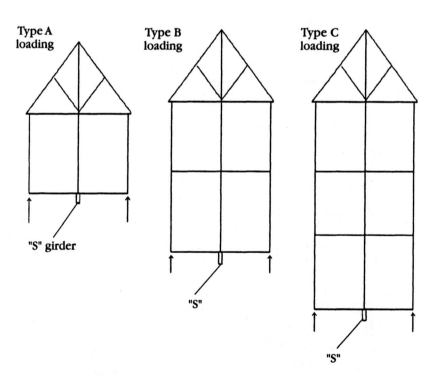

6-15 Placement of "S" girders.

LOAD COMBINATIONS

The Uniform Building Code requires every building component to be provided with strength to resist the most severe effects resulting from the following combination of loads:

- Dead + floor live + roof live (or snow)
- Dead + floor live + wind (or seismic)
- Dead + floor live + wind + snow
- Dead + floor live + snow + wind
- Dead + floor live + snow + seismic

A structure, then, must not only be of sufficient strength and stiffness to accommodate "average" living conditions, but also be able to absorb maximum loads, as when a lot of people gather in a room. An old carpenter once remarked, "You got to build 'em strong enough to hold up the expected and unexpected—like having a Thanksgiving crowd over during a blizzard!"

Look at Fig. 6-16. In conventional "stick framing," the roof loads are carried by the outer walls and the partition. This means that the girder supports the first-floor joist load, the bearing partitions, the second-floor load, the second-floor partitions, the first- and second-floor ceilings, the attic, and roof loads. Picture what would happen if the girder broke. The numbers in Fig. 6-16 are:

- First-floor dead load = 10 psf, 20 psf with plastered basement ceiling (1)
- First floor live load = 40 psf (2)
- Partition dead load = 10 psf (3)
- Second floor dead load = 20 psf (4)
- Second floor live load = 40 psf (5)

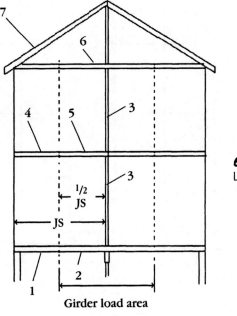

6-16
Load combinations.

Girder load area

JS = Joist span

- Attic floor live load (floored) = 20 psf when used for storage only (6)
- Attic floor dead floor (unfloored) = 10 psf (6)
- Roof dead + live load = 20 psf, maybe more depending on roofing materials (7)

When in doubt concerning local load requirements, check with the local building authority. The combined square-foot load for the house (Fig. 6-16) is:

$$
\begin{array}{r}
10 \\
40 \\
20\ (10 + 10) \\
20 \\
40 \\
10 - 30 \\
\underline{20} \\
160 - 180
\end{array}
$$

The girder must be capable of carrying a minimum load of 160 to 180 psf, depending on whether the attic is floored.

GIRDER LOADING PER LINEAR FOOT

Table 6-6 shows girder loading per linear foot under various floor loads and spans. Keep in mind that the loading area is half the distance between posts or supports. In Table 6-6, column 5 indicates that the load span is five feet (2½ feet along each side of the post). Column 6 has three feet to each side of the post, and so on. These are the "half widths."

Table 6-6 Girder loads per linear foot

Total sq. ft. floor load (pounds)	Total load per					
	5 lf	6 lf	7 lf	8 lf	9 lf	10 lf
40	200	240	280	320	360	400
50	250	300	350	400	450	500
60	300	360	420	480	540	600
70	350	420	490	560	630	700
80	400	480	560	640	720	800
90	450	540	630	720	810	900
100	500	600	700	800	900	1000

To find the total 160-psf load, add the 60 and 100 in the first column for a total of 800 pounds per linear foot for a five-foot span. For a 10-foot span, a 160-psf load is 1,600 pounds per linear foot (lf).

A 180-psf load can be found in the same manner using Table 6-6. Simply add the 80 and 100 of the first column for the span required.

THE TOTAL GIRDER LOAD

You can find the total girder load by multiplying the load per linear foot by the girder span between posts, in feet. Table 6-6 shows that a 180-psf load on a girder having a 10-lf load area (five feet to each side of the post) is 1,800 pounds per linear foot times 10, the distance in feet between supports. The total girder load is 1,800 × 10 = 18,000 pounds, which is, of course, spread equally over the full length of the girder. This is a uniformly distributed load.

ESTIMATING MATERIALS

Table 6-7 shows the board feet required for each linear foot of a built-up girder. Allow five percent for waste. Use 10d and 20d nails, as discussed earlier. Table 6-7 gives the approximate number of nails required per 1,000 lf.

Table 6-7
Materials for built-up girders

Girder size	Board feet per lf	Nails per 1000 BF
4 × 6	2	53
4 × 8	2.66	40
4 × 10	3.33	32
4 × 12	4	26
6 × 6	3	43
6 × 8	4	32
6 × 10	5	26
6 × 12	6	22
8 × 8	5.33	30
8 × 10	6.66	24
8 × 12	8	20

ESTIMATING LABOR

Allow 3.3 hours per 100 board feet for 2 × 8 built-up girders. For 2 × 10 built-ups, allow 2.5 hours per 100 board feet. Labor includes fabrication and installation.

Let's do an example. A 48-foot-long house requires a centerline girder constructed of three 2 × 10s. Table 6-7 shows that a 6 × 10 (nominal size) girder has five BF per linear foot, so a 6 × 10, 48-foot girder would be 240 BF. The hours required, therefore, are 2.4 × 2.5 = 6 hours.

7
Floor joists

Rigidity is essential in floor framing. In residential construction, you want to avoid "spring" in a floor. While most frame floors are built using solid 2-by lumber, manufactured wood floor-joist systems are widely available.

MANUFACTURED JOISTS

Manufactured joists are engineered components made up from an assortment of wood products, such as solid wood (2 × 2s or 2 × 4s) and laminated wood (plywood or OSB) with glue, staples, etc. These engineered products go by names like Gang-Lams, Inner-Seal I joists (of Louisiana-Pacific Co.), GNI joists, and wood I beams (of Georgia-Pacific Co.). Floor trusses are designed and built for long spans and heavy loads.

I joists

An I joist (Fig. 7-1) has a bottom and top flange with a plywood or OSB panel center, or *web*. The flanges can be solid wood or laminated veneer lumber (LVL). I joists

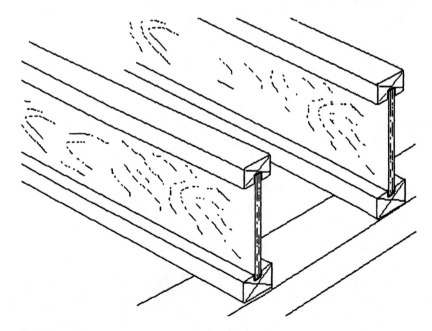

7-1 The I joist.

are available in depths ranging from 9½" to 24", depending on flange type and size. The thickness of the web can be increased to handle longer spans and greater loads.

The GNI I joist is manufactured with Gang-Lam LVL flanges and OSB webs. The joist is available in depths of 9¼", 11⅞", 14", and 16". (Depths up to 24" are available for light commercial construction.) Table 7-1 gives the span capability of a GNI having a two-inch bearing at each end.

Table 7-1 Maximum spans for I joists

oc (in)	Joist depth (inches) 9¼		11¼		40 LL + 15 DL* 14		16	
	1/360	1/480	1/360	1/480	1/360	1/480	1/360	1/480
12	18'1"	16'4"	22'1"	20'0"	26'8"	24'2"	29'7"	26'10"
16	16'4"	14'10"	20'0"	18'1"	24'2"	21'10"	26'10"	24'3"
19.2	15'5"	13'11"	18'9"	17'0"	22'8"	20'6"	25'2"	22'10"
24	14'3"	12'11"	17'5"	15'9"	21'0"	19'0"	23'3"	21'1"

* 40 lbs live load + 15 lbs dead load

Figure 7-2 shows the method of nailing joist to plate, and Fig. 7-3 illustrates installing the rim joist to each floor joist using one 10d nail per flange. When installing I joists:
- Do not cut or notch the flange.
- Do not drill the flange.

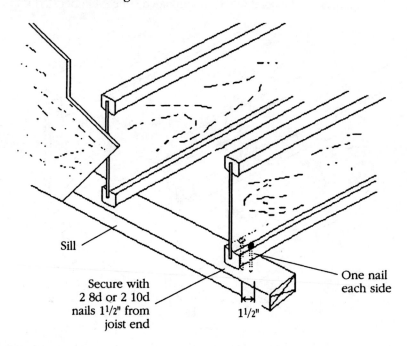

Sill

Secure with
2 8d or 2 10d
nails 1½" from
joist end

1½"

One nail
each side

7-2 Nailing the I joist.

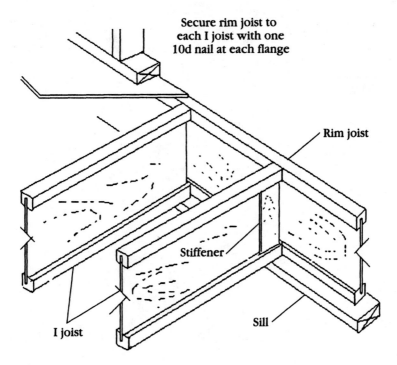

Secure rim joist to
each I joist with one
10d nail at each flange

Rim joist

Stiffener

I joist

Sill

7-3 Nailing the rim joist.

- Do not use 16d nails.
- Do not overcut the hole in the web.
- Do not cut web holes too close to the supports.

INSTALLATION TIPS

Use care when installing I joists. Most manufactured joists won't support you until properly braced to prevent "give way" of the system or buckling of the flanges. Each joist end should be secured as it's installed with continuous-closure (header) or blocking panels. Additionally, lay a 1 × 4 across the top of the joists at a right angle to the joist run. Secure the 1 × 4 brace to the top flange of each joist with two 8d nails. Lap the ends of the brace over at least two joists and locate the brace either midway between the supports or no farther apart than 12 feet. Figure 7-4 explains.

Use the upper surface of the top flange to support concentrated loads. Don't suspend loads from the bottom flange. Comply with your local code for I-joist installation and the fastening of sheathing.

A 1½-inch bearing is required for joists up to 15 inches in depth. Joists 16 inches or more in depth must have at least a two-inch bearing. Don't install I joists in contact with masonry. Make sure the joists have at least 18 inches of clearance above finish grade.

Install bridging on joists over 16 inches in depth having spans exceeding 28 feet. Panel subflooring (plywood or OSB) nailed or glued to the top flange will prevent in-service lateral movement on most styles of I joists having a depth of less than 16 inches.

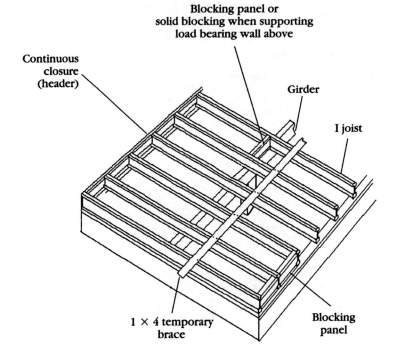

Continuous closure (header)

Blocking panel or solid blocking when supporting load bearing wall above

Girder

I joist

1 × 4 temporary brace

Blocking panel

7-4 Installing I joists.

Use two 10d nails to install plywood continuous closure to ends of joists, one nail face-driven into each flange. Use two 12d nails for solid (2-by) lumber closure.

Figure 7-5 illustrates I joists bearing on a stud wall, and Fig. 7-6 shows I joists bearing on a masonry foundation wall. Floor openings that might be required for stairs or fireplaces are shown in Fig. 7-7. Use a header beam designed for the span and load.

FLOOR TRUSSES

Open-web, flat, floor trusses are engineered components designed to support heavy loads over long spans. A well-designed open-web truss having a 20-inch depth will span 28 feet and provide a stiff floor. Trusses are commonly constructed of 2 × 4s with galvanized steel connector plates. Figure 7-8 shows an open-web flat truss. This type of truss is also used in flat roof construction. The trusses are precision-built using machinery (see Figs. 7-9 and 7-10).

Open-web floor trusses having steel diagonal members in combination with wood top and bottom flanges are also available. This truss system is effective in reducing springy floors and sag.

Floor trusses allow greater flexibility in locating bearing walls and partitions. The truss can be spaced farther apart than dimensional lumber. The 2 × 4 flanges are 3½ inches wide, providing more surface for nailing and gluing. Ductwork, wiring, and pipe can be installed through the open webs without cutting or notching (see Figs. 7-11 and 7-12).

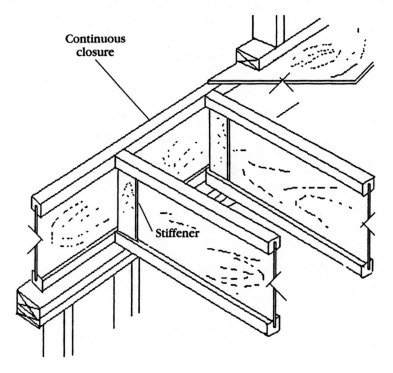

7-5 I joist bearing on a stud wall.

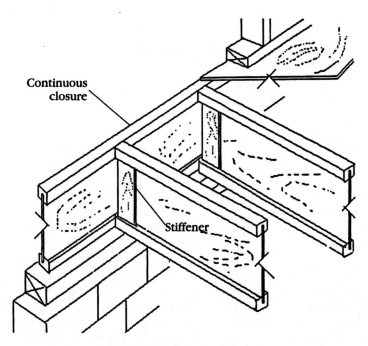

7-6 I joist bearing on a masonry foundation wall.

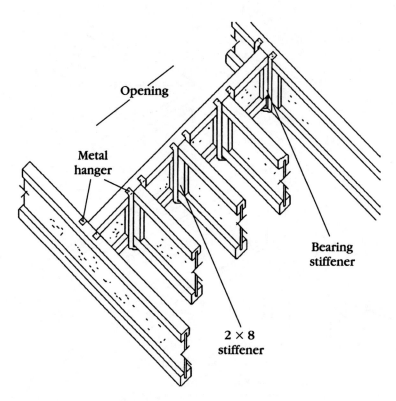

7-7 Framing the I-beam floor opening.

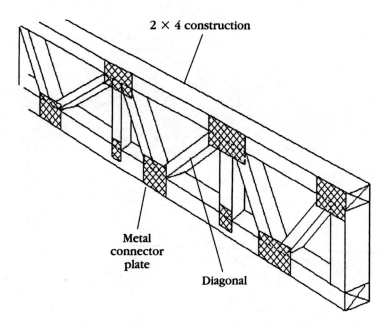

7-8 Open-web flat truss.

7-9 Preparing to install connectors.

7-10 Connectors pressed in at each joint.

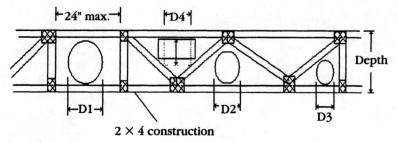

D = Duct

Depth	12"	14"	16"	18"	20"	22"
D1	9	11	13	15	17	19
D2	$7^3/8$	$8^7/8$	10	$11^1/8$	$12^1/2$	$13^3/8$
D3	$5^5/8$	$6^1/2$	$7^1/4$	8	$8^1/2$	9
D4	$13^1/2$	$13^1/2$	$13^1/2$	$13^1/2$	$13^1/2$	14
D5	4	5	6	$6^1/2$	$7^1/2$	$8^1/2$

7-11 Duct dimensions in a short web truss.

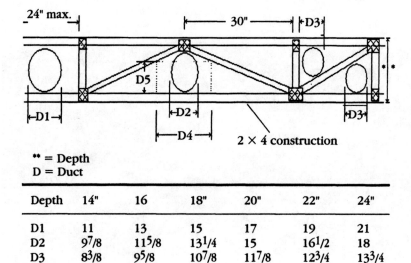

** = Depth
D = Duct

Depth	14"	16	18"	20"	22"	24"
D1	11	13	15	17	19	21
D2	$9^7/8$	$11^5/8$	$13^1/4$	15	$16^1/2$	18
D3	$8^3/8$	$9^5/8$	$10^7/8$	$11^7/8$	$12^3/4$	$13^3/4$
D4	$13^1/2$	$13^1/2$	14	14	15	16
D5	$7^1/2$	9	$10^1/2$	12	13	14

7-12 Duct dimensions in a long web truss.

Floor truss spans

An open-web truss can be designed to span most house depths without benefit of girder or wall support. A 20-inch-deep truss spaced 16 inches on center can span 32 feet. A 12-inch-deep web truss spaced 16 inches would do a good job on a house depth of 32 feet with a centerline girder. Table 7-2 shows some span capabilities of web trusses having steel diagonal members.

You can use steel truss hangers to "hang" web trusses by the bottom chord (see Fig. 7-13). Form the hanger over the top of the header or beam with four 10d nails. Face-nail the hanger to the header with eight 10d nails, four to each side. Slant-nail through the hanger with four 10d nails to penetrate through the corner of the truss into the header or beam. This is called *double-shear nailing*, as explained in Fig. 7-13.

Table 7-2 Clear spans for open-web flat trusses with steel diagonals

LIVE LOAD	40 PSF				50 PSF				80 PSF				100 PSF			
SPACING	12"	16"	19.2"	24"	12"	16"	19.2"	24"	12"	16"	19.2"	24"	12"	16"	19.2"	24"
						4 × 2 no. 2 MC 19 so, pine										
11 1/4"	20'2"	18'6"	17'10"	15'2"	18'9"	18'0"	15'5"	14'7"	16'11"	14'7"	13'6"	11'2"	14'11"	13'7"	11'2"	10'9"
12"	22'6"	19'4"	18'6"	15'5"	20'10"	18'6"	17'1"	14'11"	17'11"	14'11"	14'4"	11'4"	15'2"	14'3"	11'4"	10'10"
14"	23'10"	22'2"	19'3"	18'2"	22'6"	19'5"	18'6"	16'9"	18'10"	17'0"	14'11"	14'1"	15'9"	14'10"	14'3"	11'2"
16"	26'6"	23'1"	21'10"	18'11"	25'4"	22'1"	19'2"	18'2"	19'7"	18'4"	15'4"	14'8"	18'9"	15'3"	14'8"	13'9"
						4 × 2 no. 1 MC 19 so. pine										
11 1/4"	21'10"	18'9"	18'6"	17'4"	19'2"	18'6"	17'4"	15'3"	16'3"	14'11"	14'6"	13'10"	15'3"	14'6"	13'10"	11'3"
12"	22'6"	19'8"	18'7"	18'3"	20'1"	18'6"	18'3"	17'0"	18'3"	15'7"	14'9"	14'5"	16'10"	14'7"	14'6"	13'1"
14"	24'4"	22'6"	22'0"	19'4"	22'7"	21'9"	19'4"	18'6"	19'2"	18'6"	17'5"	14'11"	18'6"	15'7"	15'0"	14'5"
16"	26'10"	25'9"	22'10"	22'0"	26'4"	22'7"	22'6"	19'2"	22'6"	19'3"	18'6"	15'3"	19'8"	18'6"	17'2"	14'9"
						4 × 2 sel str MC 19 so. pine										
11 1/4"	22'6"	19'4"	18'6"	18'1"	20'11"	18'6"	18'0"	15'9"	18'0"	15'5"	14'6"	14'5"	15'9"	14'6"	14'5"	13'2"
12"	22'7"	21'6"	19'3"	18'6"	22'1"	19'0"	18'6"	17'7"	18'6"	17'1"	15'2"	14'6"	17'6"	15'0"	14'6"	14'0"
14"	26'6"	22'10"	22'6"	21'3"	23'4"	22'6"	21'1"	18'8"	20'0"	18'6"	18'2"	16'9"	18'7"	17'11"	15'10"	14'9"
16"	27'9"	26'6"	25'1"	22'6"	26'6"	23'4"	22'6"	21'8"	22'6"	21'2"	18'10"	18'6"	21'7"	18'8"	18'6"	17'1"
						4 × 2 no. 2 doug fir										
11 1/4"	21'5"	18'6"	18'1"	15'2"	18'10"	18'2"	15'4"	14'8"	17'0"	14'8"	11'8"	11'2"	15'0"	13'11"	11'2"	10'9"
12"	22'6"	19'4"	18'6"	16'11"	19'9"	18'6"	15'7"	14'11"	17'11"	14'11"	14'6"	13'0"	15'3"	14'6"	13'4"	10'11"
14"	23'10"	22'6"	19'4"	18'6"	22'6"	20'9"	18'8"	17'0"	18'10"	17'3"	14'11"	14'3"	18'2"	14'10"	14'6"	12'11"
16"	26'6"	23'3"	19'11"	19'0"	23'10"	22'5"	19'2"	18'5"	19'7"	18'6"	17'0"	14'8"	18'10"	15'3"	14'8"	14'0"
						4 × 2 no. 1 doug fir										
11 1/4"	21'10"	18'9"	18'6"	17'4"	19'2"	18'6"	17'4"	15'2"	17'4"	14'11"	14'6"	13'6"	15'3"	14'6"	13'8"	11'1"
12"	22'6"	19'8"	18'7"	18'2"	20'1"	18'6"	18'3"	15'4"	18'3"	15'5"	14'9"	14'0"	15'9"	14'7"	14'3"	12'9"
14"	25'9"	22'6"	22'0"	19'0"	22'7"	20'1"	19'3"	18'5"	19'2"	18'6"	15'4"	14'9"	16'4"	15'4"	14'9"	14'0"
16"	26'10"	25'9"	22'10"	21'6"	26'4"	22'7"	22'1"	18'11"	22'5"	19'0"	18'5"	15'1"	19'4"	18'4"	16'9"	14'6"

Notes: Spans include a 3 1/2" brg. each end with 10 psf dead load on the top chord and 5 psf dead load on the bottom chord.
Spans are limited to L/360 live load deflection, a length to depth ratio of 24.

Courtesy: Alpine Engineered Products, Inc.

SOLID WOOD JOISTS

Solid wood joists (dimensional lumber) will be with us a long time. It's the conventional way to frame a floor. The key to a strong, rigid floor is to know your lumber—which species, size, and span will do the job. To overspan is to create problems!

Floor joists in a multistory structure have a dual task; they must support both the floor load and the ceiling of the story below. Obviously, this requires a larger joist,

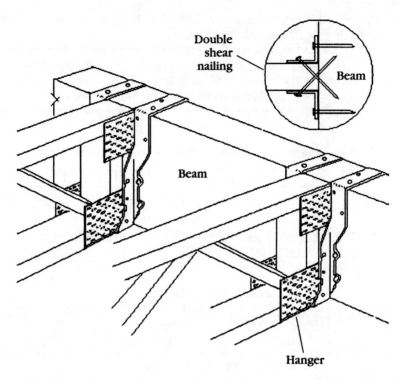

Double shear nailing

Beam

Beam

Hanger

7-13 Installing truss hangers.

such as a 2 × 10 or 2 × 12. A ceiling joist is commonly a 2 × 6 or 2 × 8, depending on the span.

In conventional framing, floor joists are doubled under partitions parallel to the joist run. The joists are also doubled under bathtubs in many plans.

JOIST SPACING

The size of subfloor sheathing panels (4' × 8') dictate the spacing of floor joists. Joist spacing of 16 inches on center is common. Other spacings are 12", 13.7", 19.2" and 24" oc. These spacings provide a joist for each end of an eight-foot panel. The panel ends fit to the center of the joists. In other joist-spacing methods, thick sheathing panels are available with span ratings up to 32 or 48 inches oc and in thicknesses up to 1⅛ inches. More on this later.

JOIST LAYOUT

With your measuring tape, begin on the left outside corner of the building, measure in 15¼ inches, mark a line, and place an X to the right of the line. The first joist will fit to the X side of the mark (see Fig. 7-14). Drive a nail on the 15¼-inch mark, hook the tape to the nail, and proceed to mark off 16 inches. Place an X on the right side of the mark and continue in this manner to the opposite end of the building. Mark XX for double joists.

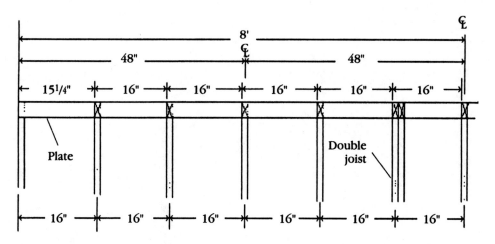

7-14 Joist layout on 16-inch centers.

If joists lap over the center girder or wall, as shown in Fig. 7-15, lay out the second section by measuring in from the outside wall 13¾ inches, mark the dimension, and continue with the layout as you did on the opposite side. Be sure to begin at the same end of the building for both layouts.

In a three-bay house, lay out bays 1 and 2 as described previously, and lay out bay 3 in the same manner as bay 1.

Floor joists don't always lap. Joist might butt the girder, as illustrated in Fig. 7-16, or butt a steel girder, as seen in Fig. 7-17. The layout for these joists are the same for each bay.

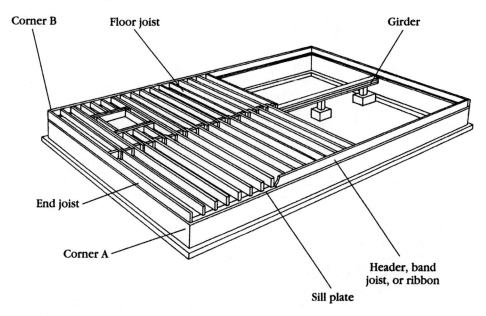

7-15 Joist overlap. American Plywood Assoc

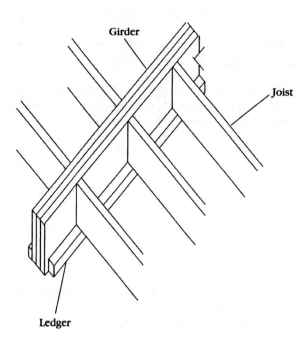

7-16
Joist butted to wood girder and supported by ledger.

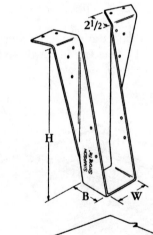

7-17
Joist butted to steel girder. Simpson Strong-Tie Co

Lay out second-floor joists in the same manner as the first-floor joists, overlapping on a load-bearing wall.

JOIST/GIRDER STRENGTH

The strength provided by joist/girder components depends on using correctly sized materials joined with precision and adequate nailing or anchoring. There's no other way to obtain a stiff, solid floor. A weak joist/girder system will result in a springy floor, which is unacceptable to any home buyer who knows how to test a floor—by jumping up and down in the center of the room. Adhering to the joist-span criteria discussed later in this chapter is essential for a strong floor. Let's look at some of the ways joists are mated to the girder.

Joists across a girder

Figure 7-15 shows floor joists resting directly on the girder. This is perhaps the simplest method of floor-joist framing. For this method, ensure that the top of the girder is flush with the top of the sill plate. A problem with this configuration is that shrinkage will be greater at the girder than at the foundation walls. A steel girder would eliminate the shrinkage problem.

Joist supports

The joists can be secured to the girder with a joist hanger or support ledger. These eliminate much of the horizontal wood that's subject to shrinkage at the girder. Figure 7-18 shows a typical saddle-hanger installation. Nail the hanger to the header with four 16d nails. Use two 10d × 1½" nails to secure hanger to joist. Figure 7-17 shows a hanger to attach a joist to a steel girder.

The standard U hanger provides a secure joist/girder installation. Apply the hanger to the header with ten 16d nails and to the joist with six 10d × 1½" nails (see Fig. 7-19).

Speed-prong joist hangers are installed using built-in prongs to secure the joist to the hanger. One hit positions the hanger for header nailing. Permanently install 2 × 10 joists to the header with eight 16d nails and two prongs. Drive the six prongs

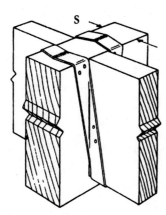

7-18
Typical saddle hanger installation.
Simpson Strong-Tie Co

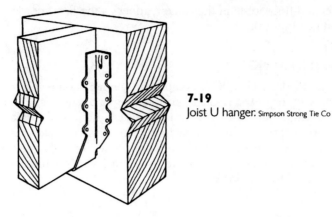

7-19
Joist U hanger. Simpson Strong Tie Co

into the joist and the installation is complete. See Fig. 7-20. Other types of framing anchors are shown in Fig. 7-21.

Joist ledger

Depending on the size of the joists and wood girder, the joists can be supported on a wood ledger strip several different ways. Each arrangement provides about equal shrinkage at the center girder and at the outer walls since the 1½-inch ledger is the same thickness as the outer wall sill. (Most framers make the ledger by ripping a 2 × 4 lengthwise down the center.) Figure 7-16 shows ledger-supported joists.

The joists must bear on the ledger. Your code might specify how to nail the ledgers. Generally, a nailing arrangement using three 16d nails, as shown in Fig.

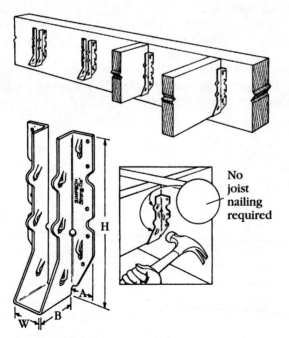

No joist nailing required

7-20
Speed-prong joist hanger. Simpson Strong Tie Co

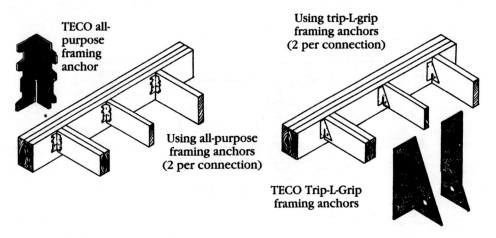

TECO all-purpose framing anchor

Using all-purpose framing anchors (2 per connection)

Using trip-L-grip framing anchors (2 per connection)

TECO Trip-L-Grip framing anchors

7-21 Framing anchors. Teco Co

7-22, will meet code requirements. In Fig. 7-23, the connecting scab at each pair of joists provides an unbroken horizontal tie and a smooth nailing surface for subflooring, where the joists are higher than the girder.

Another method uses a steel strap to tie the joists together (see Fig. 7-24).

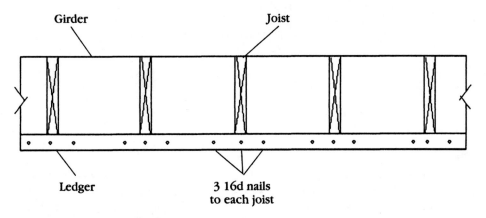

Girder

Joist

Ledger

3 16d nails to each joist

7-22 Ledger nailing arrangement.

Few floors are framed using the methods illustrated in Figs. 7-23 and 7-24 due to the extra labor and materials involved. I prefer the method I've used for 30 years, which is to butt the joists to the girder and support with a ledger, as shown in Fig. 7-16. As for tying together the joists on both sides of the girder, I prefer to use subfloor panels. Simply arrange the panel layout where panels overlap the opposing joists at the girder by at least a foot. This might involve ripping out panels for the starting row, but you'll get a solid floor tie.

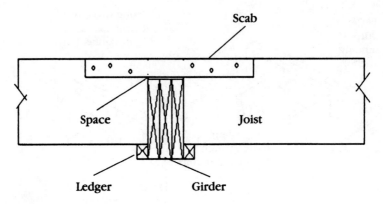

7-23 Joist scab tie.

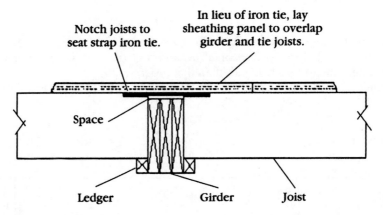

7-24 Steel strapping.

Joist blocking

Joist blocking can be used between overlapped joists resting on top of wood or steel girders. Make the blocking out of lumber the same size as the joist, and toe-nail with three 8d nails at each joist. The blocking stabilizes the joist, keeps it from twisting, and presses the overlaps together like a clamp (see Fig. 7-25).

Wood to steel

Figure 7-26 shows a steel beam supporting joists. A 2 × 4 is installed on top of the steel with bolts, and the joists are secured to the 2 × 4 with steel framing anchors.

Other methods of attaching floor joists to steel girders include supporting the joists on a wood ledger bolted to the girder (Fig. 7-27) and letting the joists rest directly on the beam's flange (Fig. 7-28). In the latter method, install blocking between the joists at the girder to prevent joist overturning.

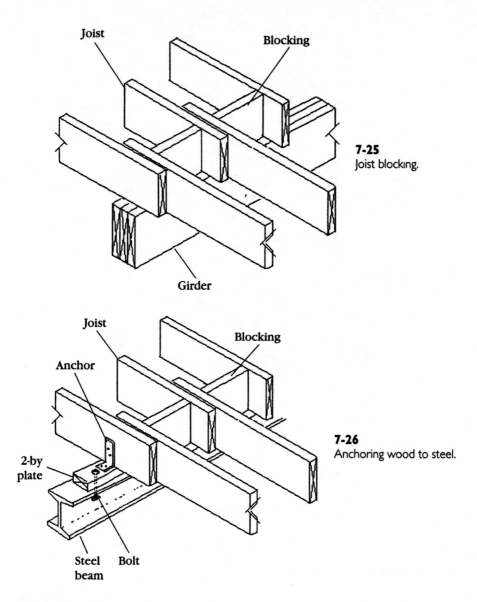

Joist

Blocking

7-25
Joist blocking.

Girder

Joist

Blocking

Anchor

2-by
plate

7-26
Anchoring wood to steel.

Steel   Bolt
beam

REQUIRED JOIST LENGTHS

The front-to-back dimension for the floor depth in a house plan is always measured between the outside surfaces of the exterior-wall studs, as shown in Fig. 7-29.

Wood joists are in length increments of two feet. You can't buy a 9- or 11-foot piece of lumber. Most pieces have a little added (up to three inches) to allow for squaring and cutting into shorter standard lengths.

A rule of thumb for finding the joist length in standard platform construction with lapped joists bearing on top of a center girder is that the length of the joist equals half the house depth minus the thickness of the band (header) joist plus the overlap of the joist at the center support. Figure 7-29 shows the rule. If you assume

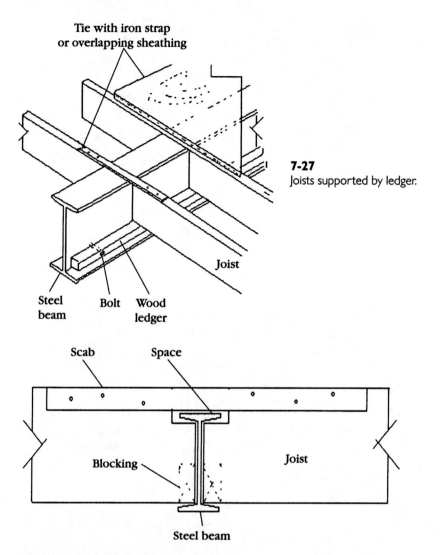

Tie with iron strap
or overlapping sheathing

7-27
Joists supported by ledger.

Steel beam   Bolt   Wood ledger

Joist

Scab   Space

Blocking

Joist

Steel beam

7-28 Joists supported by flange.

that half of the lap length is two inches, then the total joist overlap must be at least four inches. (A minimum 1½" lap length is required.)

I discussed modular building in chapter 4, and explained that joist lengths matched standard lumber sizes when the house depth is on a four-foot module of 24', 28', or 32'. Table 7-3 reveals that a 29-foot house takes as many linear feet of joists for floor framing as a 32-foot depth. Thus, there's a lot of waste. The joist material for a 29-foot depth will cost the same as for a 32-foot depth. This is a fact whether the joists are in-line or lapped.

When the allowable spans for joists exceed the spans shown in the floor plan by one foot or more, the experienced framer will recommend changing either the joist grade, joist spacing, or house depth to eliminate six to eight percent or more in waste.

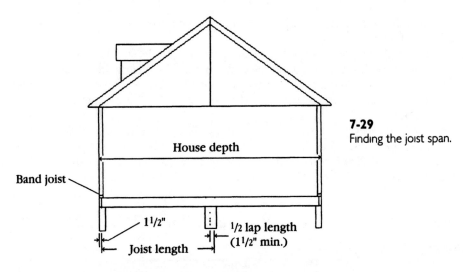

7-29
Finding the joist span.

House depth

Band joist

1½"

½ lap length
(1½" min.)

Joist length

Table 7-3 Standard lengths for floor joists

House depth (ft.)	Joist required (ft.)	Standard length (ft.)
20	10½	12
22	11	12
23	11½	12
24	12	12
25	12½	14
26	13	14
27	13½	14
28	14	14
29	14½	16
30	15	16
31	15½	16
32	16	16

ALLOWABLE SPANS

As shown in Fig. 7-29, allowable spans for lumber joists refer to the clear span between supports. Allowable spans are fixed. Builders cannot arbitrarily use just any size of joist they think will do the job. The spans are determined by:
- The working stresses for the joist grade and species
- Joist size and spacing
- The design loads specified in the building code or FHA standard

Most requirements limit joist deflection to ⅟₃₆₀ of the span under a 40-psf (or smaller) uniform live load. Joist strength must be sufficient to support the live load plus a dead load of 10 pounds per square foot.

Available lumber species and grades provide a broad range of span capabilities and a selection of joist size and spacing alternatives. Several tables later in the chapter list the most efficient joist size and grade combinations for house depths of 20 to 32 feet.

A rule of thumb for finding the clear span of joists in standard platform construction where joists bear on a center girder is that the clear span of each joist is half the house depth (measured between the outside surfaces of the exterior studs), minus the width of the sill plate, minus half the width of the bearing plate on the center support.

Figure 7-30 gives some examples. Where 2 × 4 sill plates and a 2 × 4 center bearing plate is used, the clear span of each joist is half the house depth minus 5¼ inches. Use actual dimensions of lumber and not the nominal size when computing spans. A 2 × 4 is considered to be 1½" × 3½".

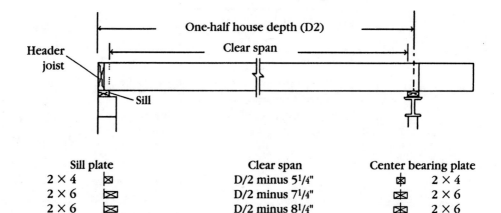

Sill plate		Clear span	Center bearing plate	
2 × 4	⊠	D/2 minus 5¹/4"	⊠	2 × 4
2 × 6	⊠	D/2 minus 7¹/4"	⊠	2 × 6
2 × 6	⊠	D/2 minus 8¹/4"	⊠	2 × 6
2 × 8	⊠	D/2 minus 10⁷/8"	⊠	2 × 8

7-30 Adjusting the clear span.

As shown in Fig. 7-30, a wider sill or center bearing plate can be used to reduce the clear span. It's possible to use a smaller joist (and reduce costs) by reducing the span.

When 2 × 6 sill plates are used in conjunction with a 2 × 4 center bearing plate, the clear span is half the house depth minus 7¼ inches. This is two inches less than if a 2 × 4 sill plate had been used.

If a 2 × 6 is used for the sill and center plates, the clear span is half the house depth minus 8¼ inches. If you use 2 × 8 lumber for both plates, the clear span is half the house depth minus 10⅞ inches, 5⅝ inches less than if 2 × 4 plates were used.

MINIMUM JOIST GRADES AND SIZES

While house plans show lumber sizes for structural components, the framer should be familiar with wood species, grades, and span capabilities. The minimum grades and joist sizes required for house depths from 20 feet to 32 feet at one-foot intervals are shown in Table 7-4 for some common species.

Table 7-4 is based on a 40-psf uniform live load, use of platform construction with center support (girder or bearing wall), a nominal two-inch-thick band joist

Table 7-4 Minimum joist grades for different house depths (for a 40-psf live load)
(Based on platform construction, nominal 2-inch-thick band joists, and, except where footnoted, nominal 2 × 4 sill and 2 × 4 center bearing plates)

Species	Joist spacing	Joist size	20	21	22	23	24	25	26	27	28	29	30	31	32	Grading rule agency
Balsam fir	16"	2 × 8	No 2	No 2	No 2	No 2	No 2 [b]	No 1 [c]								NeLMA NH&PMA
		2 × 10	No 3	No 3	No 3	No 3 [b]	No 2	No 2	No 1	No 1 [c]	No 2		No 2 [c]	No 1 [a]		
	24"	2 × 8	No 2 [c]	No 1 [a]	No 2	No 2	No 2	No 2 [c]	No 1	No 2	No 2	No 2	No 2		No 2	
		2 × 10	No 2	No 2	No 3	No 3	No 3									
California redwood (open grain)	16"	2 × 8	No 3 [c]	No 2	No 2	No 2 [a]	No 1 [b]	No 3 [c]	No 2	No 2	No 2	No 2 [a]	No 1 [a]	No 2	No 2	RIS
		2 × 10	No 3	No 3	No 3	No 3	No 3	No 3	No 3	No 3	No 3	No 3	No 3 [b]	No 2	No 2	
	24"	2 × 8	No 2	No 1 [a]	No 1 [a]	No 2	No 2	No 2	No 2 [c]	No 1 [c]	No 2	No 2	No 2	No 2 [a]	No 1 [b]	
		2 × 10	No 3	No 3 [c]	No 3	No 3	No 3	No 3 [c]	No 2	No 2	No 3					
		2 × 12		No 3	No 3	No 3	No 3	No 3	No 3							
Douglas fir-larch	16"	2 × 8	No 3	No 3	No 3	No 2	No 2	No 2	No 2	No 2	No 1 [b]	No 2	No 2	No 2	No 2	NLGA WCLIB WWPA
		2 × 10				No 3	No 3	No 3	No 3	No 3	No 2 [c]	No 3	No 3	No 3	No 3	
		2 × 12									No 3 [a]					
	24"	2 × 8	No 2	No 2	No 2	No 2	No 2	No 1 [c]	No 2	No 2	No 2	No 2	No 2 [b]	No 1 [a]	No 1 [c] DENSE	
		2 × 10	No 3	No 3	No 3	No 3 [c]	No 2	No 2	No 3	No 3	No 3 [b]	No 3	No 2	No 2	No 2	
		2 × 12				No 3	No 3	No 3								
Douglas fir-south	16"	2 × 8	No 3	No 3	No 3 [c]	No 2	No 2	No 2 [a]	No 1 [c]	No 3	No 2	No 2	No 2	No 2	No 2 [c]	WWPA
		2 × 10	No 2	No 2 [a]	No 3	No 3	No 3	No 3	No 3		No 3	No 3	No 3	No 3	No 3	
	24"	2 × 8	No 2	No 2	No 2	No 1 [c]	No 2	No 2	No 2	No 2	No 2 [b]	No 1 [c]	No 2	No 2	No 2	
		2 × 10	No 3	No 3	No 3	No 3 [c]	No 2 [b]	No 3	No 3	No 3 [a]	No 2	No 2				
		2 × 12				No 3	No 3	No 3								
Eastern hemlock-tamarack	16"	2 × 8	No 3	No 3 [c]	No 2	No 2	No 2 [b]	No 1 [a]	No 3 [a]	No 2	No 2	No 2	No 2 [a]	No 1	No 1 [c]	NeLMA NH&PMA NLGA
		2 × 10			No 3	No 3	No 3	No 3	No 2				No 3			
	24"	2 × 8	No 2	No 2 [a]	No 1 [a]	No 2	No 2	No 1	No 2	No 2 [c]	No 1 [b]					
		2 × 10	No 3	No 3	No 3 [c]	No 3	No 3	No 2								
Eastern spruce	16"	2 × 8	No 2	No 3	No 2	No 2	No 2 [a]	No 1	No 1 [c]	No 1	No 1 [b]	No 2	No 2	No 2 [c]	No 2 [c]	NeLMA NH&PMA
		2 × 10	No 3	No 1	No 1 [a]	No 3	No 3 [b]	No 2	No 2							
	24"	2 × 8	No 2 [b]	No 1	No 1 [a]	No 2	No 2	No 2 [a]	No 1	No 1	No 1 [b]	No 2	No 2	No 2	No 1	
		2 × 10	No 3 [c]	No 2		No 2	No 2									
Engelmann spruce-alpine fir (Engelmann spruce-lodgepole pine)	16"	2 × 8	No 2	No 2	No 2	No 2	No 2 [c]	No 1 [a]	No 2	No 2	No 2	No 2	No 2 [c]	No 1	No 1 [c]	WWPA
		2 × 10	No 3	No 3	No 3	No 3 [b]	No 2	No 3	No 3	No 3	No 3 [c]	No 2	No 2	No 2	No 2	
		2 × 12		No 1 [a]		No 3		No 2 [c]	No 1	No 1 [c]					No 1	
	24"	2 × 8	No 2	No 2	No 2	No 2	No 2	No 2 [c]	No 1	No 1 [c]	No 2	No 2	No 2 [c]	No 1	No 1	
		2 × 10	No 2	No 2	No 3	No 3	No 2	No 2	No 2	No 2	No 2	No 2	No 2	No 2	No 2	
		2 × 12	No 3	No 3		No 3 [c]										

Table 7-4 Continued

Species	Joist spacing	Joist size	House depth (measured between outside surfaces of exterior studs), feet													Grading rule agency
			20	21	22	23	24	25	26	27	28	29	30	31	32	
Hem-fir	16″	2 × 8	No 3[a]	No 2	No 2	No 2	No 2	No 2	No 1							NLGA WCLIB WWPA
		2 × 10		No 3	No 3	No 3	No 3	No 3[a]	No 2[c]	No 2	No 2	No 2	No 2	No 2	No 2	
		2 × 12						No 3	No 2	No 3	No 3	No 3	No 3	No 3[c]	No 3	
	24″	2 × 8	No 2	No 1	No 1	No 1[a]	No 1	No 2	No 2	No 2[c]	No 1	No 1[a]	No 1	No 2	No 1[a]	
		2 × 10	No 3	No 2	No 2	No 2	No 2	No 3[a]	No 3	No 2	No 2	No 2	No 2	No 2	No 2	
		2 × 12		No 3	No 3	No 3	No 3	No 3		No 3	No 3					
Idaho white pine or Western white pine	16″	2 × 8	No 2	No 2	No 2	No 2[a]	No 1	No 1[a]	No 2	No 2	No 2	No 2	No 1	No 1	No 1[b]	WWPA NLGA
		2 × 10	No 3	No 3	No 3	No 3[a]	No 2	No 2	No 3	No 3	No 3[c]		No 2	No 2	No 2	
	24″	2 × 8	No 1	No 1[b]	No 2	No 2	No 2[a]	No 1	No 1[a]	No 2	No 2	No 2[a]	No 1	No 1	No 1[c]	
		2 × 10	No 2	No 2	No 3	No 3[c]	No 2	No 2	No 2	No 2	No 2	No 2	No 2	No 2	No 2	
		2 × 12	No 3	No 3				No 3								
Lodgepole pine	16″	2 × 8	No 2	No 2	No 2	No 2	No 2	No 2	No 2	No 2	No 2	No 2	No 2	No 2[a]	No 1[c]	WWPA
		2 × 10	No 3	No 3	No 3	No 3	No 3	No 2	No 3	No 3	No 3	No 3	No 2	No 2	No 2	
	24″	2 × 8	No 2	No 1[a]	No 1	No 1[c]	No 2	No 2	No 2[a]	No 1	No 1[b]	No 2	No 2	No 2[b]	No 1	
		2 × 10	No 3[a]	No 2	No 2	No 2	No 3[a]		No 2	No 2	No 2		No 2			
Northern pine	16″	2 × 8	No 3[c]	No 2	No 2	No 2	No 2	No 2[a]	No 2[c]	No 2	No 2	No 2	No 2	No 2	No 2[c]	NeLMA NH&PMA
		2 × 10	No 3	No 3	No 3	No 3	No 3	No 3[c]	No 2	No 3	No 3	No 3				
	24″	2 × 8	No 2	No 2[b]	No 1	No 1[c]	No 2	No 2	No 1[c]	No 1	No 1	No 1[c]	No 2	No 2[b]	No 1	
		2 × 10	No 3	No 3[c]	No 2	No 2	No 2		No 2[a]	No 2	No 2		No 2			
Ponderosa pine-sugar pine	16″	2 × 8	No 2	No 2	No 2	No 2	No 2[b]	No 1[c]	No 2	No 2	No 2	No 2	No 2[a]	No 1[a]	No 2	WWPA
		2 × 10	No 3	No 3	No 3	No 3	No 2	No 2	No 3	No 3	No 3[a]		No 2	No 2		
	24″	2 × 8	No 2[c]	No 1	No 2	No 2	No 2	No 2[c]	No 1	No 1[a]	No 2	No 2	No 2	No 1	No 2	
		2 × 10	No 2	No 2	No 2	No 3[a]	No 3	No 3	No 2	No 3	No 3[a]		No 2	No 2	No 2	
		2 × 12	No 3	No 3	No 3				No 3							
Southern pine	16″	2 × 8		No 3	No 3	No 3	No 3	No 2	No 2	No 2[b]	No 1[c]	No 2	No 2	No 2	No 2	SPIB
		2 × 10						No 1[c] DENSE	No 3	No 3	No 2	No 3	No 3	No 3	No 3	
	24″	2 × 8	No 2	No 2	No 2	No 2	No 1[a]	No 2	No 2	No 2	No 2	No 2	No 2[c]	No 1[c]	No 2	
		2 × 10	No 3	No 3	No 3	No 3[c]	No 2	No 2	No 3	No 3[a]	No 3	No 2	No 3	No 2	No 3	
		2 × 12				No 2	No 3	No 3	No 3		No 3					
Southern pine KD (15% mc)	16″	2 × 8	No 3	No 3	No 3[c]	No 3[c]	No 2	No 2	No 2	No 2[b]	No 1[b]	No 1[c] DENSE	No 2	No 2	No 1[b]	SPIB
		2 × 10				No 3	No 3	No 3	No 3	No 3	No 3	No 3[c]	No 3	No 3	No 2	
		2 × 12										No 3			No 3	

	24"		No 2 No 3	No 2 No 3	No 2 No 3	No 2 No 3	No 1ᶜ No 2 No 3	No 2 No 3	No 2 No 3	No 2 No 2	No 1ᵇ No 2	No 1ᶜ DENSE No 2
Spruce-pine-fir, coast sitka spruce, or sitka spruce	16"	2 × 8 2 × 10 2 × 12	No 2 No 3	No 2 No 3	No 2 No 3	No 2ᵃ No 2 No 3	No 1ᵃ No 2 No 3	No 2	No 2 No 3ᵃ	No 2	No 2ᶜ No 2	No 1 No 2
	24"	2 × 8 2 × 10 2 × 12	No 2ᵇ No 2 No 3	No 1ᶜ No 2 No 3	No 1ᶜ No 2 No 3	No 2 No 3ᵃ	No 2	No 2	No 1 No 2	No 2ᵃ	No 1	No 1
Western hemlock	16"	2 × 8 2 × 10 2 × 12	No 3ᵃ No 3	No 2 No 3	No 1ᵇ No 3ᶜ No 3	No 2 No 3	No 2 No 3	No 2 No 3	No 2 No 3	No 2 No 3	No 2 No 3	No 2 No 3ᵃ
	24"	2 × 8 2 × 10 2 × 12	No 2 No 3	No 2ᵃ No 3ᵇ No 3	No 1ᶜ No 2 No 3	No 1 No 2 No 3	No 2ᵇ No 2	No 1 No 2	No 1 No 2	No 1ᵇ No 2	No 2	No 2
White woods (western woods)	16"	2 × 8 2 × 10 2 × 12	No 2 No 3	No 2ᵃ No 3ᵇ No 3	No 1ᵇ No 2 No 3	No 2ᵃ No 3	No 2ᵇ No 3ᶜ No 2	No 2ᵃ No 2	No 2 No 3	No 1ᵃ No 2	No 2	No 2
	24"	2 × 8 2 × 10 2 × 12	No 1ᵇ No 2 No 3	No 2 No 3ᵃ	No 2 No 3ᶜ	No 2 No 3	No 2ᶜ No 2	No 1 No 2	No 2 No 3	No 2	No 2	No 2
	24"	2 × 8 2 × 10 2 × 12	No 1 No 2 No 3	No 2 No 2	No 2ᵃ No 2	No 2	No 2	No 2ᵃ	No 1	No 1	No 1	No 1ᶜ

Associations (right margin): NLGA, WCLIB; WWPA; WWPA

ᵃ Nominal 2 × 6 sill plate and 2 × 4 center bearing plate, or width of sill plate plus one-half width of center bearing equal to 7¼" or more
ᵇ Nominal 2 × 6 sill plate and 2 × 6 center bearing plate, or width of sill plate plus one-half width of center bearing equal to 8¼" or more
ᵃ Nominal 2 × 8 sill plate and 2 × 8 center bearing plate, or width of sill plate plus one-half width of center bearing equal to 10¾" or more

NeLMA = Northeastern Lumber Manufacturers Association
NH&PMA = Northern Hardwood and Pine Manufacturers Association
RIS = Redwood Inspection Service
NLGA = National Lumber Grades Authority, a Canadian Agency
WCLIB = West Coast Lumber Inspection Bureau
WWPA = Western Wood Products Association
SPIB = Southern Pine Inspection Bureau
Courtesy National Forest & Paper Association

(header), and 2 × 4 sill and center bearing plates. Where use of a 2 × 6 or 2 × 8 sill or bearing plate would permit a particular size and grade of joist to be used for a larger house depth, this provision is also noted.

Here's how to use the table. Assume your house plan calls for no. 3 southern pine 2 × 12s spaced 16 inches on center for a house depth of 28 feet. You could change the floor plan to a major four-foot module of 32 feet with the same joist. Of course, more is involved in changing the floor plan than just joist considerations. You don't size a house merely on the basis of lumber lengths!

According to Table 7-4, a no. 2 Ponderosa pine 2 × 8 is adequate for a 23-foot house depth having a 2 × 4 sill and center bearing plate. By using a 2 × 6 sill and center bearing plate, the same board can be used for a 24-foot house depth.

The idea is that, with the ever-increasing cost of lumber, you should always be on the lookout for ways to reduce cost without reducing quality. For example, there are situations where you can use a more economical grade or size of lumber for your floor plan. A 28-foot house can be spanned at lower cost with no. 3 Douglas fir-larch 2 × 10s, 16 inches on center, and 2 × 6 sill plates than with no. 2 2 × 10s of the same species and spacing, but with 2 × 4 sill plates. Also, consider that using no. 1 2 × 8s 16 inches on center with 2 × 6 sill and center bearing plates might also be a more economical alternative. Yes, it can be confusing. As one old framer recently stated, "You can't build a little bird house anymore without blue prints and a calculator!"

Taking another approach, you can often reduce costs by increasing joist spacing. For example, no. 2 Douglas fir-larch or southern pine 2 × 10s can span a 28-foot house when spaced 24 inches on center as well as when spaced 16 inches on center. The cost savings will depend on the added cost of thicker subfloor panels required for 24-inch spacing.

FIELD-GLUING SUBFLOOR PANELS

A quality floor is a stiff floor. A sound floor is one that doesn't "spring." Thus, the maximum clear spans for many of the higher lumber grades are limited by lack of stiffness. In such cases, field-gluing the subfloor panels to the joists can provide additional spanning capability. The term *field-gluing* means that someone spreads glue on top of the floor joists after they're installed and nails the subflooring panels in place. Glued panels reduce floor squeaks and nail pops.

Table 7-5 outlines the minimum requirements of field-glued floor systems for house depths 20 to 32 feet. The table shows only the joist grades and sizes that can increase the maximum span. Field-glued floor system specifications, as developed by the American Plywood Association, have been accepted by HUD/FHA and most building codes.

If you compare Tables 7-4 and 7-5, it will become evident that the glue system can save material cost. For example, in Table 7-4, a no. 2 southern pine kiln-dried 2 × 12 joist can be used at 24-inch centers for a house depth of 32 feet. With glue, a no. 1 southern pine kiln-dried 2 × 10 joist can be used on 24-inch centers for the same depth having the same-sized sill and center bearing plates.

The gluing system allows you to use a smaller size joist, and you can space nails 12 inches on center (as opposed to 6 and 10 inches for the conventional method).

Table 7-5 Field-glued subfloor panels (for a 40-psf live load)
(Based on platform construction, nominal 2-inch-thick band joists and, except where footnoted, nominal 2 × 4 sill and 2 × 4 center bearing plates)

Joist Grades Having Additional House Depth Spanning Capability
Through Field-Gluing of Subfloor- Underlayment Panels to Joists

40 psf Live Load

(Based on platform construction, nominal 2-inch-thick band joists and, except where footnoted, nominal 2 × 4 sill and 2 × 4 center bearing plates)

Species	Joist spacing	Joist size	Underlayment thickness	House depth (measured between outside surfaces of exterior studs), feet												
				20	21	22	23	24	25	26	27	28	29	30	31	32
Balsam fir	16"	2 × 8	1/2, 19/32, 23/32	—	—	—	—	—	No 1	No 1[c]	—	—	—	—	No 1	No 1
		2 × 10	1/2, 19/32, 23/32	—	—	—	—	—	—	—	—	—	—	—	No 1	No 1
California redwood (open grain)	16"	2 × 8	1/2,	—	—	—	No 2	No 2	No 2[a]	No 1[b]	—	—	—	—	—	—
			19/32	—	—	—	No 2	No 2	No 2[a]	No 1[a]	—	—	—	—	—	—
			23/32	—	—	—	No 2	No 2	No 2[a]	No 1	No 1[b]	—	—	—	—	—
		2 × 10	1/2	—	—	—	—	—	—	—	—	—	No 2	No 2	No 2	No 1[a]
			19/32, 23/32	—	—	—	—	—	—	—	—	—	No 2	No 2	No 2	No 2[c]
	24"	2 × 8	19/32, 23/32	—	No 2[b]	No 1	No 1[b]	—	—	—	—	—	—	—	—	—
		2 × 10	19/32, 23/32	—	—	—	—	—	—	No 2[a]	No 1	No 1	No 1[b]	—	—	—
		2 × 12	19/32, 23/32	—	—	—	—	—	—	—	—	—	—	—	No 2	No 2[c]
Douglas fir-larch	16"	2 × 8	1/2, 19/32,	—	—	—	—	—	—	—	—	No 2	No 1 No 2[c]	No 1[c]	—	—
			23/32	—	—	—	—	—	—	—	—	No 2	No 1 No 2[c]	No 1	—	—
	24"	2 × 8	23/32	—	—	—	—	—	No 1	No 1	No 1	—	—	—	—	—
		2 × 10	19/32, 23/32	—	—	—	—	—	—	—	—	—	—	—	No 1	No 1
Douglas fir-south	16"	2 × 8	1/2,	—	—	—	—	—	No 2	No 2	No 2[a]	No 1[c]	—	—	—	—
			19/32,	—	—	—	—	—	No 2	No 2	No 2[a]	No 1[b]	—	—	—	—
			23/32	—	—	—	—	—	No 2	No 2	No 2	No 2[b]	No 1[c]	—	—	—
		2 × 10	1/2, 19/32, 23/32	—	—	—	—	—	—	—	—	—	—	—	—	No 2
	24"	2 × 8	19/32, 23/32	—	—	No 2	No 2[b]	No 1	No 1[a]	—	—	—	—	—	—	—
		2 × 10	23/32	—	—	—	—	—	—	—	—	No 2	No 2[b]	No 1	No 1	No 1[b]
Eastern hemlock-tamarack	16"	2 × 8	1/2,	—	—	—	—	—	No 2	No 2	No 2[b]	No 1[a]	—	—	—	—
			19/32,	—	—	—	—	—	No 2	No 2	No 2[a]	No 1	—	—	—	—
			23/32	—	—	—	—	—	No 2	No 2	No 2[a]	No 1	No 1[a]	—	—	—
		2 × 10	1/2	—	—	—	—	—	—	—	—	—	—	No 2	No 2	No 2[a]
			19/32, 23/32	—	—	—	—	—	—	—	—	—	—	No 2	No 2	No 2
	24"	2 × 8	19/32, 23/32	—	No 2	No 2[c]	No 1	No 1[a]	—	—	—	—	—	—	—	—
		2 × 10	19/32, 23/32	—	—	—	—	—	—	—	—	No 2	No 1 No 2[c]	No 1	No 1	No 1[c]
Eastern spruce	16"	2 × 8	1/2, 19/32, 23/32	—	—	—	—	—	—	No 1	No 1[b]	—	—	—	—	—
Engelmann spruce-alpine fir	16"	2 × 8	19/32, 23/32	—	—	—	—	—	No 1	No 1[c]	—	—	—	—	—	—
		2 × 10	19/32, 23/32	—	—	—	—	—	—	—	—	—	—	—	—	No 1
Ham-fir	16"	2 × 8	1/2,	—	—	—	—	—	—	—	No 1	No 1[a]	—	—	—	—
			19/32, 23/32	—	—	—	—	—	—	—	No 1	No 1	—	—	—	—
	24"	2 × 10	19/32, 23/32	—	—	—	—	—	—	—	—	—	No 1	No 1[c]	—	—
Lodgepole pine	16"	2 × 8	1/2,	—	—	—	—	—	—	No 1	No 1[a]	—	—	—	—	—
		2 × 10	1/2,	—	—	—	—	—	—	No 1	—	—	—	—	—	No 1
	24"	2 × 8	19/32, 23/32	—	—	No 1	No 1[c]	—	—	—	—	—	—	—	—	—
		2 × 10	19/32, 23/32	—	—	—	—	—	—	—	—	No 1	No 1[c]	—	—	—
Northern pine	16"	2 × 8	1/2,	—	—	—	—	—	—	No 1	No 1	No 1[c]	—	—	—	—
			19/32,	—	—	—	—	—	—	No 1	No 1	No 1[b]	—	—	—	—
			23/32	—	—	—	—	—	—	No 1	No 1	No 1	—	—	—	—
		2 × 10	1/2, 19/32, 23/32	—	—	—	—	—	—	—	—	—	—	—	—	No 2[b]

Table 7-5 Continued

Species	Joist spacing	Joist size	Underlayment thickness	20	21	22	23	24	25	26	27	28	29	30	31	32
	24"	2 × 8	19/32, 23/32	—	—	—	No 1	—	—	—	—	—	—	—	—	—
		2 × 10	19/32, 23/32	—	—	—	—	—	—	—	—	—	No 1	No 1c	—	—
Ponderosa pine-sugar pine	16"	2 × 8	1/2, 19/32, 23/32	—	—	—	—	—	No 1	No 1	—	—	—	—	—	—
		2 × 10	1/2, 19/32, 23/32	—	—	—	—	—	—	—	—	—	—	—	No 1	No 1
	24"	2 × 10	19/32, 23/32	—	—	—	—	—	—	—	No.1	—	—	—	—	—
Southern pine	16"	2 × 8	1/2, 19/32, 23/32	—	—	—	—	—	—	No 2	No.2	No 2	No.1a	—	—	—
		2 × 10		—	—	—	—	—	—	No 2	No 2	No 2	No 1	No 1b	—	—
	24"	2 × 8	19/32, 23/32	—	—	—	—	No 1	No 1	No 1c	—	—	—	—	—	—
		2 × 10	19/32, 23/32	—	—	—	—	—	—	—	—	—	—	—	No 1	No 1
Southern pine KD (15% mc)	16"	2 × 8	1/2,	—	—	—	—	—	—	—	No 2	No 2	No 2c	No 1c	—	—
			19/32,	—	—	—	—	—	—	—	No 2	No.2	No.2b	No.1c	—	—
			23/32	—	—	—	—	—	—	—	No 2	No 2	No 2a	No 1	—	—
	24"	2 × 8	19/32, 23/32	—	—	—	—	No.2a	No 1	No 1	No 1c	—	—	—	—	—
		2 × 10	19/32, 23/32	—	—	—	—	—	—	—	—	—	—	No 2	No 2c	No 1
Western hemlock	16"	2 × 8	1/2,	—	—	—	—	—	—	No 2	No 2b	No 1	No 1c	—	—	—
			19/32,	—	—	—	—	—	—	No 2	No 2b	No 1	No 1b	—	—	—
			23/32	—	—	—	—	—	—	No 2	No 2b	No 1	No 1	—	—	—
	24"	2 × 8	19/32, 23/32	—	—	—	—	No 1	No 1a	—	—	—	—	—	—	—
		2 × 10	19/32, 23/32	—	—	—	—	—	—	—	—	—	—	No 1	No 1b	—
White woods (western woods)	16"	2 × 8	1/2, 19/32, 23/32	—	—	—	—	No 1	No 1a	—	—	—	—	—	—	—
		2 × 10	1/2, 19/32, 23/32	—	—	—	—	—	—	—	—	—	No 2	No 1	No 1	No 1b

[a] Nominal 2 × 6 sill plate and 2 × 4 center bearing plate; or width of sill plate plus one-half width of center bearing equal to 7 1/4" or more
[b] Nominal 2 × 6 sill plate and 2 × 6 center bearing plate; or width of sill plate plus one-half width of center bearing equal to 8 1/4" or more
[c] Nominal 2 × 8 sill plate and 2 × 8 center bearing plate; or width of sill plate plus one-half width of center bearing equal to 10 7/8" or more

OFF-CENTER SPLICED JOISTS

Research by the National Association of Home Builders Research Foundation, Inc. for HUD showed that properly designed 2 × 8 spliced joists, spaced 24 inches on center with glue-nailed ⅝-inch plywood sheathing, are structurally adequate for a 28-foot-deep house with a center bearing.

This isn't just theory. NAHB actually built a demonstration house with a floor section constructed of spliced joists and a glue-nailed plywood subfloor. Full-scale loading tests showed that the floor was stiffer and stronger than a conventional floor. They preassembled full-length, 28-foot joists by splicing together two no. 2 Hem-fir 2 × 8s. One piece was 18 feet long and the other was 10 feet long. The splice was made with standard 6 × 12-inch steel truss plates on both sides.

The joists were installed 24 inches on center, with the splice alternating on either side of the center support, as illustrated in Fig. 7-31. NAHB also used a field-glued floor system with T&G ⅝-inch-thick plywood panels glue-nailed to the joists, with the T&G joint also glued. The results were good.

For house depths up to 28 feet with a center bearing, a 2 × 8 off-center spliced-joist system works well, according to these tests. For other house depths, you can make spliced joists from standard lengths of the same-quality 2 × 8 lum-

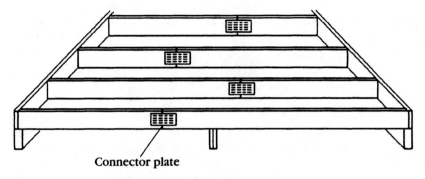

Connector plate

7-31 Off-center spliced joists.

ber. It would appear that the off-center splicing system offers all the benefits of the in-line joist system, plus an increased span capability. Figure 7-32 gives some examples.

You can make the splice with plywood or metal plates on each side of the joist. Off-center spliced joists provide structural continuity over the center support. Splicing can increase the joint stiffness by up to 40 percent.

Under theoretically uniform load conditions for common residential floor spans, the bending stress on a continuous joist is zero at a point several feet from the center support. Therefore, a spliced joint located at or near this point will have minimal bending movement.

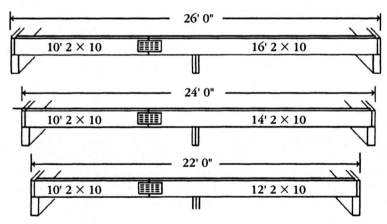

7-32 Combining short and long spliced joists.

IN-LINE FLOOR JOISTS

In-line floor joists are available at some lumber yards. The joists are preassembled and ready to install, and are available in different dimensions and lengths. It would probably cost less, however, to assemble the joists on site. Figure 7-33 shows in-line joist construction. In-line joists work well with modular floor sheathing.

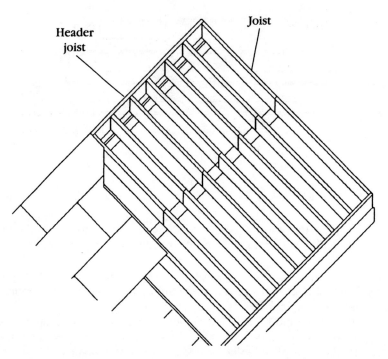

Header joist

Joist

7-33 In-line floor joists.

FRAMING OPENINGS IN FLOOR JOISTS

Stairwells and chimney holes require openings, and plumbing and ductwork also require some cutting of joists. The framing method for the openings depends on where the opening is on the floor plan. Figure 7-34 displays how a stairway opening might be framed using steel joist and beam hangers. This opening runs perpendicular to the joists, which interrupts a number of joists. An opening parallel to the joists requires cutting a minimum number of joists. A main stairway requires an opening from 8 to 10 feet long by 3 feet or more in width. Figure 7-35 shows details of a parallel opening for a stairway. Figure 7-36 illustrates the details of an opening perpendicular to the joist run.

In stairway construction, install double headers and double trimmers. For greater strength, use a steel beam and joist hangers with the special nails furnished with the hanger, or as recommended by the hanger manufacturer. The maximum double-header length is 10 feet. Anything longer should be engineered for the design load and appropriate structural strength.

Figure 7-37 is a chimney opening framed with steel joist hangers. Wood beams, joists, headers, and studs cannot be located within two inches of the outside face of a masonry chimney built partially or entirely within the dwelling, according to most codes.

Make headers and trimmers from lumber the same size as the joists. Headers in floor openings support the ends of the floor joists that have been cut off. The trimmers are the joists that support the header ends.

If stairwell partition studs support the trimmer joists, reinforcing the trimmer joist isn't necessary. See Fig. 7-38 for a joist layout with openings.

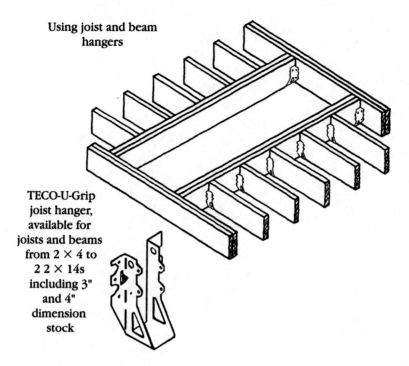

Using joist and beam hangers

TECO-U-Grip joist hanger, available for joists and beams from 2 × 4 to 2 2 × 14s including 3" and 4" dimension stock

7-34 Stairwell opening. Teco Co

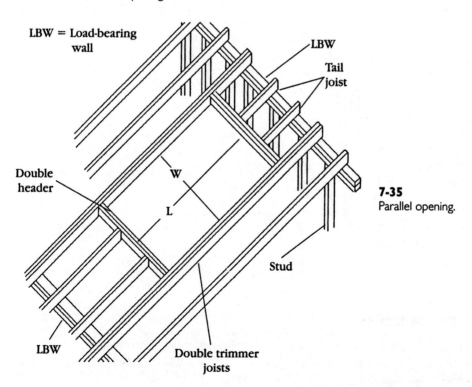

LBW = Load-bearing wall

LBW

Tail joist

Double header

W

L

7-35
Parallel opening.

Stud

LBW

Double trimmer joists

Floor joists   137

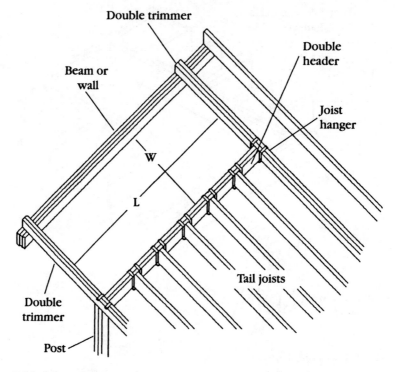

7-36 Perpendicular opening.

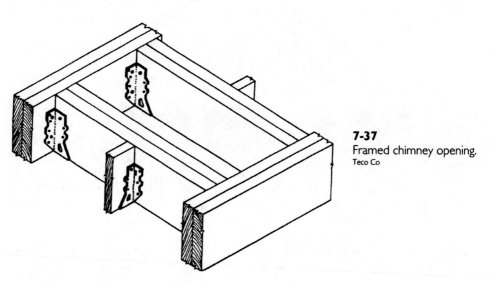

7-37
Framed chimney opening.
Teco Co

TRIMMER JOISTS

Mark the location of trimmer joists on the sill and girder when marking off the regular joists. Don't change the standard spacing of the regular joists; they're spaced as if the trimmer joists don't exist. Mark the location of the headers on the trimmers. Se-

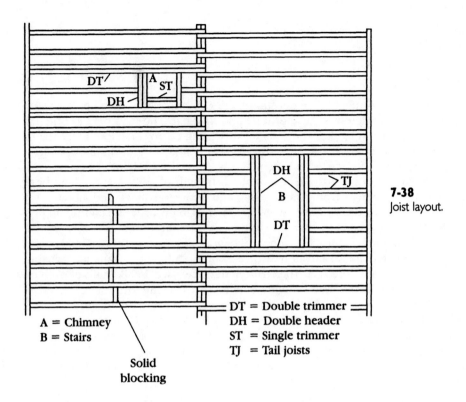

7-38
Joist layout.

DT = Double trimmer
DH = Double header
ST = Single trimmer
TJ = Tail joists

A = Chimney
B = Stairs

Solid blocking

cure the first header piece between the side trimmers with steel hangers or three 20d nails. Mark the tail joists for regular spacing and install the header to the tail joists with either end nailing and three 16d nails or steel hangers. Install the double member of the header to the first member with 16 nails. Secure it to the trimmer with three 20d nails or steel hangers.

THE LUMBER CROWN

Not all dimensional lumber arriving on a building site is fit to be used for framing. There can be pieces that form long Us and slow Ss; that is, the lumber is curved and not a true plane. A slight bow or curve can be tolerated if the crown is turned up because the weight of the floor, ceiling, or roof will often straighten the piece. But don't always count on it. Much depends on the "greenness," species, and size of the lumber.

I have, on several occasions, used a board, crown up, that refused to straighten, causing a permanent hump in the floor. The only thing to do if this happens to you is crawl under the house (or go to the basement) and cut two-thirds into the offending piece at the high point of the crown, level, and spike on a three-foot scab the same size as the joist. Any board having a crown greater than ¼ inch over a 10-foot span should be discarded, or you can rip the crown off.

To rip off the crown, place the board on saw benches and snap a chalk line from end to end at the top side for a level plane. Rip the crown off. You can tack or glue the ripped strip to the opposite edge if a true underside is required for a ceiling. Obviously, there's a limit as to how much you can rip off before affecting the span capability of the board.

BRIDGING

Cross-bridging is one of those question-mark components of framing. For many carpenters, it's considered a waste of time and material. The idea behind bridging appears to have been to prevent joists from twisting out of position. Some claim that the practice became necessary before lumber could be kiln-dried, and the green lumber warped and twisted out of plane without the bridging. Cross-bridging, or solid blocking, doesn't add to the structural strength of a floor, and it could prevent members with crowns from straightening and floors to squeak and vibrate.

In those situations or areas where cross-bridging is used, metal bridging has replaced wood, for the most part, due to the labor required to measure, saw, and toenail wood bridging. Figure 7-39 shows two types of metal bridging. The nailless type (NC) is designed for installation with a simple strike of a hammer, causing the prongs to sink into the joists. The NB style requires two 1½" 8d nails at each end.

Figure 7-40 details solid bridging between joists using same-sized materials.

Bridging is commonly installed at intervals of not more than eight feet along the joist span. The bridging is installed in a row from one side of the building to the other. Snap a chalk line across the joists to ensure a straight row.

A house having a 28-foot depth and a centerline girder has two bays with a joist span of about 14 feet. Install a row of bridging in each bay at the midpoint of the joist span.

ESTIMATING MATERIALS

Joists generally span the short dimension of a house. The size and direction are given on the house plan. The size, direction of run, and spacing of the first-floor joists are usually given on the basement plan. The second-story floor joists are shown on the second-story floor plan. The attic floor joists are also shown on the second-floor plan. Joists are supported by girders and exterior walls on the first floor and by bearing partitions and exterior walls on the second floor.

While joists in the 22- to 24-foot lengths are sometimes available, they're quite expensive. The common lengths are from 8 to 16 feet.

To find the number of joists required for a floor area, divide the spacing of the joists into the length of the wall and add one joist for the end of the span.

Conventional framing requires double joists under partitions that runs parallel to the joists. Double joists might also be required under bathtubs.

A house that's 60 feet long and 28 feet wide, and has a centerline girder will have two bays of 14 feet each. With joist spacing of 16 inches on center, it will require ¾ as many joists as the length of the bay in feet, plus one extra joist. Three quarters of 60 is 45 (60 × 0.75 = 45) plus 1 = 46 joists for each bay, for a total of 92 regular joists plus the doubles.

Table 7-6 gives the number of joists for various dimensions, with spacings of 12, 16, and 24 inches.

Don't forget to include band (header) material in your take-off. If blocking or solid bridging is used, include this material also. In the previous example, a 60-foot-

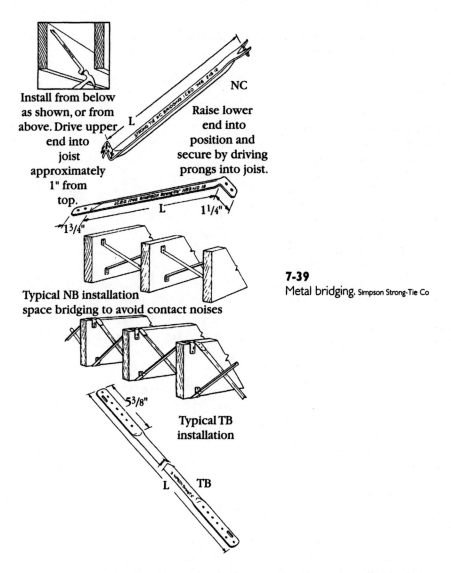

Install from below as shown, or from above. Drive upper end into joist approximately 1" from top.

L

NC

Raise lower end into position and secure by driving prongs into joist.

1 3/4"

L

1 1/4"

Typical NB installation space bridging to avoid contact noises

7-39
Metal bridging. Simpson Strong-Tie Co

5 3/8"

Typical TB installation

L

TB

long bay requires 60 linear feet (lf) of header. When estimating bridging, add the thickness of the joists and subtract from the bay's length (45 joists × 1.5" thick = 67.5 inches). Thus, about 57 lf of solid bridging is required.

For blocking between overlap joints at the girder, as shown in Figs. 7-25 and 7-26 (45 × 3 inches = 135 inches), deduct 11.25 feet for the thickness of the over-lapped joists. Thus, approximately 49 lf of blocking is required.

Conventional nailing practices for joists spaced 16 inches require 200 16d nails per 1,000 square feet of floor service area. For the example house (28 × 60), there's 1,680 square feet, which will require 340 16d box nails for 92 2 × 10 joists. There are 71 16d box nails to a pound, so order five pounds.

Solid bridging at the midspan of joists will require an additional five pounds, us-ing four nails for each member. Use 8d box nails to toe-nail joists and header to sill

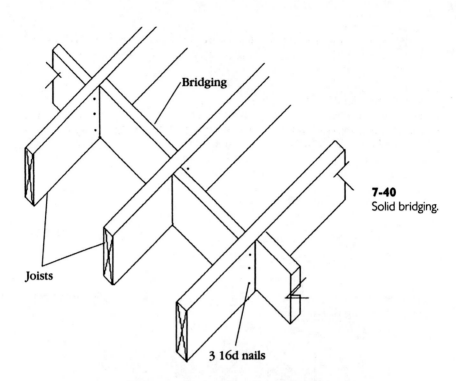

Bridging

Joists

3 16d nails

7-40
Solid bridging.

Table 7-6 Number of floor joists required

Span (feet)	Joist spacing 12"	16"	24"	Span (feet)	Joist spacing 12"	16"	24"
10	11	9	6	29	30	23	16
11	12	9	7	30	31	24	16
12	13	10	7	31	32	24	17
13	14	11	8	32	33	25	17
14	15	12	8	33	34	26	18
15	16	12	9	34	35	27	18
16	17	13	9	35	36	27	19
17	18	14	10	36	37	28	19
18	19	15	10	37	38	29	20
19	20	15	11	38	39	30	20
20	21	16	12	39	40	30	21
21	22	17	12	40	41	31	21
22	23	18	12	41	42	31	22
23	24	18	13	42	43	32	22
24	25	19	13	43	44	33	23
25	26	20	14	44	45	34	23
26	27	21	14	45	46	35	24
27	28	21	15	46	47	36	24
28	29	22	15				

and girder when the joists rest on top of the girder. About 400 nails should do the job. There are 145 8d box nails to a pound, so order three pounds.

ESTIMATING LABOR

Estimate 1.5 to 1.7 labor hours per 100 BF for 2 × 6 and 2 × 8 floor joists, and 1.3 to 1.5 labor hours per 100 BF for 2 × 10 and 2 × 12 joists. Solid bridging and blocking take about the same number of hours per 100 BF. If the example house (28 × 60) had 92 2 × 10 joists and midspan solid bridging in each bay, it would be:

Joists

One 2" × 10" × 14' floor joist = 23⅓ BF
92 × 23⅓ BF = 2146.36 BF
2147 BF (rounded off) ÷ 100 BF = 21.74 × 1.5 hrs = 32.20 hours

Headers

120 lf of 2 × 10s = 199.92 BF
200 BF × 1.5 hours = 3 hours

Solid bridging

57 lf at each bay = 57 × 2 = 114 lf = 189.92 BF
190 BF × 1.5 hours = 2.85 hours

Solid blocking

49 lf = 82 BF × 1.5 hours = 1.23 hours

Labor breakdown

Installing 92 2" × 10" × 14' floor joists	32.20 hours
Installing 120 lf of 2 × 10 header	3.00 hours
Installing 114 lf of 2 × 10 solid bridging	2.85 hours
Installing 49 lf of solid blocking	1.23 hours
Total labor hours	39.28 hours

8
Flooring panels

In platform (western) framing, the subflooring is installed once the floor joists are in place. The subfloor, or *decking*, must be in place before the wall framing can proceed. In the not-too-distant past, subflooring was 1 × 6 or 1 × 8 planks laid diagonally on top of the floor joists. Most housing tracts built during the big boom after World War II had this type of subfloor. Then things begin to change.

SUBFLOOR PANELS

A 4' × 8' panel can make short work of laying a subfloor over floor joists when compared with diagonally laid plank. Panel floor sheathing is the name of the game in house framing.

Wood panels for construction components are manufactured in a variety of ways: as plywood (cross-laminated wood veneers), oriented strand board (OSB), and composites (veneer faces bonded to OSB cores). Panels can be straightedge or tongue-and-groove.

Some grades of veneer panels are manufactured under the detailed manufacturing specifications or performance testing provisions of U.S. Product Standard PS 1-83 for Construction and Industrial Plywood, developed cooperatively by the plywood industry and the U.S. Department of Commerce. Other veneer panels, as well as an increasing number of performance-rated composite and OSB panels, are manufactured under the provisions of American Plywood Association's PRP-108, Performance Standards and Policies for Structural-Use Panels, which establishes performance criteria for specifically designated construction applications.

As most framers know, these APA performance-rated panels are easy to use because the recommended end use and maximum support spacings are clearly indicated in the APA trademark (see Fig. 8-1).

GRADE DESIGNATIONS

Panels are generally identified in terms of the veneer grade used on the face and back of the panel (A-B, B-C, etc.) or by a name suggesting the panel's intended end use (e.g., APA-rated sheathing, APA-rated Sturd-I-Floor).

Veneer grades define veneer appearance in terms of natural unrepaired growth characteristics and allowable number and size of repairs that can be made during the manufacture. The highest-quality veneer grades are N and A. The minimum grade of veneer permitted in exterior plywood is C. D-grade veneer is used in panels intended for interior use or applications protected from permanent exposure to weather.

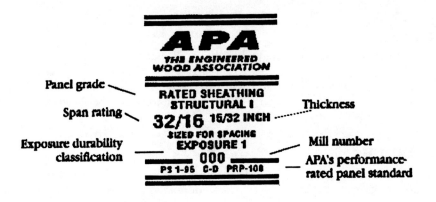

Panel grade

Span rating

Exposure durability classification

Thickness

Mill number

APA's performance-rated panel standard

8-1 APA trademark. (Typical)

Sanded, unsanded, and touch-sanded panels

Panels with B-grade or better veneer faces are always sanded smooth in manufacture since the intended use is for cabinets, furniture, built-ins, shelving, etc. APA-rated sheathing panels are unsanded because a smooth surface isn't a requirement of their intended use. Other panels, such as APA underlayment, APA-rated Sturd-I-Floor, APA C-D plugged, and APA C-C plugged, require only touch-sanding for sizing, to make the panel thickness more uniform.

Unsanded and touch-sanded panels, and panels with B-grade or better veneer on one side only usually carry the APA trademark on the panel back. Panels with both sides of B-grade or better veneer, or with special overlaid surfaces such as high-density overlay, usually carry the APA trademark on the panel edge.

EXPOSURE DURABILITY

APA trademarked panels are produced in four exposure durability classifications:
- Exterior
- Exposure 1
- Exposure 2
- Interior

Exterior
Exterior panels have a fully waterproof bond and are designed for applications subject to permanent exposure to the weather or moisture.

Exposure 1
Exposure 1 panels have a fully waterproof bond and are designed for applications where long construction delays are expected prior to providing protection, or where high moisture could be encountered in service. Exposure 1 panels are made with the same exterior adhesives used in exterior panels, but, because other compositional factors might affect bond performance, only exterior panels should be used for permanent exposure to the weather.

Exposure 2
Exposure 2 panels (identified as interior with intermediate glue under PS 1) are intended for protected construction applications where only moderate delays in providing protection from moisture are expected.

Interior

Interior panels are manufactured with interior glue and are intended for interior use only.

It's important to plan ahead and select the panel best suited for your job. You don't want to return to the job after a delay due to a long wet period to find swells and separations in the floor panels.

SPAN RATING

APA-rated sheathing, APA-rated Sturd-I-Floor, and APA-rated siding carry numbers in their trademarks called *span ratings*. These denote the maximum recommended center-to-center spacing, in inches, of supports over which the panels should be installed. Except for APA-rated siding, the span rating in the trademark applies when the long panel dimension is across supports. The span rating of siding applies when installed vertically.

The span rating in APA-rated sheathing trademarks appears as two numbers separated by a slash, such as 32/16 and 48/24 (see Fig. 8-1). The left-hand number denotes the maximum recommended spacing of supports when the panel is used for roof sheathing, with long dimensions across three or more supports. The right-hand number indicates the maximum recommended spacing of supports when the panel is used for subflooring with the long dimension across three or more supports. A panel marked 32/16, for example, can be used for roof decking over supports 32 inches on center or for subflooring over supports 16 inches on center.

The span rating in the trademarks on APA-rated Sturd-I-Floor and APA-rated siding panels appears as a single number. APA-rated Sturd-I-Floor panels are designed specifically for single-floor applications (combined subfloor and underlayment), under carpet and pad, and are manufactured with span ratings of 16, 20, 24, 32, and 48 inches on center, based on application of the long dimension across three or more supports. APA-rated siding has span ratings of 16 and 24 inches on center.

INNER-SEAL T&G FLOORING

Inner-Seal tongue-and-groove (T&G) flooring is an oriented strand board (OSB) flooring panel designed to resist moisture from the inside out. The panels are sanded on one side and are strong, rigid, and uniform. Inner-Seal panels are made primarily from small-diameter, fast-growing trees.

Inner-Seal T&G Plus flooring is an OSB flooring panel with a medium-density overlay. The panel was designed for construction in areas where standing snow, rain, or extreme humidity during construction could otherwise cause strand lifting or separation. The panel's tongue-and-groove edges have an enhanced edge seal for protection from water penetration.

INSTALLING THE SUBFLOORING

Subfloors are a double-floor system. The subfloor is installed directly to the floor joists, and provides a working platform during construction of the house. The underlayment is applied on the subfloor and the finish floor (carpet, tile, etc.) is applied on the underlayment. The subflooring can also be covered with hardwood or softwood strip flooring.

A single-floor system is possible using Sturd-I-Floor panels. The panel acts as both subfloor and underlayment.

Panels rated exposure 1 are commonly used for subflooring. Panels of this grade carry a span rating in the APA trademark stamped on the back, indicating the maximum recommended joist spacing. (A span rating of 32/16 means the panel can be installed lengthwise on rafters spaced 32 inches on center and on floor joists spaced 16 inches.) Use exposure 1 panels if construction delays will expose the flooring to the weather.

Install the panels with the best side up. Leave ⅛-inch gap at the panel edge and end joints for panel expansion. This will require end-cutting an inch or less from every third or fourth panel to ensure a center-to-center fit unless, of course, the panels are sized by the manufacturer for the proper spacing.

Panel layout

Did you install floor joists with the intent of tying the two bays together at the girder with the subflooring? If so, you must plan your subfloor sheathing layout accordingly. Also, plan for an installation with the least amount of panel cutting and handling.

If you plan to tie the bays, a good place to begin is at the corner of the house where you began the joist layout. Lay the panels out so that a panel will overlap the opposite joists by a minimum of eight inches.

If tying the bays isn't a consideration, begin your layout with a full-width (4') panel. Snap a chalk line across the joist 48 inches from the outside edge of the header joist. Start the first row with a 4 × 8 sheet set flush with the outside edge of the end joist and the long dimension across the joists. Use the chalk line to align the first row and leave space between the panel ends. Cut the last panel to fit flush with the outside edge of the end joist. It works best to have any odd-sized panels at the end of the row to cover at least two spaces between supports. The face grain must run across the supports.

Staggering the panel joints

The panel ends should *not* line up. To stagger the joints, start the second row by ripping a panel in half and beginning with the 4' × 4' piece. Be sure to leave the appropriate spacing between the edge and ends of panels. The third row begins with a full panel, the fifth row with a half panel, and so on.

Allowing for lapped joists

In conventional floor framing, joists lap at the girder. Where a joint between rows of panels falls over the lap area, the next row begins with a panel 1½ inches shorter to allow for the lap. In some cases, such as when using floor panels to tie the bays or when the panel joint doesn't fall over the lap, you have to scab a 2 × 4 on the side of a joist every eight feet to support the end of the panels. Continue to stagger the panel joints as you work the second bay. Figure 8-2 details the process of *scabbing*.

Completing the flooring

Look at Fig. 8-3. We started laying the panels at A with the gap recommended by the panel manufacturer. Since the panels in this case are a full eight feet, the fourth

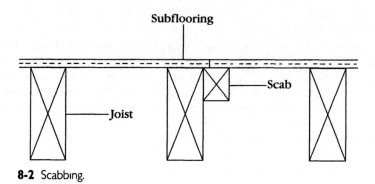

8-2 Scabbing.

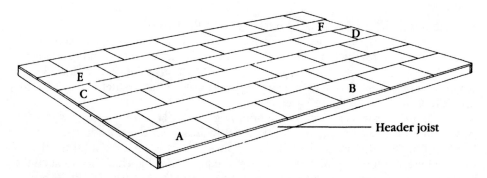

8-3 Completing the flooring.

panel (B) had to be trimmed in order for the fifth panel to fit centered on the joists. Usually, you can get by with end-trimming one panel to a row of six or seven panels. Some panel manufacturers size sheathing panels for their recommended spacing so the panel ends fall on the centerline of supports. As can be expected, not all carpenters take the time to end-trim eight-foot panels, so the spacing recommendation is obviously ignored.

In Fig. 8-3, the first row starts with a 4 × 8-foot panel, the second row with a 4×4-foot piece, and the third row with a 4 × 8 footer. The joint between the third and fourth row falls over the centerline of the girder. The first panel in the next row (C) would be four feet wide and 46½ inches long. If you want to allow for end spacing in the row, cut the panel 46¼ inches long. Panel D will probably be the only other panel in the row that has to be cut.

The fifth row starts with a 48 × 94¼-inch panel (E). You might have to end-trim the fourth panel in the row to allow for spacing and achieve bearing for the fifth panel, and a scab might be required under the end of the last panel (F). Actually, there would be a 1½-inch gap at the far end of the bay due to the joist lapping and the fact that the house length is a multiple of eight feet. I prefer installing an extra joist as a trimmer at the end of the bay to avoid scabbing.

Since the first panel was end-trimmed to 94¼ inches to allow for spacing and the lapped joists, the eight-foot panel at the end will be 1½ inches shy of a full fit. Use the scrap pieces end-trimmed from the first panel to fill this space.

Nailing the subfloor

Use 6d nails for $^{19}\!/_{32}$-inch-thick panels, and 8d nails for $^{19}\!/_{32}$-inch or $^{23}\!/_{32}$-inch panels. Place nails $\frac{3}{8}$ inch from the edge of the panel, spacing them six inches apart along all supports at the edges and ends. At butt ends, slant the nails to penetrate the floor joists. Space the nails 12 inches apart at intermediate joists. For these nail spacings on panels installed on joists spaced 16 inches on center, drive nine nails across each panel end, 17 nails along an eight-foot supported panel edge, and 5 nails along intermediate joists. See Fig. 8-4.

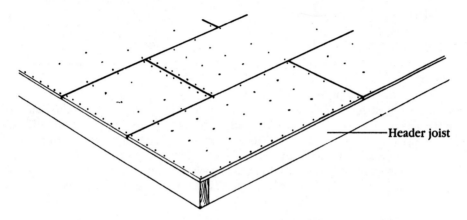

8-4 Nailing the floor panels. American Plywood Assoc

Snap a chalk line to define the center of joists to ensure the nails are driven accurately into the joists. I prefer to tack the panels at the four corners until all panels are in position, snap a chalk line over the joists, and complete the nailing.

INNER-SEAL FLOORING PANELS

Inner-Seal flooring panels are available in square edge and tongue-and-groove in $^{19}\!/_{32}$", $^{23}\!/_{32}$", 1", and $1\frac{1}{8}$" thicknesses, and in the standard 4' × 8' size. You can install the panel by nailing, screwing, and gluing techniques. A glue-nailing application is approved by the American Plywood Association for Sturd-I-Floor construction, $^{19}\!/_{32}$" for joists spaced 20 inches on center, $^{23}\!/_{32}$" for joists spaced 24 inches on center, 1" for 32-inch spacing, and $1\frac{1}{8}$" for 48-inch spacing.

Inner-Seal panels aren't sold as an exterior product, but exposure to wet weather during normal construction won't harm the panel. Before installation, allow the panels to adjust to job-site moisture conditions.

Install Inner-Seal T&G flooring to a dry, well-ventilated surface, not to rain-soaked floor framing. In crawlspace construction, a ground-cover vapor barrier is recommended.

Use conventional nailing to install Inner-Seal T&G flooring directly to joists. To produce a superior floor system, glue-nail. Use solvent-based glues conforming to performance specifications AFG-01 as developed by the American Plywood Association. Table 8-1 gives fastening specifications for Inner-Seal Sturd-I-Floor.

Table 8-1 Inner-Seal Sturd-I-Floor fastening

Joist spacing	Panel thickness	Nail size	Spacing: glue/nail		Spacing: nail only	
			Panel edge	Interior	Panel edge	Interior
16" oc	$^{19}\!/_{32}$"	*	12" oc	12" oc	6" oc	12" oc
20" oc		**				
24" oc	$^{23}\!/_{32}$"	*	12" oc	12" oc	6" oc	12" oc
32" oc	1"	***	6" oc	12" oc	6" oc	12" oc
48" oc	1⅛"	***	6" oc	6" oc	6" oc	6" oc

* 6d ring or screw-shank
** 8d common
*** 8d ring or screw-shank

When using the glue system, spread only enough glue to lay one or two panels at a time, or as specified by the glue manufacturer's instructions. Drive the nails before the glue sets to ensure bonding. Apply a continuous line of glue with a ¼-inch bead to supporting frame members. The T&G panel is sized for ⅛-inch spacing at end joints, so there will be no problem with panels catching the 96-inch center. Drive nails about ½ inch from panel edges. When installing panels with staples, use 16-gauge galvanized wire staples with a minimum ⅜-inch crown width and 1⅝-inch leg length.

APA-RATED STURD-I-FLOOR

APA-rated Sturd-I-Floor plywood panels are designed specifically for residential, single-floor applications. The floor serves as both subflooring and underlayment under carpet and pad. When glue-nailed, the floor is an exceedingly strong floor system. Use adhesives conforming to performance specifications AFG-10 and follow manufacturer's instructions.

Sturd-I-Floor panels are identified by a span rating in the APA trademark giving the maximum recommended spacing of the floor joists. Panels are available with span ratings of 16, 32, and 48 inches oc and in thicknesses ranging from $^{19}\!/_{32}$ to 1⅛ inches. Most Sturd-I-Floor panels are manufactured with tongue-and-groove edges that eliminate the need for blocking. Square-edge panels are also available. All these floor panels are moisture resistant and won't be harmed during wet weather in the course of normal construction periods. Use exterior panels if the flooring is exposed permanently to the weather or moisture.

For houses, the most common type of Sturd-I-Floor plywood is built on joists 16 and 24 inches on center. When joists are spaced 32 or 48 inches oc, select the panel rated for such spacing. There are two support spacing arrangements for Sturd-I-Floor 48 inches oc. The first is 2-by lumber joists spaced 32 inches oc; the second is 4-by girders spaced 48 inches oc. The panels are laid out and installed in much the same manner as in conventionally framed floors.

Measure the floor area and determine how the first row of panels will end at the opposite end of the floor. Follow the previous procedures for subflooring plywood panel layout. The long dimension of the panel must be perpendicular to the joists and across two or more spans between joists. Stagger the end joints of each row (see Fig. 8-5).

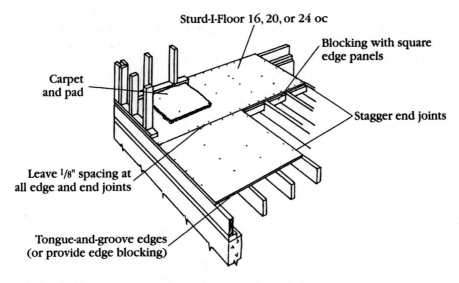

Sturd-I-Floor 16, 20, or 24 oc

Blocking with square
edge panels

Carpet
and pad

Stagger end joints

Leave ¹/8" spacing at
all edge and end joints

Tongue-and-groove edges
(or provide edge blocking)

8-5 Sturd-I-Floor. American Plywood Assoc

Begin at the outside edge of a joist header and snap a chalk line across the joints every four feet. This line will be your guide for panel alignment and gluing limits.

Now clean the top of the joist free of mud, dirt, etc., and apply a bead of glue to joists with a caulking gun. Cover only enough joists to lay one or two panels at a time, being careful to follow the instructions on the glue container. Support the edges of square-edge panels between all joists. Install 2 × 4 blocking centered to the chalk line. End-nail the blocking between the joists with two 16d nails at each joist, making sure the top of the blocking is flush with the top of the joists. Glue the edges of panels to the blocking to strengthen the floor and prevent squeaking. Blocking isn't required if a separate underlayment is used or if a structural finish floor is installed.

When installing T&G panels, lay the first panel with the tongue side to the wall and nail it in place with 6d deformed-shank nails spaced 12 inches at all supports. Apply a continuous ¼-inch bead of glue to framing members. Where panels butt on a joist, apply two beads to ensure a bead under each panel end.

Glue and nail the rest of the first row, allowing a ⅛-inch gap between the panel ends. Once the first panel row is installed, spread glue in a ⅛-inch bead that's either continuous or at three-inch intervals in the groove of one or two panels at a time.

Spread glue on the joists and other supports, and begin the second row with a half panel (4' × 4') in the same manner detailed previously for subflooring. Tap the T&G panels in place using a block to protect groove edges. Be sure the tongue-and-groove edges of mating panels are free of damage before positioning. Leave the recommended spacing between the ends and the T&G joint. (See Fig. 8-6.)

Continue installing the remaining panels in the same manner, beginning every other row with a half panel to ensure that the ends are properly staggered. Table 8-2 gives panel recommendations for APA glued-floor systems.

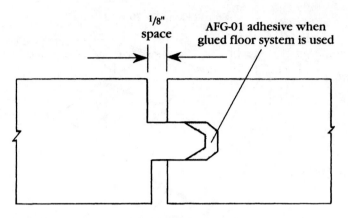

1/8"
space

AFG-01 adhesive when
glued floor system is used

8-6 Tongue-and-groove joint spacing. American Plywood Assoc

Table 8-2
Panel recommendation
for APA-glued floor system

Joist spacing (in.)	Flooring type	APA panel grade and span rating
	Carpet and pad	Sturd-I-Floor 16 oc, 20 oc, 24 oc
16	Separate underlayment or structural finish flooring	Rated sheathing 24/16, 32/16 40/20, 48/24
	Carpet and pad	Sturd-I-Floor 20 oc, 24 oc
19.2	Separate underlayment or structural finish flooring	Rated sheathing 40/20, 48/24
	Carpet and pad	Sturd-I-Floor 24 oc, 32 oc, 48 oc
24	Separate underlayment or structural finish flooring	Rated sheathing 48/24
32	Carpet and pad	Sturd-I-Floor 32 oc, 48 oc
48	Carpet and pad	Sturd-I-Floor 48 oc

Courtesy: American Plywood Assoc

THE SQUEAK-FREE FLOOR SYSTEM

A squeak-free floor is possible with properly installed components. If not properly installed, floors can squeak, buckle, and cause nails to pop up. A glued-floor system is considered a good way to eliminate squeaks.

Avoid green lumber. Dry lumber is more dimensionally stable than lumber that isn't properly cured. Green lumber tends to twist, warp, and make bumps under the finish flooring.

APA structural panels are available in a variety of grades and thicknesses. Consider floor loads, joist spacing, finish flooring, and whether the floor system is a single floor or subflooring plus underlayment. Table 8-3 is a quick guide to floor construction using APA-rated Sturd-I-Floor and sheathing.

Table 8-3 Quick guide to floor construction

Finish flooring	Subfloor[a]	Underlayment
Carpet and pad	APA-rated Sturd-I-Floor	Optional
Adhered carpet	APA-rated Sturd-I-Floor or APA-rated sheathing	Recommended
Resilient sheet goods and tile	APA-rated Sturd-I-Floor or APA-rated sheathing	Recommended
Hardwood	APA-rated Sturd-I-Floor or APA-rated sheathing	Optional
Ceramic tile	APA-rated Sturd-I-Floor or APA-rated sheathing	Recommended

(a) Edges of subfloor panels must be supported by tongue-and-groove joints or solid blocking unless covered with underlayment, lightweight concrete, or wood-strip flooring

Courtesy American Plywood Assoc

Install the panels with the recommended spacing to allow room for expansion due to changes in moisture content. Figure 8-7 is a bird's-eye view of what makes a squeak-free floor.

ESTIMATING MATERIALS

Estimate subflooring panels by dividing the square feet of the floor area by the square feet in one panel. For example, if a house is 28' × 64' (1,792 square feet) and you're using 4' × 8' flooring panels (32 square feet), then you'd need 56 panels (56 × 32 = 1,792).

Deduct only large openings when estimating floor panels. Any opening smaller than 4' × 8' shouldn't be considered. A four-foot module structure as in the example will have little, if any, waste. If the dimensions are on a two-foot module, waste can be as much as five percent.

Estimate nails at 1.5 nails per square foot of floor space for joists spaced 16 inches oc. In the example house of 1,792 square feet, 2,688 nails are required to install 56 panels.

If you're using 8d common nails, there are 106 nails to the pound, so 25.36 pounds would be needed to install 56 panels on 16-inch spaced joists. Estimate 181 6d common nails to the pound and 14.85 pounds to install 56 panels.

Note:
Provide adequate
ventilation and use
ground cover vapor
retarder in crawlspace.
Panels must be dry
before applying
finish floor.

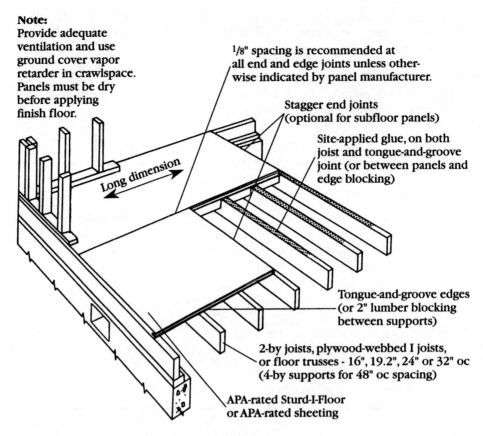

$^1/_8$" spacing is recommended at
all end and edge joints unless otherwise indicated by panel manufacturer.

Stagger end joints
(optional for subfloor panels)

Site-applied glue, on both
joist and tongue-and-groove
joint (or between panels and
edge blocking)

Long dimension

Tongue-and-groove edges
(or 2" lumber blocking
between supports)

2-by joists, plywood-webbed I joists,
or floor trusses - 16", 19.2", 24" or 32" oc
(4-by supports for 48" oc spacing)

APA-rated Sturd-I-Floor
or APA-rated sheeting

8-7 Squeak-free floor system. American Plywood Assoc

ESTIMATING LABOR

As a rule of thumb, estimate installing 4' × 8' subflooring panels on joists spaced 16 inches oc at 10 to 12 hours per 1,000 square feet. Add additional time for T&G panels. Glue-nailing will require approximately 15 to 18 hours per 1,000 square feet.

9
Wall framing

Wall framing begins with the bottom (sole) plate and ends with the top plate. The sole plate is also referred to as *mud sill* or *rat sill*. The studs are the vertical members and rest directly on the bottom plate in platform construction. In balloon framing, the studs rest on the sill plate (see Fig. 4-8). Door headers, window headers, and window sills are horizontal components.

The plates and studs in conventional framing are commonly 2 × 4s. The headers over doors, windows, and other openings in load-bearing walls are constructed of larger pieces of lumber. Many builders use 2 × 10s in combination with a 2 × 4 for all door and window headers, as shown in Fig. 9-1. In an eight-foot-high wall, this header provides the correct rough door-opening height of 6'10" to 6'11" above the subfloor. Also, since most windows are installed at the same height as the doors, the header provides a solid nailing surface above the windows. The need for cripples above the header is eliminated for most window placements. Figure 9-2 shows a typical wall framing.

9-1 Conventional header.

9-2 Typical wall framing.

STARTING OUT RIGHT

Careful framers closely examine their house plans to ensure they don't contain errors and that the wall layout carefully follows the plan. They want to know if the dimensions are drawn to the middle or outside of walls. A few inches can mean a big difference and can be costly, if not impossible, to correct later. The dimensions of rough openings for doors and windows should be verified with the actual size of the door and window units to be installed. If you assume that all wood-frame, double-hung windows of the same size require the same-sized rough opening, then you might find yourself changing the opening when it comes time to install the windows. When in doubt, it's wise to either physically measure the window or have the manufacturer's documented rough-opening requirements on hand before framing the openings.

SNAPPING THE WALL LINES

The house plan will show where each wall is located. Measure and mark the wall location and snap a chalk line the length of the wall. On exterior walls, snap a line 3½ inches from the outside edge of the platform if the studs are to be flush with the platform's (or slab's) outside edge. If the wall sheathing is to be flush with the outside edge of the platform (or slab), allow 3½ inches plus the thickness of the sheathing for the line. Figure 9-3 explains. The chalk line ensures that the bottom plate is installed straight.

Snap the exterior walls first. Then measure and snap the interior walls, longer walls first. Mark an X on the side of the chalk line the plate will go. Some framers

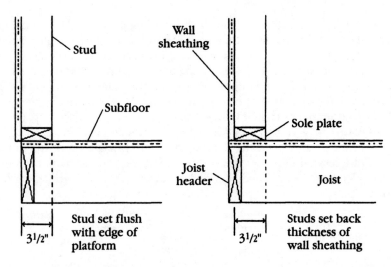

9-3 Snapping the exterior wall line.

prefer to snap a second line 3½ inches from the first to indicate both sides of the plate. This, of course, ensures that you'll always consider the width of the plate when taking measurements from either side of the wall.

CEILING HEIGHTS

Most houses are built with an eight-foot ceiling height even though a slightly lower ceiling is permitted by most codes. An eight-foot ceiling allows easy use of 4' × 8' building materials. Precut 2 × 4 studs make wall framing in platform construction easier than using standard eight-foot-long 2 × 4s. Precuts are 7'8⅝" long and, when used with a 2 × 4 bottom plate and double 2 × 4 top plate, they'll give you a wall height of 97⅛ inches from the subfloor.

PLATFORM CONSTRUCTION

In platform construction, build the wall framing flat on the subfloor and then tilt it up into position. Raise the exterior walls first, then build the center load-bearing wall and tilt it into position. The partition walls come last.

Some framers put together the single top plate and studs, and tilt it onto a bottom plate nailed into position. Then they toe-nail the studs to the bottom plate with four 8d box nails. Other framers nail all the components together, including the framed door and window openings, and raise them into position.

Large crews might install the sheathing while the frame is on the deck and then raise the wall. This method can cause problems, however, unless the floor is completely level and the wall framing exactly square. Most framers prefer to tilt the wall frame into position, plumb it, and brace it before applying the sheathing.

Laying out the plates

After snapping the wall lines, begin by laying out the bottom plate for the exterior walls with 16-foot-long 2 × 4s. Of course, if the studs are 2 × 6s the plates will be

2 × 6s as well. Extend the side-wall plates the full length of the floor to the outside edge of the platform or to the sheathing line, depending on the sheathing installation method (Fig. 9-3). Position the bottom plates for the end walls between the side-wall plates. Tack the bottom plates in place, butting the ends firmly. Use only three or four nails since all you intend for the moment is to hold the plate in position for marking the wall components such as stud placement, openings, and partition intersections.

With the bottom plates tacked in place to the subfloor, lay the top plate directly beside the bottom plate and tack in place. Use 16-foot lengths where possible. The next step is to locate and mark the centerline of window and door openings, and the location of intersection partitions and studs. Use a square to mark both the bottom and top plate at the same time. Figure 9-4 shows how your marking might look.

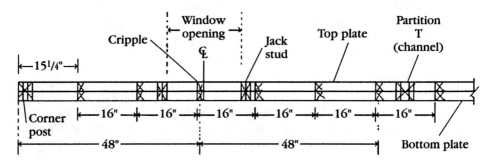

9-4 Marking the plates.

Stud spacing

In conventional framing, the stud layout will generally be 16 or 24 inches on center. The 24-inch spacing is used on many houses, and you saw in chapter 4 how you can reduce labor and material costs with this method. To mark off the stud layout, the determining factor is the width (48 inches) of most structural wood sheathing, siding panels, sheet rock, interior paneling, etc. The dimensions from the outside of the corner to the centerline of the first stud from the corner should be 16 inches, or 24 inches when studs are spaced 24 inches on center (see Fig. 9-5).

Corner post construction

How the components are cut, laid out, and nailed together depends on the crew size, preference of methods, and whether it's an assembly-line job in a tract where several houses are framed simultaneously.

A three- to five-member framing crew is typical. Such a crew might proceed in the manner so far discussed and, with the stud layout marked, begin with putting together the corner posts. This is my method. Yours might be to begin by building the window and door framing. Another crew might proceed to cut all the cripples, jacks, headers, etc., and lay them out with the precut studs on the deck in position and ready to nail. Since we have to start someplace and because one way is probably as good as another, let's do it my way this time.

A corner post must be constructed to serve as a nailing surface for exterior and interior materials, and the post must be rigid enough to do the job. The two most

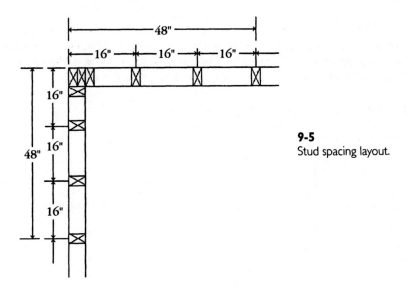

9-5
Stud spacing layout.

common styles use three 2 × 4s (see Fig. 9-6). The B post also uses three 2 × 4 blocks, or *separators*, about 12 inches in length. Locate the blocks flush with the ends of the studs, or a couple inches from the ends and at the midpoint of the post. Nail it to a stud with three 10d box nails and nail the opposite stud to the blocks with three 16d nails. Be sure the two studs are flush at the ends.

Face-nail the third member of the post to the blocked studs with 16d nails spaced 12 inches apart. Face-nail the stud at each block with one 16d nail. Tie the three studs of post A together, as shown in Fig. 9-6, using 10d nails spaced 12 inches apart. Be sure the ends of the members are flush. Construct a corner post for each corner in the outside walls and each corner in the interior walls.

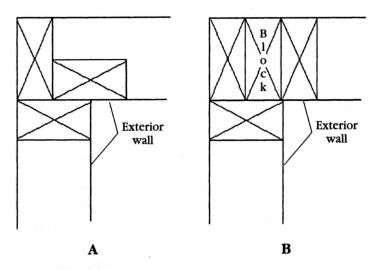

A

B

9-6 Typical corner posts.

Interior wall T construction

Look at Fig. 9-7. The partition T is used when an interior wall intersects another wall, whether it's an exterior wall or another interior wall. Its purpose is to provide a nailing surface for wall materials at corners. The T requires three studs. Nail the studs together as shown, with 10d box nails spaced about 12 inches apart. Be sure the ends are flush.

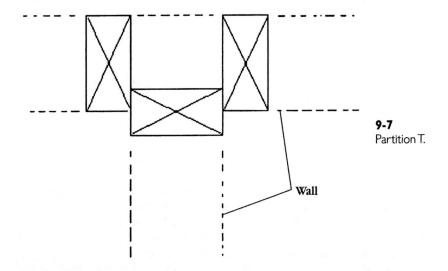

9-7
Partition T.

Wall

Stud materials

Studs for platform framing can be precut and ready to install or can be cut on the job from standard 2 × 4s. The precuts are 7'8⅞" for standard ceiling heights. If you're cutting your own studs for the floor-to-floor ceiling height on a plan, add one inch for underlayment and ceiling material thickness and subtract 4½ inches for the thickness of a 2 × 4 bottom plate and a double 2 × 4 top plate. For higher or lower ceilings, the studs are generally cut on the job from standard-length stock.

When cutting studs on the job, select a straight 2 × 4, measure it, and cut it. Mark it "PAT" for stud pattern and use it to measure all exterior and interior studs of the same height.

Tilt-up framing

Tilt-up framing is possible when there's a floor surface on which the wall can be assembled and then raised into position. Tilt framing is possible in platform construction and on concrete slabs.

Build the long exterior walls first. Sixteen-foot-long bottom and top plates are a good length to work with. A longer wall is hard to lift up with a small crew.

Remove the bottom and top plates you tacked to the floor and marked for stud layout. Move the top plate toward the center of the floor about 10 feet from the outside edge. Lay all full-length studs in position between the bottom and top plates. Then lay the jack studs, headers, cripples, and sill in position, as appropriate for door and window framing. Do *not* place corner posts and partition Ts in position.

These will be installed after the wall is tilted into position. This is necessary because the dimension (thickness) of the T and post is greater than the wall studs. (When the bottom plate is installed first and the wall tilted onto it, the corner posts can be nailed to the bottom plate, plumbed, and braced before the wall is raised.)

Assemble the window and door framing using 16d nails. Face-nail studs to each header member larger than a 2 × 4 with three 16d nails. Figure 9-8 shows the components of a conventionally framed window opening. Door openings are framed using the same header material and method.

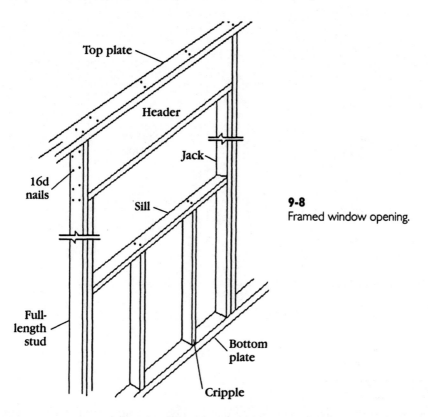

9-8
Framed window opening.

With the door and window openings framed, you can begin nailing the pieces of the wall together. Tilt the bottom and top plates on edge. Nail the studs in place through the bottom and top plates with two 16d nails at each end. Secure the window and door framing in place using the same nailing method. Additionally, face-nail the top plate to each header member with 16d nails spaced 12 inches apart. Cut the top plate to center over a stud. Continue assembling the complete wall in 16-foot or shorter sections.

Let-in bracing

Before you tilt the wall into position, cut the notches for let-in bracing. Many framers nail 4' × 8' plywood or other structural panels at each exterior corner to brace the wall. The let-in brace is, however, the favorite method of many framers and it requires a little more expertise than simply nailing up a 4 × 8 panel. All exterior walls and main cross-stud partitions must be braced at each end (or as near the end as possible) at every 25 feet of wall length. A let-in can be a 1 × 4 or 1 × 6 installed at approximately a 45-degree angle. Here's how:

1. Square, to a reasonable degree, the corner section of the wall framing while it lies horizontally on the deck.
2. Lay the 1 × 4 or 1 × 6 plank at about a 45-degree angle from the bottom plate to the top plate. The plank must be one continuous piece (see Fig. 9-9).

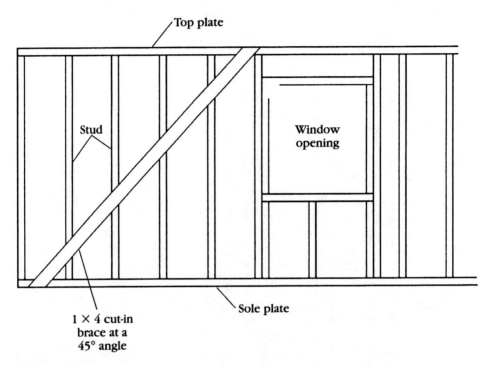

9-9 Fitting the cut-in brace.

3. Set your saw blade to a 1½-inch depth, slide it along the top of the brace, and cut into the studs on each side of the brace.
4. Saw off the brace top and bottom flush with the plates, or mark the studs on each side of the brace and saw them to a ¾-inch depth.
5. Reset the saw blade to full depth and rip out a ¾-inch notch between the saw kerfs just made in the studs.
6. Position the brace in place and check to make sure it fits flush with the surface of the studs.
7. Set the let-in brace in place and nail it to the bottom plate with three 8d box nails.
8. Tack the brace to the top plate. Do *not* attempt to square the frame on the floor and nail the brace in place. It works best to square the wall and secure the brace after the wall is in position. Otherwise, a slight variance in the floor level could cause problems.

9. Lift the wall into place, lining up the bottom plate with the chalk line.
10. Face-nail the bottom plate to each joist through the subflooring with two 16d nails and to the joist header at 16-inch intervals with 16d nails.

Temporary bracing

Temporarily brace the wall with 2 × 4s and nail the braces to blocks nailed to the floor, as shown in Fig. 9-10. On-slab construction requires many temporary braces long enough to extend from the bottom of one wall to the top of an opposite wall (see Fig. 9-11). Don't place the temporary braces where they'll interfere with the building and the tilt-up of end walls or interior partitions.

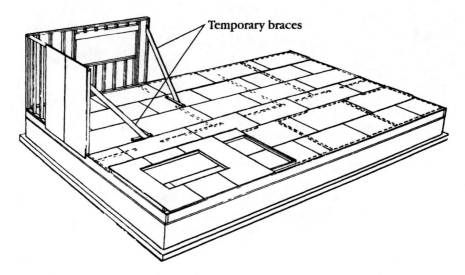
Temporary braces

9-10 Lifting wall section into place and bracing. American Plywood Assoc

Setting the corner posts

After the wall is tilted up and temporary braces are in place, it's time to install the corner posts. The post is fitted flush with the outside edge and end of the bottom and top plates (see Fig. 9-14). Toe-nail the post to the bottom plate with five 8d box nails. Face-nail the top plate to the post with four 16d nails.

Square and plumb the wall with the temporary braces (Fig. 9-12) and nail the let-in braces in place at each stud and top plate with three 8d box nails.

Figure 9-9 illustrates fitting a let-in brace with the complete wall, framed horizontally. When the tilt-up is with a wall consisting of the top plate and studs onto an already installed bottom plate, the let-in brace fits at the bottom, as shown in Fig. 9-13. The let-in brace rests on top of the bottom plate and is nailed to blocking installed between the studs. The let-in can be installed on the exterior or interior side of the wall. Leave as many temporary braces in place as you can during construction until the roof is framed and sheathed.

9-11 Long braces needed for on-slab construction.

9-12 Plumb and square wall before nailing in the let-in bracing.

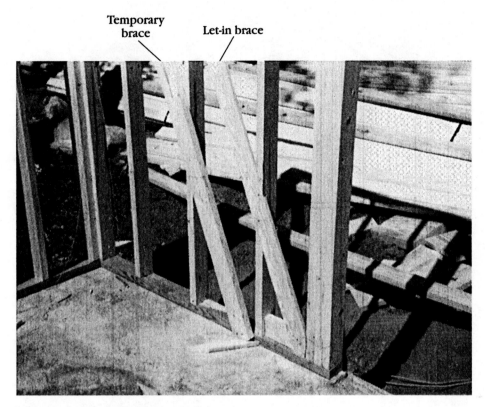

Temporary brace   Let-in brace

9-13 Another method of fitting a let-in brace.

End-wall framing

The end wall is framed in the same manner as the side walls. Cut and fit the pieces for window and door openings and build the frames. Lay out the studs and nail on the top and bottom plates. Prepare the necessary let-in braces and raise the wall. The bottom plate end fits under stud no. 3 of the corner post (Fig. 9-14). It's often a tight fit and you'll have to tap it into position with a hammer. At the same time, the top plate of the end wall fits on top of the no. 3 stud (see Fig. 9-15).

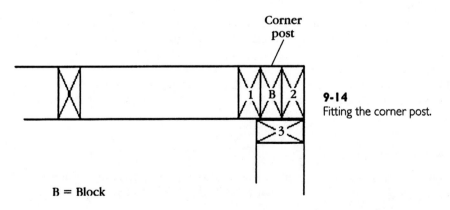

Corner post

1 B 2

3

9-14
Fitting the corner post.

B = Block

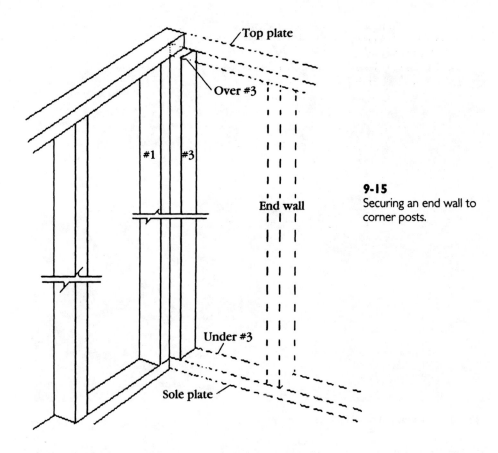

9-15
Securing an end wall to corner posts.

Face-nail the bottom plate through the flooring to the floor joist or stringer joist with 16d nails spaced 16 inches apart. Secure the top plate to the no. 3 stud of the corner post with two 16d nails. Plumb the wall with temporary braces. Locate the braces so as not to interfere with the framing and tilt-up of other walls. Before nailing the let-in braces, check the plumb of the side walls.

Installing the wall Ts

The wall Ts can now be installed in the side and end walls. Look at your wall layout, indicated by the chalk lines on the floor. A T goes wherever an interior wall intersects the exterior wall.

Place the T on the bottom plate over the T channel mark and toe-nail with five 8d box nails. Line the T up with the T channel mark on the top plate and check it with a level. The T should be plumb for both walls. Face-nail the top plate to the T with four 16d nails.

Partition wall framing

Partition walls can also have corner posts and wall Ts. Start framing interior walls with the longest wall. This is generally the load-bearing wall at or near the center of the house. There might be more than one load-bearing wall, depending on the house depth and design.

The interior walls are laid out the same as exterior walls, except for window openings. Begin by fitting the bottom and top plates. Lay them side by side on the floor at the chalk line and tack them in place.

Begin the stud layout by measuring the first stud 16 inches (or 24 inches, depending on the stud spacing) from the interior surface on the intersecting wall. With your measuring tape, mark for the first stud at 15¼ inches from the face of the bottom plate on the exterior wall. Draw a line perpendicular across both plates and place an X to the right side of the line. See Fig. 9-16.

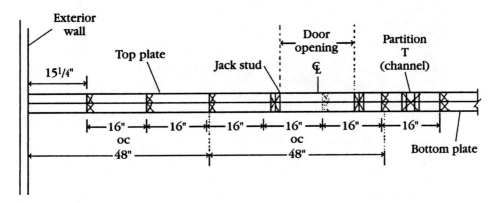

9-16 Marking stud layout for an interior wall.

Mark the plates for door openings and any other special framing specified by the plan. Separate the plates, placing them on edge on the floor approximately nine feet apart. Cut and arrange the pieces for openings. Lay the studs in place and start nailing the pieces together. Cut for let-in braces as required. Then tilt-up the wall and face-nail the bottom plate to the floor joists through the subflooring with two 16d nails at each joist.

Use temporary braces to plumb the wall. Nail to the exterior wall Ts at the intersections. Do not nail in the let-in braces of the interior walls yet. Continue building and raising the interior walls, working the longer walls first. Figure 9-17 shows how the maze of framing might look at this stage.

Top plate alignment

Before installing the top member of the top plate, you must make the top of the wall as straight as possible. To do this, use a taut gauge string and ¾-inch-thick blocks, as shown in Fig. 9-18.

Tack a block to the side of the top plate near each end of the wall. Near the block, closer to the end of the plate, drive a 16d nail about two-thirds of the way into the plate. Pull a taut string from nail to nail over the top of the blocks. Insert a ¾-inch-thick block between the string and the plate at various places along the plate to determine if the plate is straight. To adjust the top plate in or out, use temporary braces. Nail the brace to the side of a stud immediately under the top

9-17 Wall framing in place and braced.

plate, force the wall into alignment, and nail the other end of the brace to a block tacked to the deck. Figure 9-19 shows a top plate that's straight and ready for the next framing stage.

Installing top member of top plate

The top member (cap) of the top plate is the same size as the top plate. The 2 × 4 cap ties all the walls together. The butt joints in the plate and cap are offset, occur

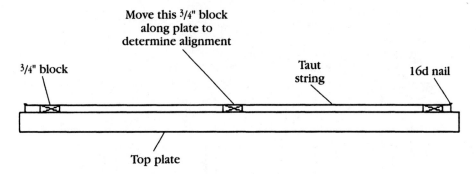

Move this 3/4" block
along plate to
determine alignment

3/4" block

Taut
string

16d nail

Top plate

9-18 Stringing the top plate.

9-19 A straight top plate is absolutely essential.

over wall studs, and are lapped at all intersecting walls. Figure 9-20 explains. The cap of each intersecting wall is overlapped, or *eared* into the other wall, as shown in Fig. 9-21.

Second-floor framing

In platform (western) construction, the second floor is framed much the same way as the first floor, building on top of floor joists. When the walls of the first floor have been framed, the floor joists of the second floor (which are also the first-floor ceil-

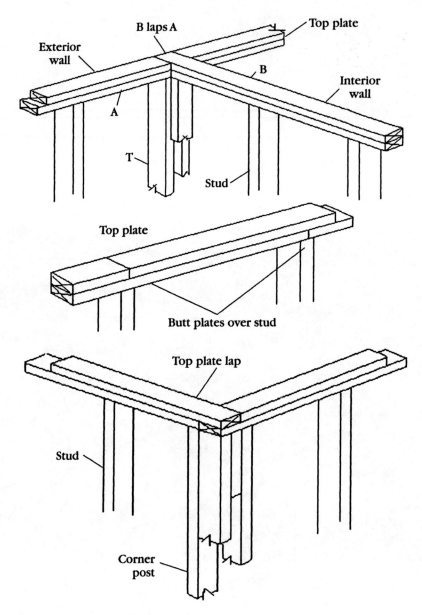

9-20 Tying the wall system together.

ing joists) are installed directly on top of the double top plate of the first floor (see Fig. 9-22). Also, see Figs. 4-1 and 4-4. Figure 9-23 shows the second-floor platform framing over a bearing partition.

Construct the second-floor walls horizontally on the subfloor and tilt them up the same way you built the first-floor walls. Be sure you have sufficient help when raising the walls. Think safety when working at second-floor heights. Figure 9-24 illustrates framing the end wall of a second floor for platform construction.

9-21 Locking the framed walls together with the top-plate cap.

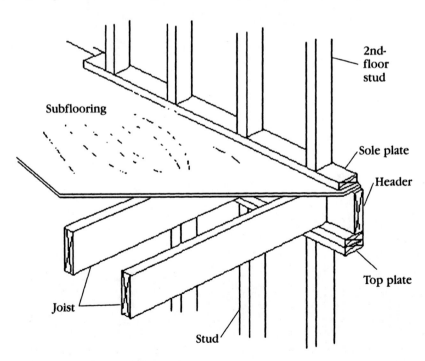

9-22 Second-floor framing.

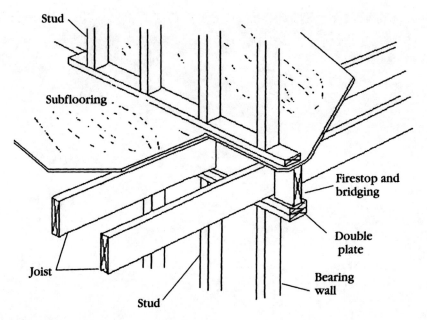

9-23 Platform framing over a bearing wall.

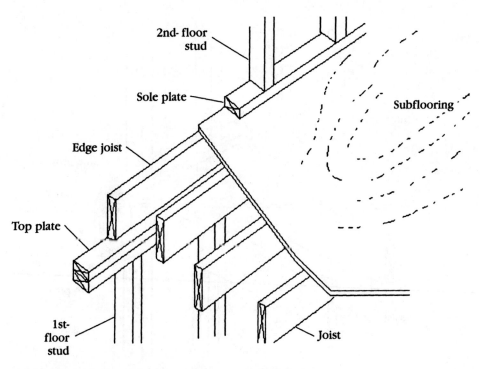

9-24 Platform framing of the second floor at an end wall.

You can use platform construction on a second floor without using full-length studs. High and steep-slope rafters and knee walls can be the complete second-floor framing. See Fig. 9-25.

9-25 Another way to frame a second floor.

STORM-RESISTANT CONSTRUCTION

While there's little you can do to completely protect a structure against the more violent forces of nature, such as tornadoes, hurricanes, floods, and earthquakes, you can strengthen a frame house against high winds and the less violent forces away from the center of a storm.

Nails alone can resist only so much pressure. Structural framing members will generally pull away at the joints before breaking. Metal framing anchors are required by code in many areas. A second floor secured with floor-tie anchorage, as shown in Fig. 9-26, will resist a great deal more pressure than conventional nailing.

Figure 9-27 illustrates one method of anchoring framing components to the foundation, and Fig. 9-28 shows another way to tie together the first and second floor framing. Studs can be anchored to the bottom and top plates with steel angles (see Fig. 9-29). Another style of framing anchors is shown in Fig. 9-30.

Use nails furnished with the anchors or as recommended by the anchor manufacturer. Rafters, as you'll see later on, can also be secured with anchors. Various types of steel-band diagonal-wall bracing are also available and can often be substituted for let-in wood members.

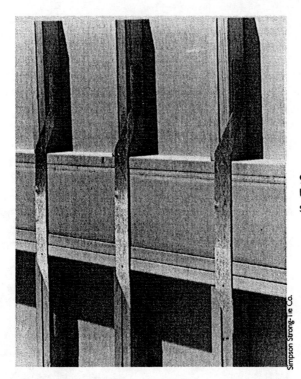

9-26
Using steel anchors to tie the second floor.

Simpson Strong-Tie Co.

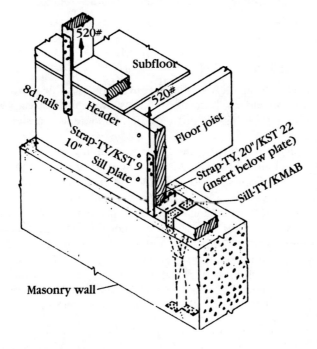

520#

Subfloor

8d nails

Header

520#

Floor joist

Strap-TY/KST 9
10"

Strap-TY, 20"/KST 22
(insert below plate)

Sill plate

Sill-TY/KMAB

Masonry wall

9-27
Anchoring framing components to the foundation. Teco Co

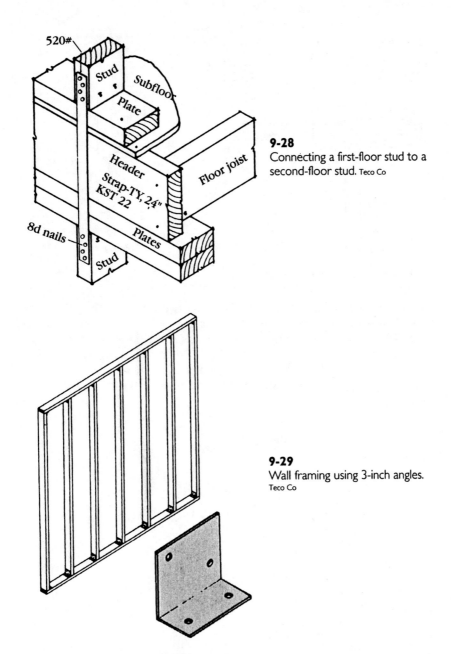

9-28
Connecting a first-floor stud to a
second-floor stud. Teco Co

9-29
Wall framing using 3-inch angles.
Teco Co

BALLOON CONSTRUCTION

The balloon framing method is shown in Fig. 4-8 back in chapter 4. Balloon framing allows less shrinkage in exterior walls. For some, it's the preferred method for two-story houses having a stone or brick veneer.

The framing method uses a two-inch-thick (nominal) wood sill on the foundation wall, and the joists and studs rest directly on the sill. The studs are nailed to the joists

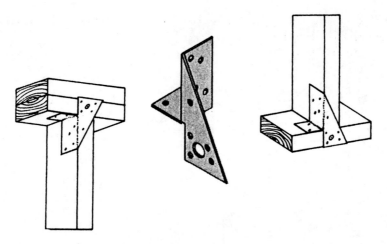

9-30 Trip-L-Grip framing anchors. Teco Co

with three 12d nails and toe-nailed to the sill with two 8d nails. Then the joists are toe-nailed to the sill with three 8d nails. Framing anchors are recommended in high-wind areas. A firestop is installed between the studs at the floor line. See Fig. 9-31.

Horizontal shrinkage is limited to the sill. Where a 2-by sill is used on top of a steel centerline girder, the horizontal shrinkage is equal at all sills. In a two-story structure, the exterior-wall studs extend to the top plate of the second story.

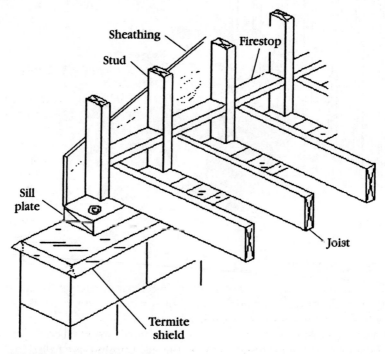

9-31 Balloon framing method.

The second-floor joists are supported by a ribbon let into the exterior-wall studs and nailed to the studs with three or four 12d nails (see Fig. 9-32). Firestopping is installed between the studs at each floor level (see Fig. 4-8). The center load-bearing partition is generally constructed with single-story-height studs with a single top plate, as shown in Fig. 9-33.

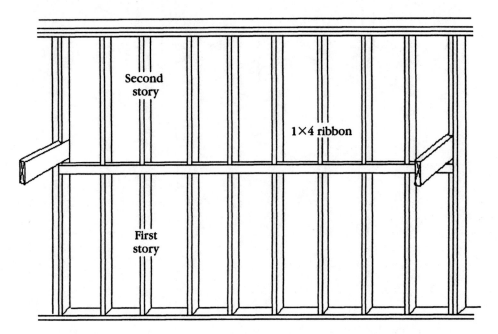

9-32 Let-in ribbon.

The joists at the exterior end walls that run parallel to the wall on both the first and second floors are nailed to each stud with three 12d nails. Figure 9-34 explains.

Diagonal 1 × 4 let-in braces can be installed at the corners of the wall of each story after the walls have been erected and plumbed. You can cut the notches with a power saw. If an opening is near the corner, you can locate the diagonal brace back from the corner near the opening. Plywood, OSB, and other kinds of structural panels can be used to brace the wall in lieu of let-ins. Many framers prefer using 4' × 8' × ½" plywood at corners and on long walls for bracing. Other structural sheathing, such as fiberboard, gypsum, exterior particleboard, and hardboard, is approved for bracing when the thickness, size, and application comply with building codes.

Balloon walls are not generally tilt-ups. A two-story wall is difficult to raise unless you have a crane or lift available.

CANTILEVER FRAMING

Cantilever framing for the second floor provides an overhang of the second-story exterior wall. The framing method is basically platform construction except the second story floor joists extend beyond the exterior wall a short distance.

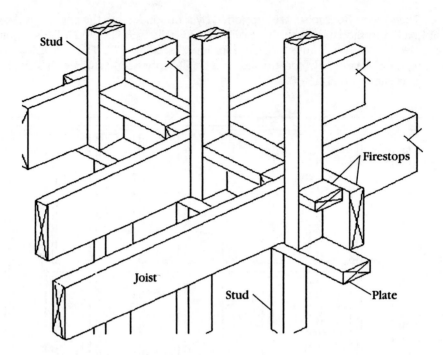

9-33 Balloon framing at a load-bearing wall.

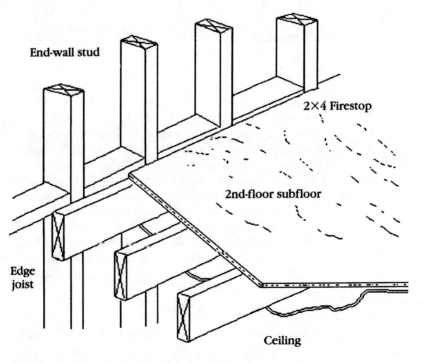

9-34 End-wall framing for balloon construction.

With cantilever framing, the joists can run at right angles to the supporting wall (Fig. 9-35) or the overhang can be constructed with lookout joists when the main joists run parallel to the supporting wall, as illustrated in Fig. 9-36.

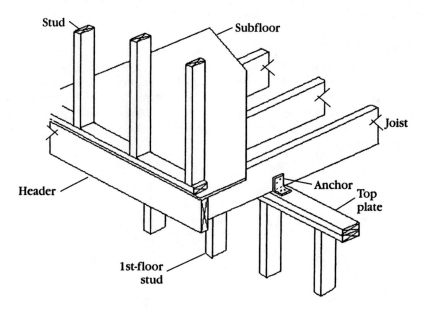

9-35 Cantilever framing using regular joists.

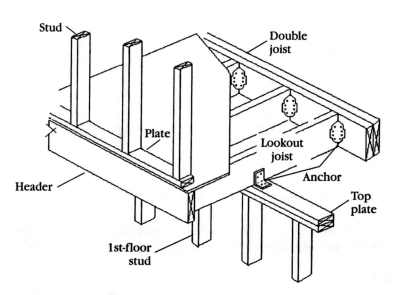

9-36 Cantilever framing using lookout joists.

The projection of the second floor can be to accommodate brick or stone veneer of the first floor or solely for architectural effect. The overhang can be 16 inches or more.

When the overhang parallels the second floor joists, as shown in Fig. 9-36, locate the double joist back from the wall a distance about twice the overhang dimension. Use framing anchors to secure the lookout joists to the double joist and to the wall plate.

FRAMING OPENINGS

Door and window openings can be framed in different ways. Often, the type of framing for openings is purely the preference of the framer, who might construct the opening with 2 × 4 or 2 × 6 header material, as shown in Fig. 9-37. Short upper cripples are used over the header to continue the stud spacing and provide a nailing surface for finish material. Whatever the method, the header must be of sufficient strength to support the imposed load.

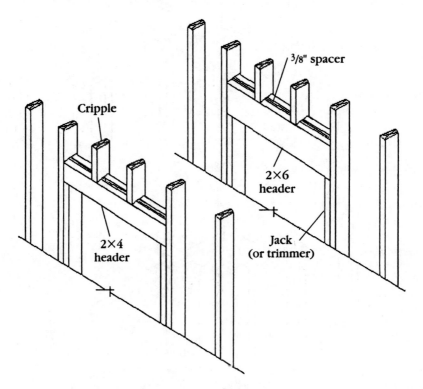

9-37 Window opening using 2 × 4 or 2 × 6 headers.

Look back at Figs. 4-26 and 4-32 in chapter 4 to see other framing methods. Figure 9-38 provides the basic formula for sizing window and door openings.

Header size criteria

The framing members used over window and door openings are called heads or headers. As the span of the opening increases, the depth of the header must also in-

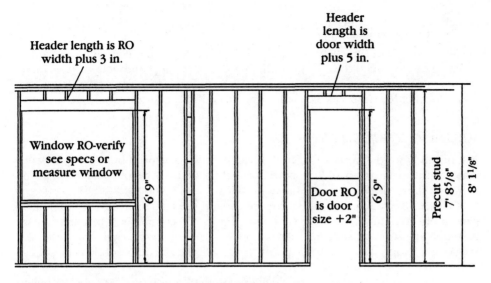

Header length is RO width plus 3 in.

Header length is door width plus 5 in.

Window RO-verify see specs or measure window

6' 9"

Door RO is door size +2"

6' 9"

Precut stud 7' 85/8"

8' 11/8"

9-38 Sizing formula for window and door openings.

crease because the wider the span, the heavier the load imposed by the ceiling and roof. Headers are generally built-up with two-inch nominal (1½" actual thickness) members and can be spaced ⅜ inch apart with plywood or OSB panels cut the same length and depth as the header. The panel is sandwiched between the 2-by members. The panel gives added strength to the header. Most framers, however, merely space the header members without using any spacing material.

The header is generally supported at the ends by the inner (jack) studs, also called *jamb* or *trimmer* studs. The header rests on the jack studs, which is nailed directly to a full-length stud.

The species used for floor joists is generally strong enough to use for average headers in a house. Table 9-1 provides a guide for header sizes. Wide openings might require specially designed trussed headers.

Table 9-1 Header size guide

Maximum span (feet)	Header size (inches)
3½	Double 2 × 6
5	Double 2 × 8
6½	Double 2 × 10
8	Double 2 × 12

LOW-COST WALL FRAMING

You can achieve low-cost wall framing by reducing the materials and labor required to construct the walls. Modular wall framing on 24-inch centers can reduce wall-framing costs considerably. Likewise, nonmodular construction with stud spacing on

24-inch centers can reduce material costs 20 percent or more. Refer to chapter 4 and compare Figs. 4-27 and 4-28.

Mid-height blocking between wall studs is generally unnecessary and can be eliminated unless required by your building code. The top and bottom plates provide adequate firestopping, and ½-inch sheet rock installed horizontally doesn't require blocking for support when studs are spaced 24 inches or less.

BUILDING STRAIGHT WALLS

One of the keys to a successful framing career is the ability to build straight walls. Straight walls make it possible to have a straight roof, and without straight walls the interior and exterior walls won't finish properly.

Crooked lumber is a curse on carpenters, and the curse is worse on some jobs than others. Avoid using excessively bowed lumber in components that are difficult to straighten, such as wall top plates and top plate caps. A 16-foot-long, badly bowed, 2 x 4 top plate can be most difficult to straighten. The best rule is to not use such lumber in the first place.

To ensure straight walls, use a chalk line on the floor to which the bottom plate can be aligned, as previously discussed. And always use a gauge line to align the top plate.

ESTIMATING MATERIALS

The materials required to frame a wall are primarily studs, plates, headers, nails, and framing anchors.

Studs for western framing

Unfold the house plan. Begin at one corner of the building and measure the linear feet all the way around the outside walls. Next, measure the linear feet of the inside stud partitions running in one direction. Then measure the partitions running at right angles. Follow the same procedure for all walls on the second floor. If the basement and attic have partitions, measure them also.

Walls without openings
For a wall without openings, with studs spaced 16 inches on center, multiply the length of the wall in feet by ¾ (0.75) and add one stud. Table 9-2 gives the number of wall studs required for 16-inch spacing.

Walls with openings
For a wall with openings and with studs spaced 16 inches on center, estimate one stud for each linear foot of wall. This allows for doubling studs at corners and window and door openings. Table 9-3 gives coverage estimates for standard stud walls.

The following rule of thumb can often offer a fairly accurate estimate. Try this on your next house: The number of studs required in platform framing 16 inches on center approximates the total square feet of floor (not counting the basement) divided by three. Thus, a 1,600-square-foot house will require about 533 studs for all exterior and interior walls.

Table 9-2
Studs required for 16-inch spacing
for walls without openings

Length of partition in feet	Number of studs required	Length of partition in feet	Number of studs required
5	5	17	14
6	6	18	15
7	6	19	15
8	7	20	16
9	8	21	16
10	9	22	17
11	9	23	18
12	10	24	19
13	11	25	19
14	12	26	20
15	12	27	21
16	13	28	22

Table 9-3
Board feet of studs per square foot of wall

Size of studs	Spacing oc	BF per sq. ft. of area	Lbs. nails per 1000 BF
Exterior-wall studs (Includes an allowance for corner bracing)			
	12"	1.09	
2 × 4	16"	1.05	22
	24"	94	
	12"	1.66	
2 × 6	16"	1.51	15
	24"	1.38	
Partition-wall studs (Includes an allowance for plates, end studs, blocks, framing around openings, and waste)			
	12"	1.22	
2 × 4	16"	1.12	19
	24"	1.02	
2 × 6	16"	1.48	16
	24"	1.22	

Top and bottom plates

To estimate the material for plates, multiply the linear feet of all walls and multiply by three. If a single member is used for the top plate, multiply by two.

Studs 24 inches on center

Estimate studs for interior partition walls without openings by dividing the length of the wall in feet by two and adding one stud. For example, a wall 18 feet long will be computed as:

$$18 \div 2 = 9 + 1 = 10 \text{ studs}$$

Figure a partition wall with openings the same way, except add two extra studs for each opening. Materials for exterior walls are estimated the same as for partitions, with one added stud for each corner. For example, a wall 52 feet long with four windows and one door would be computed as:

$$52 \div 2 = 26 + 1 = 27$$

$$
\begin{array}{l}
 27 \\
+ 2 \text{ (studs for two corners)} \\
+ 8 \text{ (studs for four window openings)} \\
+ \underline{2} \text{ (studs for door opening)} \\
 39 \text{ (for 24" oc)}
\end{array}
$$

Additional pieces might be required for corner posts and partition Ts, depending on your framing method.

Firestops

Firestops are the same size as the studs, which are generally 2 × 4s. Determine the linear feet of all walls requiring firestopping to find the linear feet of required firestops. For firestopping at the mid-height of walls, subtract the combined width of all openings. The result will equal the number of firestops. To fine-tune your estimate, deduct the thickness (1½") of each stud in the wall. If a wall has 39 studs, deduct 58.5 inches (39 × 1.5").

Corner bracing

Corner bracing, as you know, provides rigidity to the building by protecting against lateral forces such as wind. Plan to use 12-foot-long 1 × 4s for an eight-foot wall. You'll need two for each corner and one along every 25 feet of long walls. Bracing is required for each story.

If you're using panels for bracing, figure a panel for each corner and at every 25 feet of long walls. Where panels are used for exterior corner bracing, let-ins are used in interior walls—requiring bracing unless the finish wall is considered structural.

Studs for balloon framing

Most studs in balloon framing are long, extending from the sill plate to the top plate of the second story. The total number of board feet is essentially the same as for platform construction. Full-length studs are required for exterior walls and for all double studding at openings. Shorter lengths can be used under and over the openings, such as from the top of a first-floor opening to the top plate of the second story. The inside partition studs are estimated the same as for platform construction. Add 10 percent when estimating stud requirements to allow for waste and rejects.

Ribbon

The amount of required ribbon is the total linear feet of the two exterior side walls supporting the second-floor joists.

Nails

Nail requirements are listed in Table 9-3.

ESTIMATING LABOR

Estimate 21 skilled and 6 unskilled labor hours for exterior wall framing per 1,000 BF. Partition framing will require about 20 skilled and 5 unskilled hours per 1,000 BF.

A house 24' × 52' with an eight-foot ceiling height and stud spacing 16 inches on center has 1.05 board feet of wall area (see Table 9-3).

A 52-foot wall has 416 square feet of wall area and requires 436.8 board feet of lumber. Exterior wall studding requiring 21 skilled and 6 unskilled hours per 1,000 BF equals to 2.1 skilled and 0.6 unskilled hours per 100 BF. This means that:

$$2.1 \times 436 \text{ BF} = 9.16 \text{ hours}$$
$$0.6 \times 426 \text{ BF} = 2.62 \text{ hours}$$

So a total of 9.16 skilled and 2.62 unskilled hours are required to frame the 52-foot wall.

Partition studding requires 2 skilled and 0.5 unskilled hours per 100 BF. A partition with eight-foot ceilings and studs spaced 16 inches on center has 1.12 BF per square foot of wall area (Table 9-3). A 24-foot partition has 192 square feet and requires about 215 BF of lumber. The results are as follows:

$$215 \text{ BF} \times 2 \text{ skilled hours} = 4.3 \text{ skilled hours}$$
$$215 \text{ BF} \times 0.5 \text{ unskilled hours} = 1 \text{ unskilled hour}$$

10
Wall sheathing

Most wall sheathing used today are panels. Wall sheathing covers the exterior side of studs, bottom and top plates, and door and window headers to provide a smooth, flat surface for the exterior finish materials. The "hard" or structural panels also serve to provide strength and rigidity to the wall, eliminating the need for diagonal corner bracing.

PLYWOOD SHEATHING

Plywood is made from thin sheets of veneer wood peeled from a softwood or hardwood log. The sheets, after drying, are bonded under heat with adhesive, with the grain of each ply running at right angles to the adjacent ply. The end product is a strong and durable panel.

The C-D grade of plywood is used for wall, floor, and roof sheathing. The panel is unsanded and is available with exterior glue. The standard size is 4' × 8', although other sizes, such as 4' × 9' and 4' × 10', are also available. APA-rated plywood sheathing meets building code requirements for bending and racking strength without let-in corner bracing. APA-rated sheathing corner panels can be used in lieu of let-in bracing when nonstructural fiberboard sheathing is used. Building paper is not required over plywood wall sheathing with brick veneer or masonry if air space is provided between the sheathing and the masonry. Building paper (15-pound felt) is, however, required under stucco.

For 16-inch stud spacing, the minimum plywood thickness of ⁵⁄₁₆ inch can be used, but a ⅜-inch or thicker panel is desirable when the exterior finish is nailed directly to the sheathing. Table 10-1 gives specifications for APA panel wall sheathing. Table 10-2 shows plywood stapling recommendations.

Panel sheathing can be carried to the subfloor, as illustrated in Fig. 10-1, or to the foundation wall, as shown in Fig. 10-2. When the sheathing panel extends to the foundation wall, the wall is tied to the floor system. This results in a house frame that will stand up better against outside forces.

Corner panels

Plywood has long been recognized by framers as being a desirable corner bracing component. I use ½-inch-thick C-D grade panels on each exterior corner when installing ½-inch gypsum or fiberboard sheathing on the wall. Attach the plywood to the framing members with 8d common nails spaced six inches on center along panel edges, and 12 inches on center at intermediate supports. See Fig. 10-3.

Table 10-1 APA wall sheathing specifications

Panel span rating	Maximum stud spacing (inches)	Nail size***	Nail spacing***	
			Panel edges	Intermediate
12/0, 16/0				
20/0 or wall 16" oc	16*	6d for panels ½" thick or less, 8d for thicker panels	6"	12"
24/0, 24/16, 32/16	24**			

Note: APA-rated sheathing panels continuous over two or more spans

*Apply panels less than ⅜" thick with face grain across studs when exterior covering is nailed to sheathing

**Apply 3-ply panels face grain across studs 24" oc when exterior covering is nailed to sheathing

***Common, smooth, annular, spiral-thread, or galvanized box, or T-nails of same diameter as common nails (0 113" dia for 6d, 0 131" for 8d) can be used Staples also permitted at reduced spacing.

Table 10-2 Sheathing stapling recommendation

Panel thickness (inches)	Staple leg length (inches)	Spacing around entire perimeter of sheet (inches)	Spacing at intermediate members (inches)
⁵⁄₁₆	1¼	4	8
⅜	1⅜	4	8
½	1½	4	8

Notes: Values are for 16 ga. galvanized wire staples with a minimum crown width of ⅜ inches.

Staples aren't recommended for attachment of APA-rated siding.

Installation

Use APA-rated sheathing 24/0 over studs spaced up to 24 inches on center. Sheathing can be applied vertically or horizontally. Some building codes require blocking behind horizontal joints. (Vertical application is the long side parallel to the studs. Horizontal application is the long side perpendicular to the studs.)

For a vertical application, position the first panel with the long edge flush with the outside edge of the corner post. Flush the bottom of eight-foot panels with the subfloor, as shown in Fig. 10-1. If you're using precut studs 92⅝ inches in length and a double top plate, the wall height will be 97⅛ inches from the subfloor to the top of the double plate. Thus, a full eight-foot panel will be 1⅛ inches shy of the top of

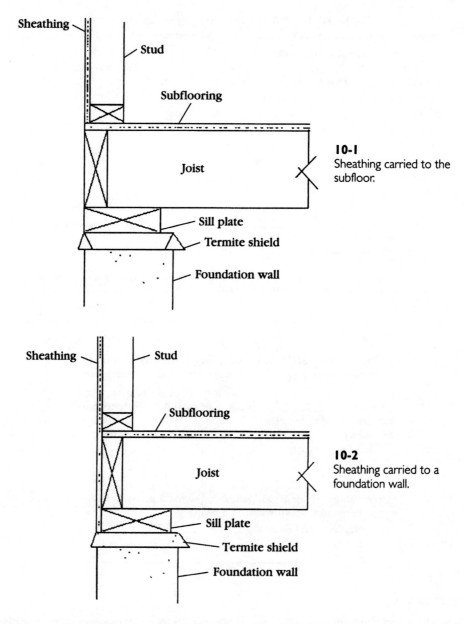

10-1
Sheathing carried to the subfloor.

10-2
Sheathing carried to a foundation wall.

the top member of the top plate, allowing space to fit the heel cut of the rafter directly against the top plate (see Fig. 10-4).

When applying sheathing with the face grain across the studs (horizontal application), rest the long edge on or flush with the subfloor, the same as with a vertical installation. Stagger the vertical joints at least one stud space.

Nail the sheathing to the framing members with 6d common nails spaced six inches apart along edges and 12 inches apart over intermediate studs. Leave ⅛ inch at all panel edge and end joints. See Fig. 10-5.

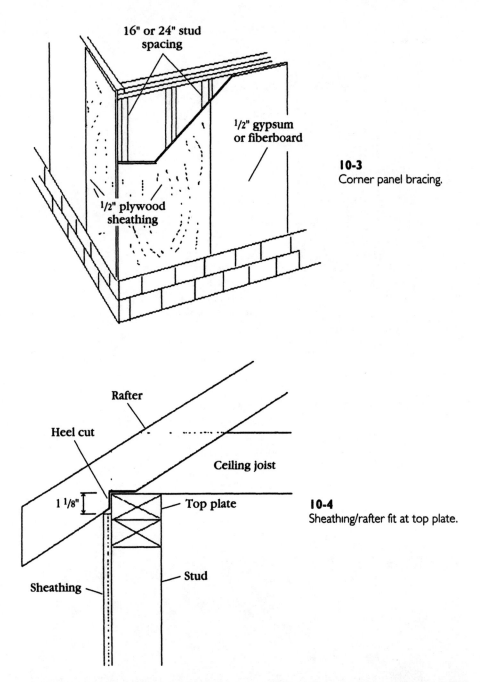

16" or 24" stud spacing

1/2" gypsum or fiberboard

1/2" plywood sheathing

10-3
Corner panel bracing.

Rafter

Heel cut

Ceiling joist

1 1/8"

Top plate

Stud

Sheathing

10-4
Sheathing/rafter fit at top plate.

Where the outside surface of the studs are flush with the outside surface of the floor framing, as shown in Fig. 10-2, you can use sheathing filler strips, as shown in Fig. 10-5. Nail the filler strip to both header joist and sill to tie the two. Use 6d nails spaced six inches apart.

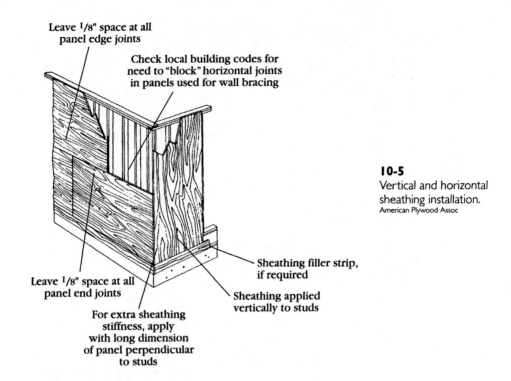

Leave ¹/8" space at all
panel edge joints

Check local building codes for
need to "block" horizontal joints
in panels used for wall bracing

10-5
Vertical and horizontal
sheathing installation.
American Plywood Assoc

Sheathing filler strip,
if required

Leave ¹/8" space at all
panel end joints

Sheathing applied
vertically to studs

For extra sheathing
stiffness, apply
with long dimension
of panel perpendicular
to studs

ORIENTED STRAND BOARD

APA-rated OSB panels are structural panels suitable for all types of sheathing. Like plywood, OSB can be used for corner bracing. Figure 10-6 shows OSB panels used as corner bracing in conjunction with fiberboard sheathing.

10-6 OSB panels used for corner bracing.

OSB panels are available in various thicknesses and in standard 4' × 8', 4' × 9', and 4' × 10' sizes. The 7⁄16-inch-thick panel can be used on studs spaced up to 24 inches on center, with panels applied either vertically or horizontally. You want to stagger the vertical ends at least one stud space when applying the panels horizontally.

Install the panels with at least 1⁄8 inch of space between all edges. Use 6d nails spaced six inches apart along all edges and 12 inches apart on intermediate supports.

FIBERBOARD SHEATHING

Fiberboard is manufactured from wood fibers and various bonding agents. Fiberboard sheathing has about twice the insulating value as plywood and is often referred to as insulating board. Structural fiberboard is probably the most economical sheathing material. The panel is coated or impregnated with asphalt to make it water resistant, which makes it a good dry-in material because it will never become rain-soaked. The three common types of fiberboard used for sheathing are regular-density, intermediate-density, and nail-base.

Regular-density fiberboard is available in 1⁄2-inch and 25⁄32-inch thicknesses, and in 2' × 8', 4' × 8', and 4' × 9' panels. Intermediate-density and nail-base sheathing are denser, available only in 1⁄2-inch thickness and 4' × 8' and 4' × 9' panels.

Regular-density, 2 × 8-foot panels with matched edges are applied horizontally, while 4 × 8- and 4 × 9-foot panels are generally installed vertically.

Install diagonal, let-in braces at corners when applying panels horizontally and 1⁄2-inch regular-density sheets vertically. You don't generally need diagonal let-ins for 25⁄32-inch-thick regular-density board or for intermediate-density and nail-base sheathing installed vertically (see Fig. 10-7). Instead of let-in bracing, 1⁄2-inch-thick plywood or OSB panels can be used at corners for bracing.

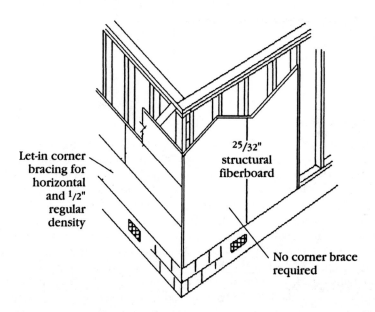

Let-in corner bracing for horizontal and 1/2" regular density

25/32" structural fiberboard

No corner brace required

10-7 Vertical and horizontal fiberboard sheathing.

Position the panel bottom at or flush with the subflooring, and the edge flush with the outside edge of the corner post. Secure ½-inch panels with 1½-inch galvanized roofing nails. For ²⁵⁄₃₂-inch fiberboard sheathing, use 1¾-inch nails.

In stapling applications where corner bracing is omitted, use 1½-inch, 16-gauge, galvanized wire staples with ⁷⁄₁₆-inch crown and divergent chisel points.

Generally, you want to install fiberboard sheathing vertically to the framing, allowing ⅛ inch between panels. The sheathing is cut scant to allow for spacing.

When installing fiberboard sheathing without diagonal corner bracing, nail or staple the panel first to intermediate framing members at six inches on center, and then fasten along all edges with nails three inches apart and not less than ⅜ inch from edge. Drive the nails flush, and shoot staples so the crown slightly depresses the sheathing surface and the staples' crown width is parallel to the sheathing edge. See Fig. 10-8.

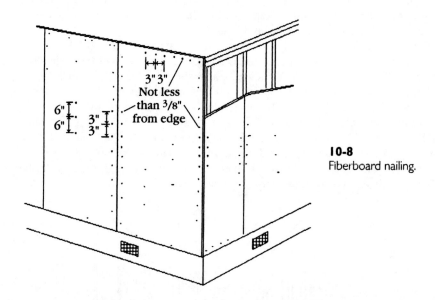

10-8
Fiberboard nailing.

GYPSUM SHEATHING

Gypsum sheathing is available with a silicone-treated gypsum core, surfaced with inorganic fiberglass facings. This "paperless" gypsum withstands warping and deterioration and on-site damage more effectively than paper-faced gypsum. These panels are manufactured in a four-foot width and in eight-, nine-, and 10-foot lengths, and can be installed vertically or horizontally.

Install ½-inch paperless gypsum sheathing on framing spaced 16 inches or less with 1½-inch, hot-dip, 11-gauge, galvanized nails with ⁷⁄₁₆-inch heads, or the equivalent. Space the nails a maximum of four inches apart on center along the perimeter and eight inches apart in the field of the board. When studs are spaced 24 inches on center, apply ⅝-inch-thick panels with nails 1¾ inches in length. Drive nails flush with the panel surface. Don't dimple. Stagger vertical joints when applied horizontally.

Gypsum sheathing cannot be used as a nailing base for other materials. Diagonal corner bracing is necessary.

When wood shingles or shakes are installed over gypsum and regular-density fiberboard, apply 1 × 3-inch wood furring strips over the gypsum sheathing, spaced to correspond to the shingle exposure. Nail the strips to the framing with a minimum of one nail at each stud. The nails must be long enough to penetrate a minimum of one inch into the studs. See Fig. 10-9.

Regular gypsum sheathing is also available in ½- and ⅜-inch thicknesses and in four-foot widths 8 to 16 feet in length, with square edges.

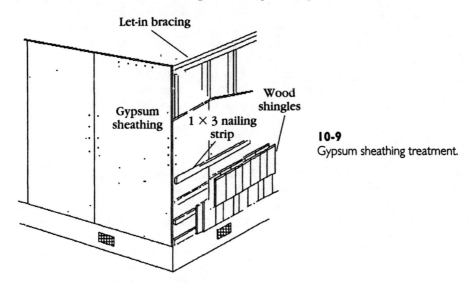

10-9
Gypsum sheathing treatment.

INSULATING FOAM-PLASTIC SHEATHING

Insulating foam-plastic sheathing panels are used when a high insulating value is required. Expanded polystyrene and other rigid foam-plastic panels with aluminum foil facing are sold by many different manufacturers under various trade names. The panels are available in thicknesses ranging from ½ to three inches, and in 4 × 8- and 4 × 9-foot sizes.

Foam-plastic sheathing is not a structural panel, and corner bracing must be provided. In addition, in areas immediately adjacent to or above combustion equipment (such as chimneys or furnaces) or other surfaces that could reach high temperatures, foam-plastic sheathing and other combustibles must be shielded. Consult your local code. In attached garages, the insulated walls and ceiling separating the garage from the living area must comply with building codes concerning fire resistance. At a minimum, ½-inch gypsum board should be installed to both sides of the frame wall. Type X (fire-resistant) gypsum panels are recommended for ceilings.

Installation

Be careful to avoid puncturing the panel's foil face during handling and installation. The aluminum foil protects the insulation from ultraviolet light, which will harm the foam. You can repair small tears and punctures in the foil face with aluminized tape. Repair larger holes or tears with appropriately sized pieces of the sheathing held in place with aluminized tape.

Some foam sheathing requires venting in colder climates to avoid trapping water vapor within the stud wall. Follow the manufacturer's instructions when installing the sheathing. Plastic vent strips are available for placement between the top plate and sheathing.

Install foam-plastic sheathing vertically, with the long edge in moderate contact with the adjacent panel and bearing directly on the framing members.

Apply the sheathing with galvanized roofing nails with ⅜-inch heads that are long enough to penetrate the framing a minimum of ¾ inch. Use 16-gauge wire staples with a minimum of ¾-inch crown and a leg length long enough to penetrate the framing ½ inch. Shoot the staples with the crowns running parallel to the direction of the framing. Nails and staples should not be overdriven so as to tear the foil facing.

Cut the panel with a sharp utility knife using a straightedge.

Wear sunshades over your eyes to protect against the glare when installing sheathing in the sunlight. Wall sheathing is generally not installed until all the framing is completed.

STURD-I-WALL

Sturd-I-Wall is a plywood panel that can be applied directly to the framing as a combination siding and structural sheathing. Use APA-rated siding. See Fig. 10-10.

Sturd-I-Wall panels are available ⅜- to ¾-inch thick, in 4' × 8', 4' × 9', and 4' × 10' lengths. You can install the panels vertically, with the long dimension running parallel to the studs, or horizontally. The vertical application is the predominate method. The allowable stud spacing is marked on the back of the panel. Panels marked "24 oc" can be installed vertically to studs spaced 16 or 24 inches on center. Panels marked "16 oc" can be installed vertically over studs spaced no more than 16 inches on center. Textured 1-11 siding can be applied vertically to studs arranged 16 inches on center.

Any APA-rated siding can be used on studs spaced 24 inches on center when hung with the long dimension horizontal, if blocking is provided at the horizontal joints (see Fig. 10-10).

Corner bracing isn't necessary with panel siding. In some cases, depending on the house plan and window type, the windows might have to be positioned and secured to the framing prior to siding installation. No building paper is required if panel joints are shiplapped or are going to be covered with battens. Use building paper for unbatten square butt joints and horizontally hung grooved-panel siding. Panel the side walls first and then work the end walls.

Installing the panels

Figure 10-11 shows how to fit the panel. Allow for a one-inch minimum overlap on top of the foundation wall, and finish flush with the top of the top plate.

Begin panel installation at a corner, flushing the panel edges with the outside edge of the corner post. Use hot-dip galvanized, aluminum, or other nonstaining nails to prevent staining the siding. Secure ½-inch-thick panels with 6d siding or casing nails. For thicker panels, use 8d nails. Space nails six inches along panel edges and 12 inches at intermediate supports. Leave ⅛ inch between panels (see Fig. 10-12). Install solid-lumber blocking to support all panel edges. Maintain a ⅛-inch space between panels.

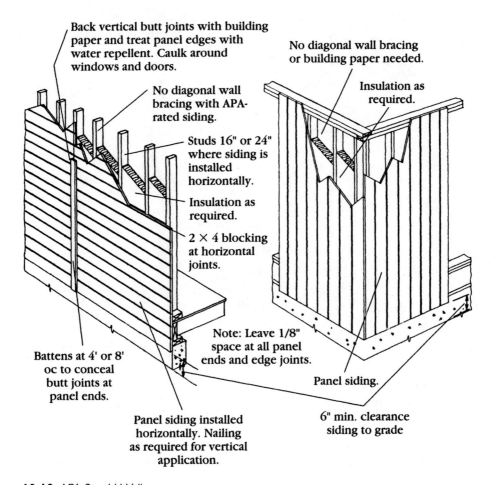

Back vertical butt joints with building paper and treat panel edges with water repellent. Caulk around windows and doors.

No diagonal wall bracing with APA-rated siding.

No diagonal wall bracing or building paper needed.

Insulation as required.

Studs 16" or 24" where siding is installed horizontally.

Insulation as required.

2 × 4 blocking at horizontal joints.

Battens at 4' or 8' oc to conceal butt joints at panel ends.

Note: Leave 1/8" space at all panel ends and edge joints.

Panel siding.

Panel siding installed horizontally. Nailing as required for vertical application.

6" min. clearance siding to grade

10-10 APA Sturd-I-Wall. American Plywood Assoc

Place the panel in position, maintaining proper spacing, and tack at each corner. Drive the first row of nails next to the preceding panel, from top to bottom. Now remove the tacking nails, hold the panel firmly against the first intermediate stud, and nail from top to bottom. Repeat this action at the next stud and then nail the opposite edge. Complete the installation by nailing at the top and bottom plates.

The end-wall corner panel overlaps the side-wall panel edge, as shown in Fig. 10-13. Install trim molding to dress out the corner.

Caulking the joints

Shiplapped joints don't require caulking. Neither do joints backed up by building paper. You must, however, caulk butt joints at all inside and outside corners using high-performance butyl, polyurethane, or thiokol caulks. Apply the caulk in accordance with the manufacturer's instructions.

When you install the panels horizontally, treat the edges of the panels with a good water repellent. Use building paper for grooved panel siding installed hori-

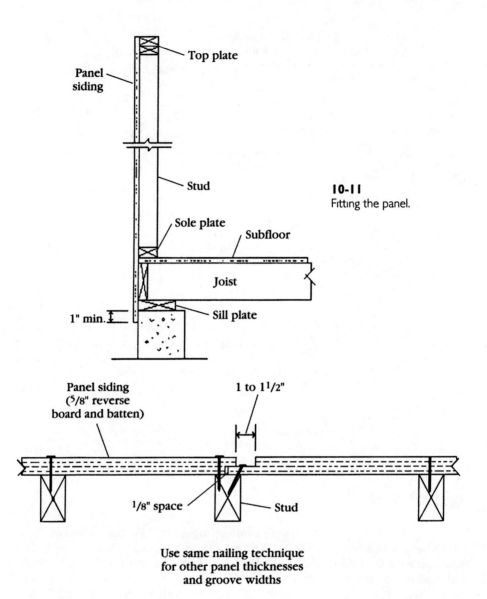

10-11
Fitting the panel.

Labels in figure: Top plate, Panel siding, Stud, Sole plate, Subfloor, Joist, Sill plate, 1" min.

Panel siding
(⁵/₈" reverse
board and batten)

1 to 1¹/₂"

¹/₈" space — Stud

Use same nailing technique
for other panel thicknesses
and groove widths

10-12 Nailing a shiplapped panel. American Plywood Assoc

zontally, and for ungrooved panels when vertical joints aren't covered with battens. Be sure to caulk around doors and windows.

Install battens to cover the vertical butt joints at panel ends of siding that's applied horizontally. Use nails long enough to penetrate the studs a minimum of one inch.

ESTIMATING MATERIALS

Calculate the total linear feet of the exterior walls on each floor and multiply by the wall height to find the gross area in feet. You can deduct or not deduct for average-

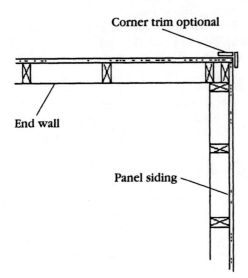

Corner trim optional

End wall

Panel siding

10-13
Fitting the corner panel of the end wall. American Plywood Assoc

sized window openings, depending on your method of installation. To save labor hours, many framers run the sheathing over the openings and cut out the opening when the windows are installed. This protects the interior from blowing rain in the event there's a delay in window installation.

If gables require sheathing, multiply the rise from the plate to the ridge by the width of the gable, and divide by two. Calculate the area of each gable if they're a different size, and add the totals.

Now add all areas to find the total panels required. If you deduct for openings, subtract the total area of the openings from the total wall and gable area. This gives the total net area of sheathing required. Divide the net area by the square feet of the panel size to find the number of panels required. (There are 32 square feet in a 4' × 8' panel and 36 square feet in a 4' × 9' panel.)

Let's do one. The house is 62' × 28', rectangular in shape. The gable is eight feet from the top plate to the ridge, and both gables are the same size. For the walls:

$$62 + 62 + 28 + 28 = 180 \text{ lf}$$
$$180 \text{ lf} \times 9' \text{ (sheathing length)} = 1,620 \text{ square feet}$$

and for the gables:

$$8 \times 28 = 224 \div 2 = 112 \text{ square feet per gable}$$
$$112 \text{ sq. ft.} \times 2 = 224 \text{ sq. ft.}$$
$$224 + 1,620 = 1,844 \text{ sq. ft.}$$
$$1,844 \text{ sq. ft.} \div 36 \text{ sq. ft.} \text{ (4' × 9' panel)} = 51.22 \text{ (round off to 52)}$$

Nails

For plywood and OSB 4 × 8 panels installed on studs spaced 16 inches on center, use 6d common nails spaced six inches at edges and 12 inches intermediate, which equals 62 nails per panel. There are 181 6d common nails to the pound.

For 4 × 8 fiberboard installed on studs spaced 16 inches on center, use 1½-inch, 11-gauge, galvanized roofing nails with 7⁄16-inch heads, spaced three inches at edges and six inches intermediate, which equals 124 nails per panel. There are 186 nails to the pound.

For 4 × 8 gypsum sheathing installed on studs spaced 16 inches on center, use 1½-inch, 11-gauge, galvanized roofing nails with 7⁄16-inch heads, spaced four inches at edges and eight inches intermediate, which equals 94 nails per panel.

Assuming the house requires 52 4 × 8 sheathing panels, the nails required for plywood or OSB would be:

$$3,224 \text{ 6d common nails} = 17.81 \text{ pounds}$$

for fiberboard:

$$6,448 \text{ 1½-inch roofing nails} = 34.66 \text{ pounds}$$

and for gypsum board:

$$4,888 \text{ 1½-inch roofing nails} = 26.28 \text{ pounds}$$

ESTIMATING LABOR

Estimate 4 × 8 plywood or OSB installation labor at 10 to 12 hours per 1,000 square feet. Add 20 percent for fiberboard and gypsum sheathing due to the extra nailing required. Thus:

52 4 × 8 plywood or OSB panels = 52 × 32 sq. ft. = 1,664 sq. ft.

Therefore, 1,664 sq. ft. ÷ the labor unit (1,000 BF per 10–12 hours) = 16.64 labor hours per 10-hour unit, or 19.97 labor hours per 12-hour unit.

Here's a pretty good rule of thumb for estimating sheathing labor: Multiply the number of 4 × 8 panels required to cover the wall in 25 minutes. Use ⅔ of the sum for skilled labor and ⅓ for unskilled labor. Using this rule of thumb, multiply 52 panels by 25 minutes for the sum of 1,300 minutes, or 21 hours and 40 minutes. Apply ⅔ (14 hours and 26 minutes) for skilled labor and ⅓ (7 hours and 14 minutes) for unskilled labor.

11
Ceiling joists

In conventional "stick framing," ceiling joists lock the framework together, securing the walls and roof as a unified component. Ceiling joists support the finish ceiling while also acting as the floor joists for the attic above. Ceiling joists are installed after the walls are permanently braced and the top plates installed. Figure 11-1 shows a ceiling-joist installation in progress.

Ceiling joists normally run across the width of the house in conjunction with the rafter run. Most house plans locate the interior walls to use standard-length joists in 10-, 12-, 14-, and 16-foot lengths, avoiding excessive lumber waste, which can add up amazingly fast if a building isn't properly planned.

Glue-laminated beams can be used in association with 2-by ceiling joists for architectural and esthetic reasons, allowing longer spans and greater spacing between members. Figure 11-2 shows a laminated beam in place and supported by a post made up of three studs.

11-1 Ceiling joist installation in progress.

11-2 Laminated beams allow longer spans and wide spacing.

Glue-laminated beams are built with a slight crown to allow the beam to absorb heavy load stresses without excessive deflection. Note the slight crown in the beam awaiting installation in Fig. 11-3. The crown, of course, is always turned up. Keep beams off the ground and protected from the weather pending placement.

11-3
Laminated beams have a slight crown, which is turned up when installed.

TYPICAL JOIST TIE-IN

Ceiling joists are generally made from 2-by lumber. In houses with no appreciable attic space, 2 × 6 joists are typical. A 2 × 8 or larger joist can be used where attic space is of a dimension to allow storage or occupancy.

Joists are nailed to the plate at both outer and inner walls. Joists are also nailed together, either directly or with wood or metal cleats. The cleats are secured to the joists where they cross or join at load-bearing partitions, as shown in Fig. 11-4. Later, when the rafters are raised, the joists are nailed directly to the rafters with five 10d nails. See Fig. 11-5. In the meantime, toe-nail the joists to the upper plate with two 8d box nails.

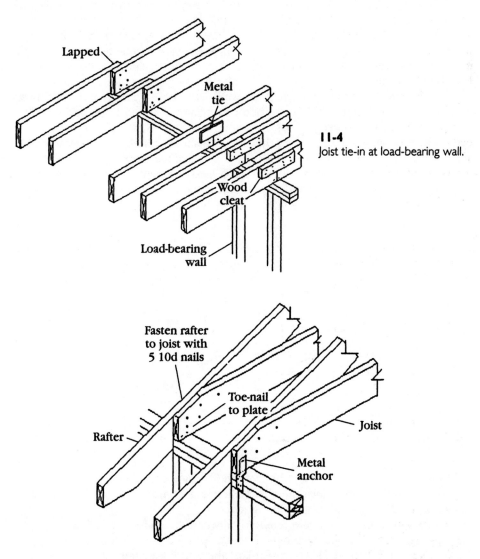

11-4 Joist tie-in at load-bearing wall.

11-5 Joist tie-in at exterior wall plate.

Cleats are necessary only when the joists butt in-line over the partition. When the joists lap over the partition, face-nail them with four 16d nails. Use 8d box nails to toe-nail the joists to the partition top plate.

CEILING-JOIST LAYOUT

Laying out the ceiling joist is generally accomplished with the rafter position in mind. That is, the ceiling joist and rafters are laid out at the same time since both should be on the same spacing and in contact with each other. The joists and rafters need not line up over the studs, but most framers prefer to line up the components when both have the same spacing. Joists and rafters can, however, be 24 inches on center while the studs are spaced 16 inches on center.

If you recall the procedure for laying out the floor joist, then laying out the ceiling joists will be a snap because both are done in much the same manner. You mark each joist and rafter location on both outside wall plates and also on the interior load-bearing plate.

The joist tie-in at the center bearing wall determines your layout. If the joists butt in-line at the partition, the layout of the joist/rafter position at the outside plates will be identical. The procedure for the layout is different when the joists lap at the center. Rafters on opposite sides of the structure should frame opposite each other at the center ridge. To ensure that the rafters line up at the ridge, install a filler block the same thickness of the rafters between the lapped joists at the center (see Fig. 11-6). Thus, the ceiling joists lapped at the center are separated by the block, which occupies the "rafter space," ensuring accurate rafter fitting.

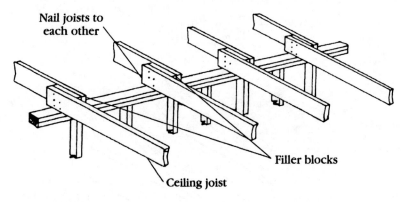

Nail joists to each other

Filler blocks

Ceiling joist

11-6 Joist filler blocks. American Plywood Assoc

In houses with a depth requiring two load-bearing partitions, a filler block isn't required since the middle joist member (extending from interior load-bearing wall to interior load-bearing wall) will fill this slot.

Additionally, filler blocks are required between the end rafter and the end joist since the end rafter outside face must fit flush with the outside wall and won't lap the end joist (see Fig. 11-7). You can place the end joists after the gable end has been framed, as shown in Fig. 11-8.

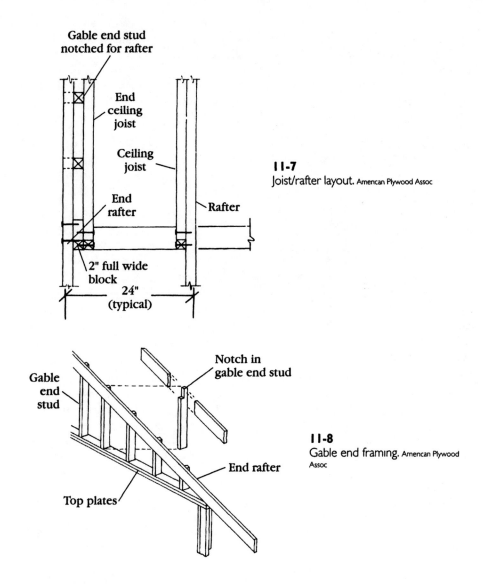

11-7
Joist/rafter layout. American Plywood Assoc

11-8
Gable end framing. American Plywood Assoc

Begin installing the ceiling joists by placing the first joist, crown up, to lap the first interior roof rafter location marked on the exterior wall plate, which will have its centerline 24 inches (or 16 inches) in from the face of the end wall. Install the rest of the ceiling joists on the spacing selected.

You must trim the outside top corner of the ceiling joist to match the rafter slope at the outside wall plate. You can do the trimming either on saw benches before being handed up or after the rafters are installed. It's much easier, however, to trim joists on the benches.

The ceiling joists fit flush with the outside face of the exterior wall and overlap at least four inches at the center unless the joists butt at the center, in which case they extend to the center of the plate. Toe-nail the joists to the top plates with three 8d nails.

Secure each joist to the center filler blocks with four 16d nails. Nonload-bearing walls that run parallel to the ceiling joists can be secured with backing blocks, as illustrated in Fig. 11-9.

Attic-access scuttle and stairway openings are framed in the ceiling the same way floor openings are framed. Double headers, double stringers, and metal anchors are appropriate for stairwells and openings larger than 3' × 3'.

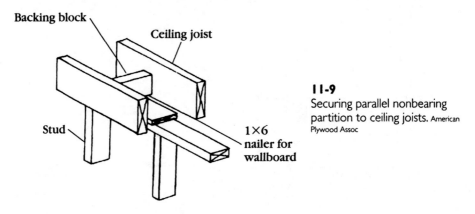

11-9
Securing parallel nonbearing partition to ceiling joists. American Plywood Assoc

LATH NAILERS

Lath nailers are framing components that provide a backstop to fasten finishing materials such as wallboard, plaster lath, and furring strips at the inside corners. Generally, horizontal lath nailers are installed at the ceiling and wall junction in one of three ways. You can install double ceiling joists above the wall, as shown in Fig. 11-10, or use a 1 × 6 or pieces of 2 × 6 scrap for nailers, as shown in Fig. 11-9. Other sizes of scrap lumber, such as 2 × 8 or 2 × 10, can also be used. Secure 1 × 6 nailers with 8d nails and 2-by pieces with 16d nails. Stagger nails 10 to 12 inches apart.

For walls running at right angles to the ceiling joists, install 1-by or 2-by nailers between the joists, as shown in Fig. 11-11.

It's important to attach nailers securely when attaching material to them to avoid knocking them loose. A solid backer in the form of nailers is necessary to ensure a professional finish.

FLUSH CEILING FRAMING

A flush beam allows for a flush ceiling over a large span, as might be required in a living room/dining room configuration (see Fig. 11-12).

The flush beam eliminates the requirement for a load-bearing post or wall for the area. A beam built on the site with two, three, or more 2-by members of the required load-bearing capacity will support the ends of the ceiling joists.

The joists can be toe-nailed to the beam with four 10d nails and supported by a 2 × 2 ledger, as shown in Fig. 11-13. Face-nail the ledger to the beam with 16d nails spaced no further than eight inches apart. Flush the ledger with the bottom edge of the beam. Notch the joists to fit on the ledger and flush with the bottom edge of the ledger.

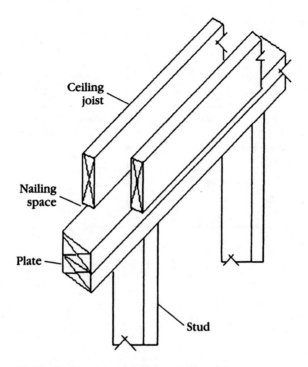

11-10 Double ceiling joists at a parallel wall.

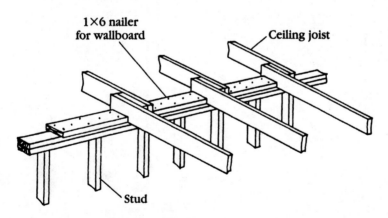

11-11 Lath nailer on a perpendicular wall.

The flush beam is also useful when the direction of joist runs change over a wide span, with one set running perpendicular to another set, as shown in Fig. 11-14. Joist installation is in process here as the second set (parallel to the beam) is being placed.

Ceiling joists can be anchored to the beam with metal joist hangers (Fig. 11-15). Secure the anchors with the nails that come with the anchors or as recommended by the hanger manufacturer. 8d 1½-inch nails are generally used with the hanger type shown in Fig. 11-15.

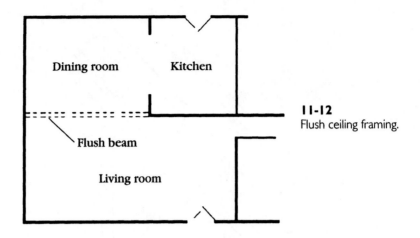

11-12
Flush ceiling framing.

11-13 Flush ceiling framing, beam with ledger.

JOINING PITCHED AND HORIZONTAL CEILINGS

Ceilings of different types can be joined over a long span with a beam. The pitched and level joists can be secured to the beam with framing anchors, or supported on a ledger and toe-nailed to the beam. See Fig. 11-16.

Joist   Beam

                                              2×2
                                              ledger

                                              Joist

11-14 Flush beam used to change the direction of a joist run.

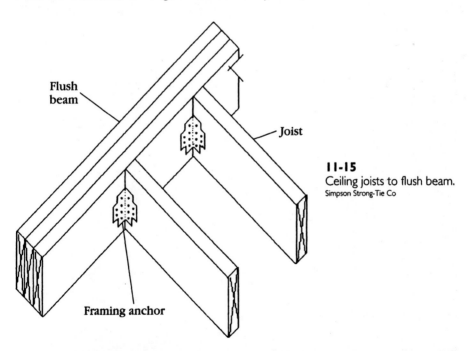

Flush
beam

                                    Joist

11-15
Ceiling joists to flush beam.
Simpson Strong-Tie Co

Framing anchor

The ends of ceiling beams must be supported at both ends by a load-bearing wall capable of transferring the load to the foundation. To ensure adequate support for heavy ceiling loads, reinforce the wall framing directly under the beam. Figure 11-17 offers an example.

Pitched joist

Beam

2×2 ledger

Joist

Bearing wall

11-16 Joining ceilings of different types.

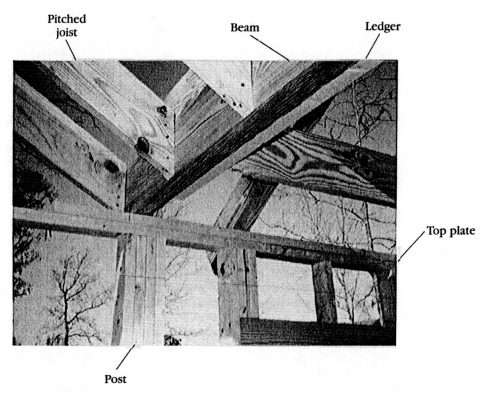

Pitched joist

Beam

Ledger

Top plate

Post

11-17 Reinforcing wall framing under the beam.

PLANK-AND-BEAM CEILINGS

Plank-and-beam construction was discussed in chapter 4. The ceilings of these houses are generally the underside of the roof decking. The roof is usually flat or low-pitched.

Interior exposed ceiling beams have been around a long time. Log cabins built with an attic or second floor generally had exposed beams. Contemporary houses often accent exposed beams to enhance the interior design. Beams are frequently used to replace interior load-bearing walls. Plank-and-beam structures can have large open areas.

The roof can have a conventional joist-rafter combination, or a thick wood decking spanning between the beams. For the deck construction, the top plate is supported by a post that can be solid or split, as illustrated in Fig. 11-18. Metal anchors are used to secure the connections.

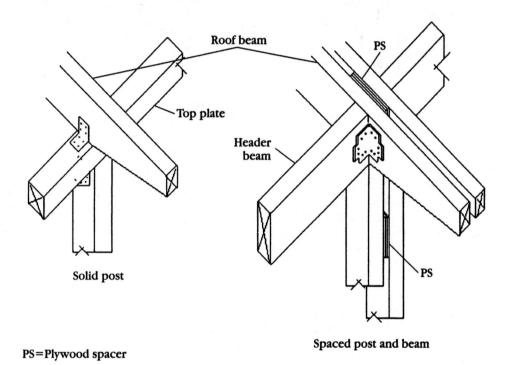

PS=Plywood spacer

11-18 Post-and-beam ceiling/roof components tie-in with metal anchors.

The spaced beam and post are sandwiched together with ⅜-inch or thicker plywood cleats extending between the spaced members to tie the joints. The cleats can be nailed or glue-nailed to the members.

Thick wood T&G planks are frequently used for beam spacings up to 10 feet. The planks are 3" × 6" or 4" × 6". Toe-nail and face-nail the planks directly to the beams, and edge-nail the planks to each other with long nails (see Fig. 11-19). The underside of the decking can be the finish ceiling.

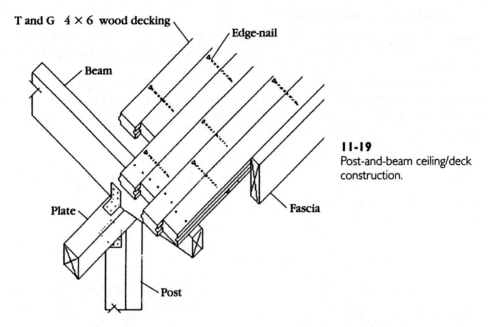

T and G 4 × 6 wood decking

Edge-nail

Beam

Plate

Fascia

Post

11-19
Post-and-beam ceiling/deck
construction.

There might not be ceiling "joists" as such in a plank-and-beam house. The spaced beams and planking together make up the ceiling joists, rafters, ceiling, and roof decking.

HIP-ROOF CEILING JOISTS

The ceiling joists in hip-roof construction change directions. The regular joists stop short of the end wall, and short joists are installed perpendicular to the regular joists. This allows clearance for the hip and jack rafters. The length of the short joists is determined by the slope of the rafters. See Fig. 11-20.

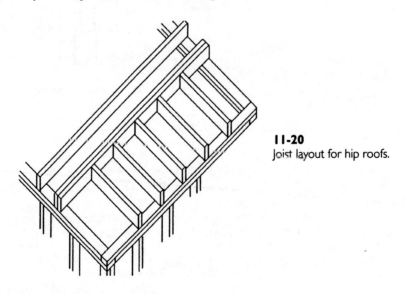

11-20
Joist layout for hip roofs.

JOIST SPANS

The size and species requirements for ceiling joists depend on several factors, the main one being the span. The next is whether there's limited or no attic storage.

Limited attic storage

Limited attic storage is when the attic space won't permit future addition of rooms (or a stair isn't provided), even though the slope of the roof is over 3 in 12.

Ceiling joists must meet the total design load for both stress and deflection: 30 psf (20-psf dead load plus 10-psf live load). The amount of deflection should not exceed ⅟₂₄₀ of the clear span up to 15 feet, or ¾ inch for lengths over 15 feet.

No attic storage

No attic storage space is considered to exist when the roof slope is 3 in 12 or less. A 3/12 slope is when the rafter rises three inches for each 12 inches of run. I'll get into roof pitches and rafter cutting in detail in a later chapter.

The ceiling joist must meet the total live and dead load requirements for both stress and deflection of 15 psf. The deflection cannot exceed ⅟₂₄₀ of the clear span up to 15 feet, and ¾ inch for lengths over 15 feet.

Floors of attic rooms

Where a permanent or disappearing stair is provided or where space permits development of future rooms, the ceiling joists must be capable of carrying a 30-psf live load, the same as floor joists.

Figure 11-21 provides a quick view of the span capabilities of various lumber species and sizes in the construction grade. Your local building code might specify the joist size, span, and spacing. Most lumber yards will have joist tables on the species they sell.

ESTIMATING MATERIALS

The floor plan of a house will show the direction the ceiling joists run, as well as the required span and size. The plan will also show the dimensions of rooms. The joists generally span the shorter distance. The direction of the joist run and the room dimension reveals the length of the joist.

Most stick-built houses have a load-bearing partition near the center of the structure. As I've explained, the ceiling joists rest on this wall and are secured to it. (Trusses span the entire width of the building. Joists seldom do.)

To estimate ceiling-joist requirements for 16-inch spacing, multiply the linear feet of the wall by 0.75 and add one joist for the end. For 24-inch spacing, multiply the linear feet of the wall by 0.50 and add one joist.

Toe-nail the ceiling joists to the top plate with three 8d nails at each plate, and face-nail the joist overlap at the bearing wall with four 16d nails. (When the rafters are installed, the joists will be fastened to the rafter with five 10d nails.) Box nails will do the job nicely, although you can use metal framing anchors, of course, to better secure the joists. In some areas, metal anchors are required.

Species (construction-grade)

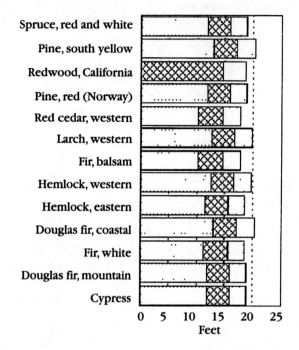

2×6 2×8 2×10

Ceiling joist span 16" o.c. limited attic storage

11-21 Span capabilities of various species of lumber.

Joists

A 60' × 28' house with load-bearing partition centerways will have two joist bays with a 14-foot span. Assuming 16-inch on-center spacing, your joist calculation would be:

$$60' \times 0.75 = 45 + 1 \text{ end joist} = 46$$
$$46 \times 2 \text{ bays} = 92 \text{ joists}$$

Nails

Each joist requires six 8d nails and two 16d nails, so:

$$92 \text{ joists} \times 6 = 552 \text{ 8d nails}$$
$$92 \text{ joists} \times 2 = 184 \text{ 16d nails}$$

There are 106 8d common and 145 8d box nails to a pound. The 8d common nail is 0.131 inch in diameter, and the 8d box nail is 0.115 inch in diameter. So about 5.20 pounds of 8d common nails or 3.80 pounds of 8d box nails are required.

There are 49 16d common and 71 16d box nails to the pound. The 16d common nail is 0.165 inch in diameter, and the 16d box nail is 0.134 inch in diameter. Thus, about 3.75 pounds of 16d common nails or 2.6 pounds of 16d box nails are required.

Table 11-1 shows the board feet of lumber required for ceiling and floor joists per square feet of surface area.

Table 11-1
Floor joist BF required for
100 sq. ft. of surface area

Joist size	12" oc	16" oc	24" oc
2 × 6	115	88	63
2 × 8	153	117	84
2 × 10	194	147	104
2 × 12	230	176	126

ESTIMATING LABOR

Estimating labor for installing ceiling joists is generally done by the board feet of lumber used. Figure 65 board feet per hour for 2 × 6 and 2 × 8 joists, and 70 board feet per hour for 2 × 10 and 2 × 12 joists. Using the previous 60' × 28' house, requiring 92 14-foot joists, as an example:

$$14 \text{ BF} \times 92 \ 2 \times 6 \times 14\text{-foot joists} = 1,288 \text{ BF}$$
$$18\tfrac{2}{3} \text{ BF} \times 92 \ 2 \times 8 \times 14\text{-foot joists} = 1,717\tfrac{1}{3} \text{ BF}$$
$$23\tfrac{1}{3} \text{ BF} \times 92 \ 2 \times 10 \times 14\text{-foot joists} = 2,146\tfrac{2}{3} \text{ BF}$$
$$28 \text{ BF} \times 92 \ 2 \times 12 \times 14\text{-foot joists} = 2,576 \text{ BF}$$

Joist sizes of 2 × 6 and 2 × 8 can be installed in 26.41 hours (1,717 BF ÷ 65 BF per hour = 26.41 hours). Joist sizes of 2 × 10 and 2 × 12 can be installed in 36.8 hours (2,576 BF ÷ 70 = 36.8 hours).

12
Roof trusses

The modern roof truss used in house construction is a fairly recent development. The truss concept, however, has been around since 1560 when Andea Palladio, an Italian architect, designed wood trusses to be used in bridge construction. The truss has since evolved into a scientifically engineered component designed for long spans and heavy loads.

It wasn't until the early 1940s that roof trusses became popular for house construction in a few sections of the country. It was found that roof trusses resisted wind thrusts better than conventional roofs. At the time, plywood gussets or split rings fastened with nails and glue were used to secure the truss joints. In the 1950s, metal-plate connectors (many nails, or *gang nail*, on a plate) were developed, replacing the split ring and plywood gusset.

The size and grade of the lumber used, as well as the size of the connectors and the number of spikes it has, determines the strength of the truss. A truss built according to the engineered design will do its intended job.

A roof truss contains a pair of rafters and the ceiling joist. When a truss is raised, the rafters and ceiling joist are installed as a unit, cutting labor hours as much as 50 percent in some instances. Another advantage is that roof trusses can span longer dimensions without an interior bearing wall. The two exterior walls support the truss. Trusses are generally constructed with 2 × 4s spaced 24 inches on center.

TRUSS TYPES

Roof trusses can be designed and built for almost any type roof or ceiling shape. The four basic designs for residential construction are:
- W type (Fig. 12-1)
- King post (Fig. 12-2)
- Scissor type (Fig. 12-3)
- Attic type (Fig. 12-4)

There are literally thousands of truss configurations possible. Where a vault ceiling is called for, a truss can be designed to provide the raised ceiling within the span area, as shown in Fig. 12-5. The mansard-style roof truss is shown in Fig. 12-6. Stub and monopitch (Fig. 12-7) are trusses that are occasionally used in house construction.

All trusses have a top chord, bottom chord, and web members. Most trusses used in houses are made with 2 × 4 lumber fastened with metal connector plates.

Trusses are designed to consider the combined load factors of snow, wind, and roof weight. Generally, the lesser the slope the greater the stress, which might require larger members and stronger connectors.

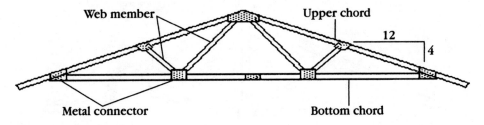

12-1 W-type truss.

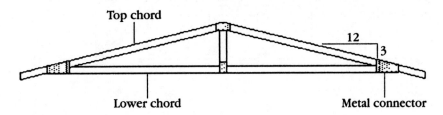

12-2 King post truss.

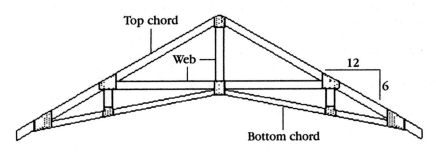

12-3 Scissor truss.

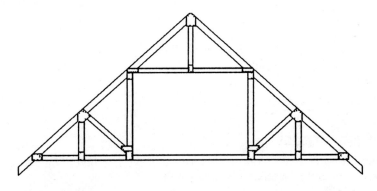

12-4 Attic truss.

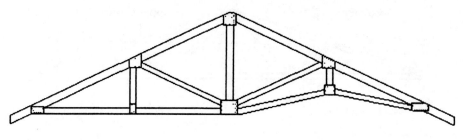

12-5 Vault truss.

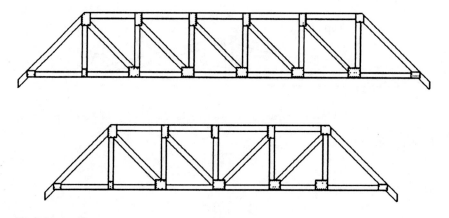

12-6 Mansard truss.

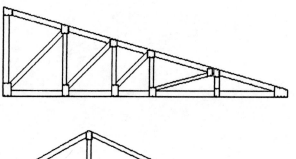

12-7
Monopitch-and-stub truss.

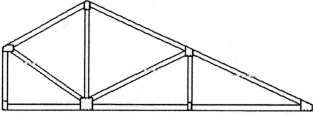

THE COMMON TRUSS

The common truss is a variation of the basic W type. It's the configuration for the most widely designed roof shapes (see Fig. 12-8).

A common truss having 2 × 4 bottom and top chords, a 5/12 pitch, and spaced 24 inches on center will meet most house spans and roof loading. For example, a

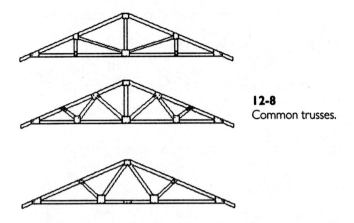

12-8
Common trusses.

span of 44 feet is allowed for a shingle roof and a 40-psf live load. Where the pitch is 2/12, the span is limited to 24 feet.

THE MONOPITCH TRUSS

Monopitch trusses are used for roofs sloped in one direction. Such a truss having 2 × 4 bottom and top chords, a 4/12 pitch, and spaced 24 inches on center will meet most house spans and roof loading. For example, a span of 35 feet is allowed for a shingle roof and a 40-psf live load. The span is limited to 24 feet for a 2/12 pitch.

THE SCISSOR TRUSS

Scissor trusses are designed for structures with sloping roofs, such as houses with vaulted or cathedral ceilings. This truss has, of course, two pitches. It's most economical when the difference in the slope between the top and bottom chords is a minimum of 3/12, or if the pitch of the bottom chord is half the pitch of the top chord (i.e., a 6/12 top chord and 3/12 bottom chord).

A scissor truss made with 2 × 4 bottom and top chords, a 6/12 to 3/12 pitch, and spaced 24 inches on center will span 33 feet when a shingle roof is used and the live load is 40 psf. A 40-foot span is allowed when the pitch is 6/12 to 2/12.

FLAT TRUSSES

Flat trusses, as the term implies, are used for flat roofs. Figure 12-9 shows a four-panel and six-panel flat truss. The most economical flat truss is considered to be when the depth of the truss in inches is equal to about seven percent of the span in inches. For example, a 28-foot-depth house would require:

$$28' \times 12 = 336 \text{ inches} \times 0.07 = 23.52$$

Thus, a flat truss spanning 28 feet should have a depth of 23 to 24 inches. This assumes 2 × 4 top and bottom chords and spacing of 24 inches on center.

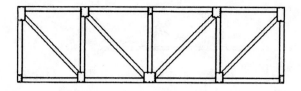

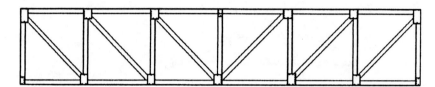

12-9 A four-panel and six-panel flat truss.

THE KING-POST TRUSS

The king-post roof truss has a lower and upper chord, and a center vertical post. Allowable spans are less than those of the previous truss types because of the unsupported length of the upper chord. For short and medium spans, the king-post truss is probably more economical because it requires fewer pieces. Excessive deflection of the top chord under roof loads is possible, however.

TRUSS FRAMING TECHNIQUES

The roof truss is supported by the two exterior walls, and the bearing point is the top plate of the wall. Figures 12-10 through 12-17 show how different types of trusses fit at the bearing point and beyond.

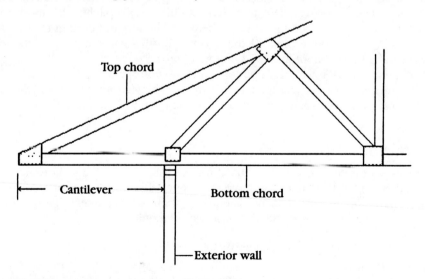

12-10 Pitched truss with cantilever extension.

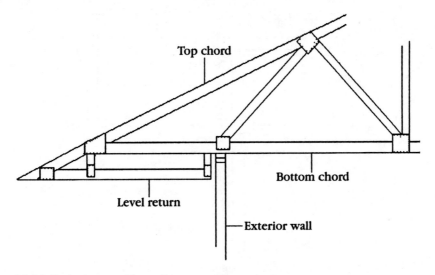

12-11 Pitched truss with cantilever extension and return.

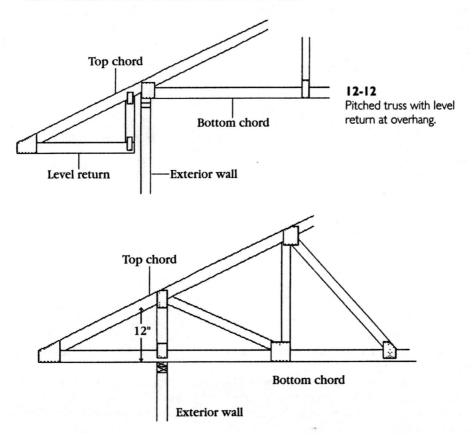

12-12
Pitched truss with level return at overhang.

12-13 Cantilever (or stub) truss designed for 12-inch insulation in an energy-efficient structure.

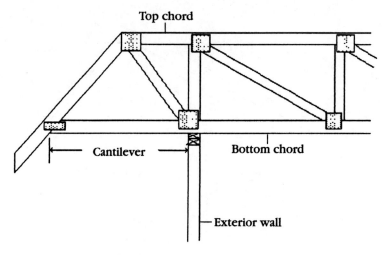

12-14 Mansard truss with cantilever extension.

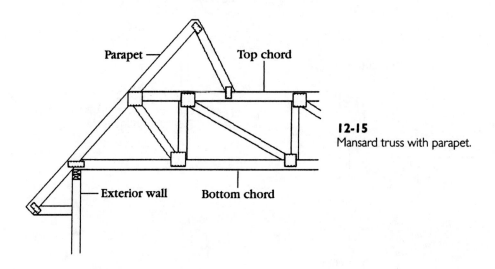

12-15
Mansard truss with parapet.

INSTALLING ROOF TRUSSES

Roof trusses arrive on the site in banded packages, which contain as few as six and as many as 12 or more trusses, depending on truss size and the shipper's method of delivery. While a package can be hoisted by crane to the top of the wall, few framers have access to such equipment and, therefore, must manually lift the trusses up into position.

While a truss is a strong component when installed in the upright position, it's a flimsy "twig" in a flat position. I recommend that you use three people, one at each end and one in the center, when handling trusses to guard against excessive bending in the center.

For a simple roof, it doesn't make any difference at which end of the house you start. You can even begin raising the trusses in the middle of the structure. Regard-

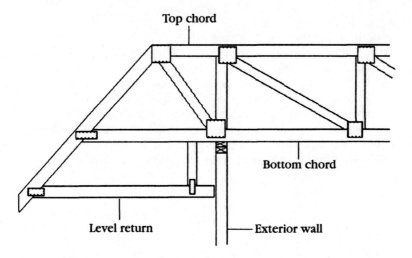

12-16 Mansard truss with level return at overhang.

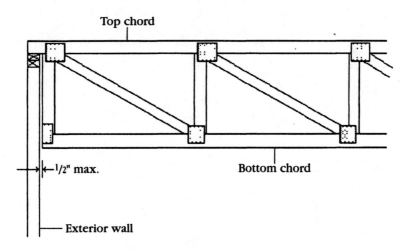

12-17 Flat truss with top-chord bearing.

less of where you start, the truss positions should be marked on the top plate at the appropriate spacing, commonly 24 inches.

The key to safe truss installation is bracing. The first truss raised or *rolled* is braced in position to the building wall or floor. Use 2 × 4s to ensure a strong brace. You might need scaffolding for workers to stand on. Make sure the truss is plumb and centered on the structure. Do this:

1. Mark each truss position on the top plate. Also, mark the exact position on each truss if there's a specific place for that truss. While many framers raise the gable-end truss first and use spacers to position the balance of the trusses, it's still a good idea to first mark off the truss layout—unless you're experienced at installing roof trusses.

2. Hand up the truss. Rest one end of the assembly, peak down, in its position as marked on the top plate. See Fig. 12-18.
3. Move the other end to its position on the opposite wall, as shown in Fig. 12-19.
4. Rotate or roll the truss into an upright position at the peak. See Fig. 12-20.
5. Locate the truss on the layout mark on the top plate and fasten it to the plate with two 10d nails on each side of the heel joint. For better construction or as required by code, secure the truss to the plate with truss tie-down anchors. Figure 12-21 gives an example. Also see Figs. 12-22 and 12-23 for additional ties against uplift created by strong winds.

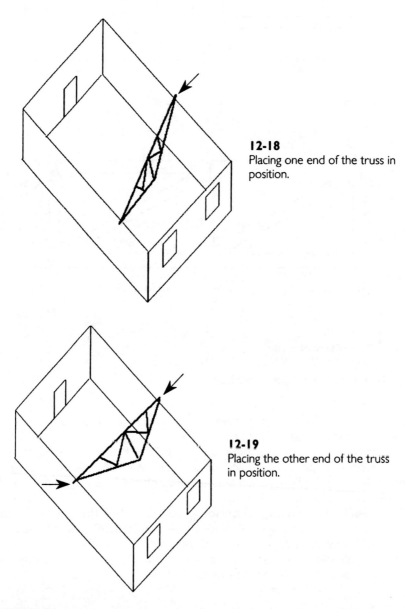

12-18
Placing one end of the truss in position.

12-19
Placing the other end of the truss in position.

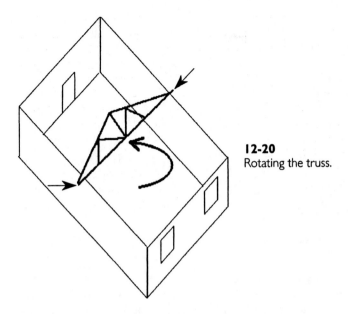

12-20
Rotating the truss.

6. Raise and fasten three trusses into position, ensuring that each truss is properly centered between the bearing walls. If spacer blocks are required between the trusses at the bearing walls, install them as you go. For 24-inch on-center truss spacing, 2 × 4 spacer blocks are cut 22½ inches in length. The same-length 2 × 4 spacer blocks are installed between the trusses at the peak to form the ridge board and ensure the proper truss spacing at the

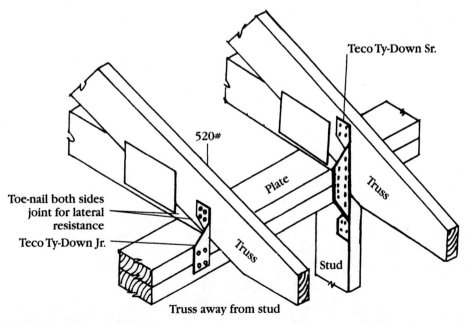

12-21 Tie-down anchors. Teco Co

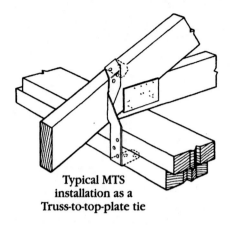

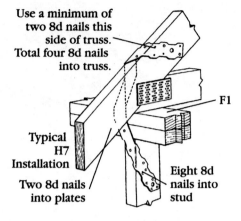

Use a minimum of two 8d nails this side of truss. Total four 8d nails into truss.

F1

Typical H7 Installation

Two 8d nails into plates

Eight 8d nails into stud

Typical MTS installation as a Truss-to-top-plate tie

12-22 Twist straps. Simpson Strong-Tie Co

12-23 Hurricane ties. Simpson Strong Tie Co

top. Check your plan to determine if the spacer blocks at the plate should be set vertically flush with the outside edge of the plate or as a frieze block, set square with the truss and extending out from the top plate. Figure 12-24 explains. Spacer blocks with vents are available from the truss manufacturer and are installed between the trusses as specified by the house plan. Use two 12d nails at each truss to secure the blocks.

7. With the three trusses in position, nail 1 × 6 braces across the top of the trusses and over additional assemblies as they're raised. See Fig. 12-25.

8. The gable-end truss generally has 2 × 4 studs 16 inches on center built into the component. The studs are installed flush (flat side out) with the truss framing. Align the outside edge of the truss's bottom chord to the outside edge of the top plate, and toe-nail it to the plate with 16d nails spaced about 16 inches apart. You want the end truss to line up vertically with the wall. Nail a long, straight 2 × 4 to the wall with the end extended up near the center of the end truss and fasten it to the truss. Leave the 2 × 4 brace in place until all the trusses are installed and braced, and the roof sheathing is applied.

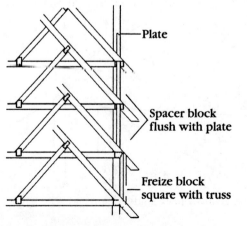

Plate

Spacer block flush with plate

Freize block square with truss

12-24
Spacer block details.

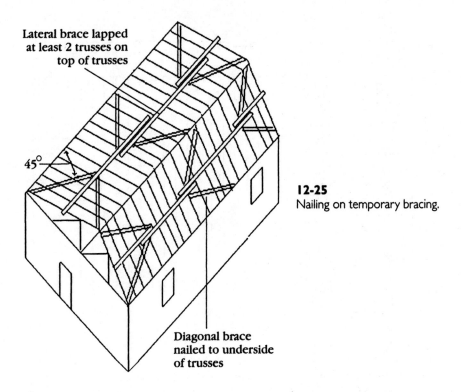

Lateral brace lapped at least 2 trusses on top of trusses

45°

Diagonal brace nailed to underside of trusses

12-25
Nailing on temporary bracing.

Most framers begin truss installation with the gable-end assembly and work toward the opposite end, bracing firmly as work progresses.

HIP TRUSSES

In a hip roof, the regular joists end half the dimension of the building width from the end wall. Thus, a 64-foot-long house that's 28 feet wide will have the regular trusses begin 14 feet from one end wall and stop 14 feet from the opposite end wall. These joists are usually doubled. See Fig. 12-26.

A hip-roof package for each end arrives on the job with the truss package. The set of jack rafters running perpendicular to the regular trusses have the lower chords (ceiling joists) attached.

Make sure the double trusses are exactly positioned, or you're going to have trouble fitting the hip package. Install the hip members, which extend from the center of the double truss to the building corners. Fill in with the jacks furnished along the hip members (spacing each with 22½-inch-long spacer blocks) from the top plate to the hip and attach the bottom chord to the hip member. Your truss supplier can furnish installation instructions for the hip package.

JOINING ROOFS OF DIFFERENT PLANES

Figure 12-27 happens when one roof plane meets a roof that has a different plane. First, install roof sheathing on roof B. Use a long straightedge (2 × 4) or string along the top of roof A, and extend it horizontally until it intersects roof B. The two valleys will

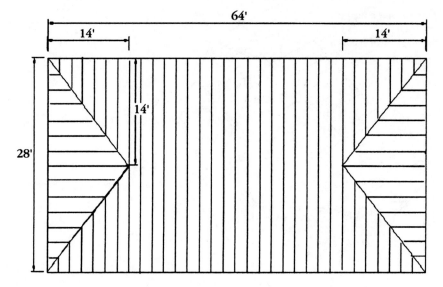

12-26 Hip-roof layout.

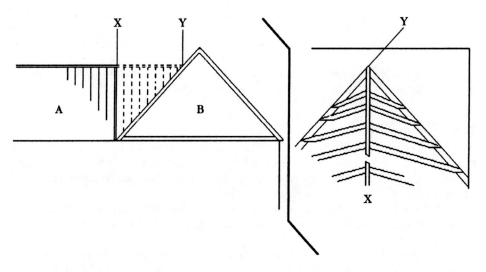

12-27 Joining roofs of different planes.

begin at this point and run to the intersection of roof A at the bottom. Mark this position. Snap a chalk line from the top mark to the bottom mark. This is the valley line.

Now nail down a 1 × 6 valley board, dropping back from the chalk line about 1½ inches to allow the sheathing to merge with its top side to the line. The sheathing thickness will determine how far to drop the valley board back from the line. To determine the exact position for the valley board, run a straightedge along the top of the trusses of roof A to the valley chalk line. Then move the 1 × 6 valley board up the roof toward the chalk line until it touches the straightedge. This is the distance the valley board should be from the valley chalk line in order for the roof sheathing to properly plane.

The distance from position X to position Y (see Fig. 12-27) is the length of the ridge board you'll need. Cut the board to fit the roof slope of roof B and nail it in place, making sure it aligns with the ridge of roof A.

If the truss supplier didn't furnish the jack rafters for joining the two roofs, cut them for the same spacing as the trusses (24 inches on center).

STABILIZING MEMBERS

The stabilizing members for trusses are horizontal runners (catwalks) and diagonal braces in the attic space between the top and bottom chords. Use a 1 × 6, 1 × 8, or a 2 × 6 across the top of the bottom chord for the length of the house, perpendicular to the joist run. Generally, a catwalk is installed on each side of the middle truss member about half the distance to the exterior wall.

Tie a 2 × 4 diagonal brace from each end of the catwalk to the gable-end top chord. Position the diagonal brace at about a 45-degree angle. These stabilizing members will strengthen and tie the roofing trusses together.

HOW TO BUILD A TYPICAL TRUSS

Designing and building roof trusses isn't something the average framer is concerned with; it's more profitable to devote your time to the actual building process. Designing a truss is an engineering function, but carpenters have long been improvising designs and putting together various trusses for different on-site situations. A number of professional carpenters have built and installed roof trusses with excellent results. Most were W-type trusses, as shown in Fig. 12-28.

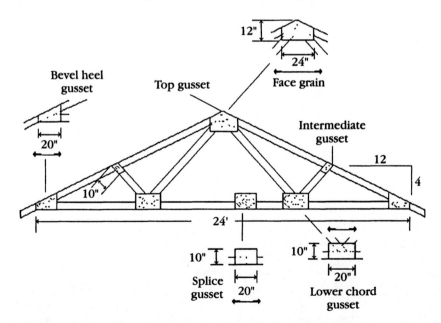

12-28 24-foot W-type truss.

A truss must be built for the area. It must allow for snow, ice, and wind loads. A truss used in Maine must be capable of handling snow loads up to 80 pounds per square foot. The truss must also allow for the roof weight, taking into consideration the slope of the roof.

All truss manufacturers now use metal connector plates made of structural-grade A446 steel with punched-out teeth designed to grip and hold. These plates are placed on both sides of the joint and mechanically pressed into the wood.

You can, however, build a truss using plywood gussets. While it's not recommended to build such a truss for a house, it could be used in a shed or small barn.

The nail-glued gusset truss shown in Fig. 12-28 spans 24 feet with a 4/12 pitch. The allowable roof load is 40 psf, sufficient for a moderate-to-heavy snow-belt area. Use quality 2 × 4s with a moisture content of 15 to 19 percent, then follow these steps:

1. Cut gussets from ⅜- or ½-inch exterior-grade plywood sheathing. Follow the cut-out size of the gussets for glue-nailing, as shown in Fig. 12-28.
2. Use a resorcinol glue for the gussets in areas of high humidity. A casein or similar glue works well in other areas. Always follow the glue manufacturer's instructions.
3. Spread the glue on clean surfaces. Both the gusset and truss members must be clean. Use nails to apply pressure while the glue sets. Nails and glue used in combination provide greater holding power than either used alone.
4. Fasten ⅜-inch plywood gussets with 4d nails spaced three inches on center. Use 6d nails and four-inch spacing for ½- to ⅞-inch plywood gussets. Use two rows of nails spaced ¾ inch from the edges. If the truss members are six inches wide, use three rows of nails.

ESTIMATING MATERIALS

To estimate the number of roof trusses spaced 24 inches on center, multiply the length of the building by 0.50 and add one truss. Do this for each section of the structure where there's a break in the roof line.

List hip-roof assemblies the same way, basing your calculation on a dimension of one-half the house depth for each hip end.

Determine the number of metal anchors by multiplying the anchors required for each truss times the number of trusses.

ESTIMATING LABOR

The truss length and height, lumber size used in the truss, building height, number of stories, and weather are some of the things to consider when estimating labor hours. Consider, too, if spacer blocks will be used at the plates. Installing framing anchors or ties will require additional labor time.

Generally, two carpenters and two laborers can place and install a 20-foot, 2 × 4, W-type truss with a 2/12 to 5/12 pitch in three labor hours. Add 0.30 labor hours for installing spacer blocks and framing anchors. Table 12-1 gives labor hours for installing roof trusses.

Table 12-1
Labor hours for installing roof trusses*

Span in feet	Unit	Labor hours for placement	
		1 story	2 stories
Raised by hand			
20	each	3.0	4.0
26	each	3.5	4.5
30	each	4.0	5.0
32	each	4.3	5.3
Raised by crane			
34 to 40	each	3.0	4.0

* Crew size of two carpenters and two laborers for hand placement, and one operator and two to three men on guy lines for crane placement. (Add 0.30 labor hours per truss for plate-spacer blocks and framing anchors.)

13
I-beam rafters

Engineered components made up of an assortment of wood products, such as 2-by lumber and OSB panels glued or nailed or stapled together, are used for rafters as well as for floor joists.

I-beam rafters have a bottom and top flange with a plywood or OSB center called the *web*. The flanges can be solid wood or laminated veneer lumber (LVL). These manufactured components are available in depths from 9½ to 24 inches. The thickness of the web can be increased to carry heavy loads over a long span.

A typical I beam will have a ⅜- or ⅝-inch plywood or OSB web fitted into 2 × 2, 2 × 3, or 2 × 4 flanges. Figure 13-1 shows an I beam you might use as a rafter over an 18-foot span when spaced 24 inches on center for a roof with a 20-psf live load and 15-psf dead load.

MEASURING RAFTERS FOR PITCHED ROOFS

In a gable roof, the rafter span is the distance from the outside surface of the top plate to the centerline of the building depth. To find the required length of the rafter, you must use a particular ratio for each pitch (see Table 13-1).

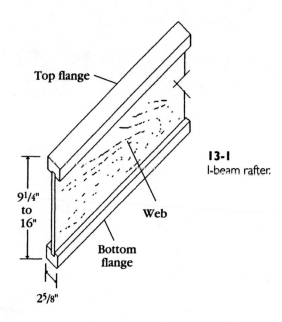

Top flange

9¼"
to
16"

Web

Bottom
flange

2⅝"

13-1
I-beam rafter.

Table 13-1
Multiplying factor
of common rafters*

| Common rafters | | Hip-and-valley rafters | |
Rise	Ratio	Rise	Ratio
3	1.03	3	1.43
4	1.05	4	1.45
4.5	1.07	4.5	1.46
5	1.08	5	1.47
6	1.12	6	1.50
7	1.16	7	1.53
8	1.20	8	1.56
9	1.25	9	1.60
10	1.30	10	1.64
11	1.26	11	1.69
12	1.41	12	1 73

* Slopes in 12

The rise of a rafter, also called the *slope*, is expressed as the rise in inches per 12 inches of run. Thus, a rise of 9 inches per 12 inches of run is written as "9 in 12" or simply "9/12". How does the ratio factor in? Assuming a span of 16 feet and rise of 9/12:

$$16' \text{ span} \times 1.25 \text{ (ratio)} = 20'$$

Thus, a 20-foot rafter is required to extend from the roof ridge to the exterior face of the top plate. However, you must allow for the plumb cut at the ridge and the overhang at the eaves. Figure 13-2 explains. Table 13-2 gives the required length for the plumb cut for various rafter depths.

ALLOWABLE SPANS

Your supplier of I-beam rafters will have span charts for various roof-load requirements. For a typical I-beam, like the one shown in Fig. 13-1, with a depth of 9¼ to 16 inches, the allowable spans are shown in Table 13-3. A 30-psf live load, plus 15-psf dead load, and L/180 total deflection are assumed.

I-beam rafters are available that can span any size roof and any required loads for any house you'll be asked to frame.

THINGS YOU SHOULD AND SHOULD NOT DO

There are some definite restrictions and requirements involving the installation of I-beam rafters. Here are a few:
- Do not stack the rafters on the ground. Keep the material dry while awaiting installation. Be sure the units are stacked level so as to prevent bending.
- Do not cut a birdsmouth or notch in the bottom flange along the midpoint for knee walls or at the peak to fit a support or ridge board (Fig. 13-3).

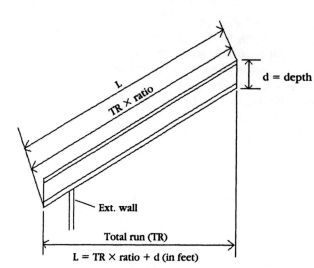

13-2
Finding the rafter length.

$$L = TR \times ratio + d \text{ (in feet)}$$

Table 13-2
Rise factor and length required
for plumb cut (in feet)

Rise	Ratio factor	9.25"	*Joist depth* 11.25"	12"	14"	16"	18"
3	1.03	0.19	0.23	0.25	0.29	0.33	0.38
4	1.05	0.26	0.31	0.33	0.39	0.44	0.50
5	1.08	0.32	0.39	0.42	0.49	0.56	0.63
6	1.12	0.39	0.47	0.50	0.58	0.67	0.75
7	1.16	0.45	0.55	0.58	0.68	0.78	0.88
8	1.20	0.51	0.63	0.67	0.78	0.89	1.00
9	1.25	0.58	0.70	0.75	0.88	1.00	1.13
10	1.30	0.64	0.78	0.83	0.97	1.11	1.25
11	1.36	0.71	0.86	0.92	1.07	1.22	1.38
12	1.41	0.77	0.94	1.00	1.17	1.33	1.50

Table 13-3
I-beam rafter allowable span
(30 psf LL + 15 psf DL, L/180
deflection)

Beam depth	12" oc	16" oc	24" oc
9.25"	23'00"	19'11"	16'03"
11.25"	26'03"	22'08"	18'06"
14"	30'00"	26'00"	21'03"
16"	32'07"	28'02"	23'00"

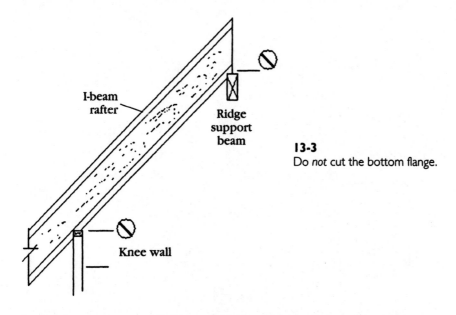

I-beam
rafter

Ridge
support
beam

13-3
Do *not* cut the bottom flange.

Knee wall

Instead, place a continuous wedge or appropriate framing anchor at these points to support and fasten the rafter. See Fig. 13-4. You can cut a birdsmouth at the exterior wall top plate, but make it a shallow cut in the flange. A cant strip fastened to the top plate as a bearing for the rafter beam is preferable. See Fig. 13-5.

* Do not support the rafter on the web, as illustrated in Fig. 13-6.
* Where the rafters butt to a ridge board at the peak, use anchor straps or hangers to secure. The maximum pitch for I-beam rafters is 12/12. See Fig.

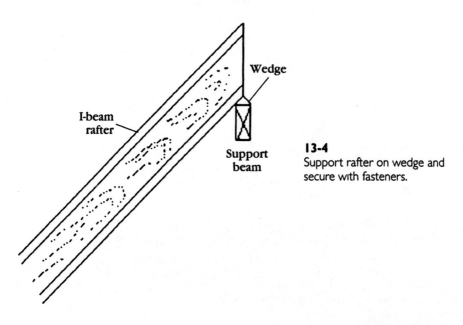

Wedge

I-beam
rafter

Support
beam

13-4
Support rafter on wedge and secure with fasteners.

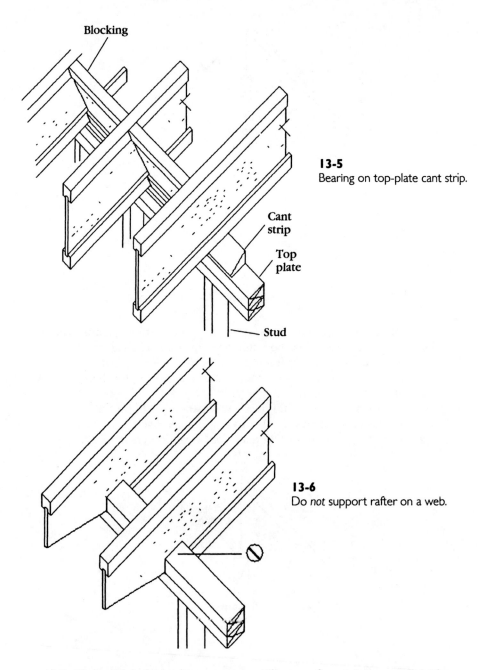

Blocking

13-5
Bearing on top-plate cant strip.

Cant
strip

Top
plate

Stud

13-6
Do *not* support rafter on a web.

13-7. Figure 13-8 shows how to secure I-beam rafters joining over a ridge beam. Install ²³⁄₃₂-inch plywood or OSB fillers and scabs on both sides of the rafter with the face grain horizontal.

• The tail end of the rafter can be cut plumb, as shown in Fig. 13-9. For a horizontal soffit, cut the component as shown and reinforce with 2 × 4 scabs fastened with 8d box nails spaced six inches apart.

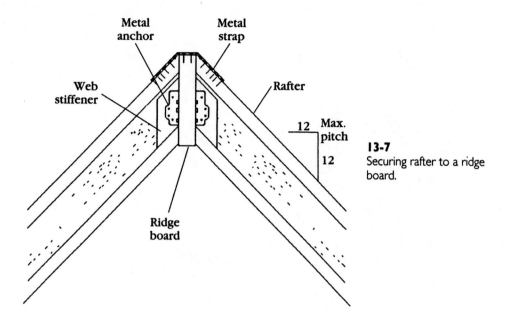

Metal
anchor

Metal
strap

Web
stiffener

Rafter

12 ⌐ Max.
       pitch
   12

13-7
Securing rafter to a ridge
board.

Ridge
board

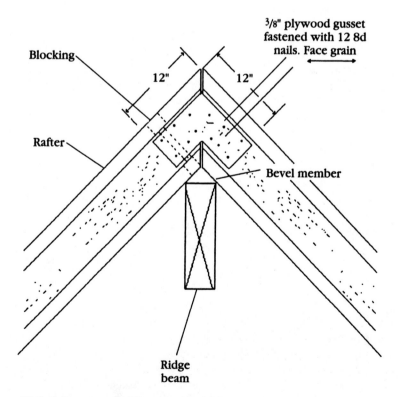

Blocking

³/₈" plywood gusset
fastened with 12 8d
nails. Face grain

12"   12"

Rafter

Bevel member

Ridge
beam

13-8 Rafter supported by a beam at peak.

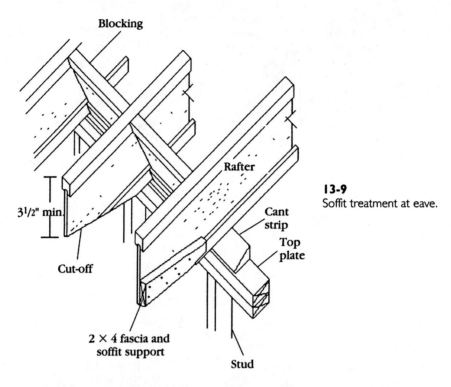

Blocking

Rafter

3½" min.

Cant strip

Cut-off

Top plate

13-9
Soffit treatment at eave.

2 × 4 fascia and soffit support

Stud

• At the roof overhang at the gable end, construct the ladder and rake outrigger as shown in Fig. 13-10. The maximum overhang is two feet. A 2 × 4 filler is fastened to the I-beam rafter with 8d box nails spaced six inches on center. Position the ladder members 24 inches on center.

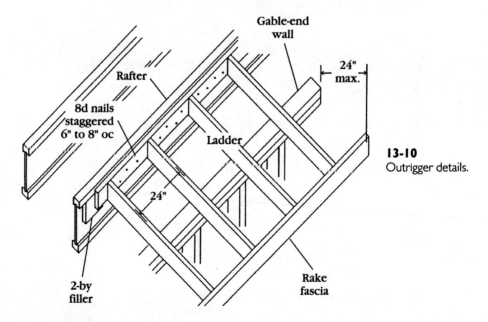

Gable-end wall

Rafter

24" max.

8d nails staggered 6" to 8" oc

Ladder

13-10
Outrigger details.

24"

2-by filler

Rake fascia

Other restrictions prohibit cutting, notching, or drilling holes in the flanges. Don't knock holes in the web unless a knock-out is provided, don't hammer on the flanges, and don't use 16d nails. Use 8d or 10d box nails instead.

Wood I-beam components make a structurally sound roof, but, as evidenced in these instructions, their erection can be time-consuming as compared to the installation of trusses or conventional rafters.

14
Conventional roof framing

The conventional rafter is a 2-by solid piece of lumber cut to fit and fastened with nails. In hurricane-prone areas, the rafter might be required by code to be secured with metal framing anchors designed to resist uplift and separation of the rafter from the top wall plate (see Fig. 14-1). Trusses and fabricated rafters such as I beams, discussed in chapter 13, are also required to be so anchored in these areas.

Of course, if the top plate isn't securely tied to the studs, the uplift caused by high winds can force the separation at that point. Anchoring all components, as shown in Fig. 14-2, will correct the problem.

ROOF SLOPES

If a roof is made of straw, it had better have a steep slope to shed water. A flat roof would be a hazard in heavy snow country, but is acceptable in arid regions. A number of things, such as the climate, availability of materials, and, of course, the home-

14-1 Conventional rafter fastened to a top plate with metal anchors.

14-2 Framing secured to prevent uplift and separation.

buyer's preference, have a lot to do with the slope of roofs. In the case of wood shingles, a reasonably steep roof is recommended to quickly remove the water. However, by doubling the underlay (building paper) and decreasing the exposure dimensions of the shingle, a roof slope as low as 3/12 is possible.

You can have a flat or slightly pitched roof, an intermediate slope, such as 6/12, or a steep slope in a contemporary house. The two basic roof types are labeled "flat" and "pitched." In a typical flat roof, one member serves as both roof and ceiling support. Pitched roofs have both rafters and ceiling joists.

The pitch of a roof is expressed as the number of inches of vertical rise in 12 inches of horizontal run. The rise is expressed first. For example, 6 in 12 means that the roof rises 6 inches in each 12 inches of horizontal run.

For most conventional rafters, a no. 2 grade of softwood framing lumber will do the job provided you stay within the span tables, which are shown in the chart in Fig. 14-3.

FLAT ROOF CONSTRUCTION

In addition to the flat roofs associated with plank-and-beam construction, there's the conventional flat roof. Such a roof is either level or has a slight pitch to provide for drainage. A slight pitch will eliminate puddling of water on the roof.

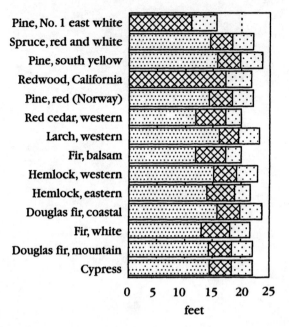

Species (construction grade)

14-3
Rafter spans for roof pitch over 3/12.

[Chart showing rafter spans in feet (0 to 25) for various species:]

Pine, No. 1 east white
Spruce, red and white
Pine, south yellow
Redwood, California
Pine, red (Norway)
Red cedar, western
Larch, western
Fir, balsam
Hemlock, western
Hemlock, eastern
Douglas fir, coastal
Fir, white
Douglas fir, mountain
Cypress

feet

☐ 2 × 6 ☒ 2 × 8 ☐ 2 × 10

Flat roofs have a single framing component that supports the roofing and ceiling materials. This member carries a heavy load and must be of a larger dimension than rafters in a pitched roof.

Flat roofs commonly overhang exterior walls 18 to 24 inches or more. To provide an overhang on all sides of the flat roof, lookout rafters are used (Fig. 14-4). For end-wall and side-wall overhangs more than 36 inches, use the layout in Fig. 14-5.

Nail the lookout rafters to a double header. Before installing the second member of the header, face-nail the single member to each lookout with three 16d nails. Install the second member of the header with 10d nails staggered 12 inches apart. Toe-nail the lookout to the wall plate with three 8d nails. The installation of metal framing anchors securing the rafters to the header and top plate will significantly strengthen the roof.

Make the distance from the double header to the top plate twice the overhang dimension. Install a nailing header on the rafter ends to act as a "straightener" of the rafter ends and provide a base for the soffit and finish fascia board. Venting a flat roof is essential and is best provided with a continuous vent strip in the soffit.

GABLE ROOF CONSTRUCTION

The gable roof has been around a long time and is a popular style throughout the world. A simple gable roof (see Fig. 14-6) is the simplest form of the pitched roof, requiring both ceiling joists and rafters. Attic space is created between the joists and rafters.

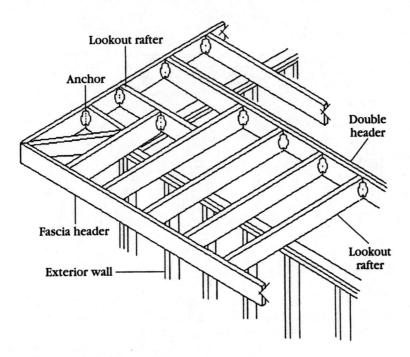

14-4 Lookout construction for medium overhang.

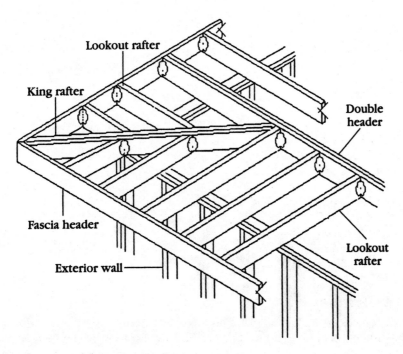

14-5 Lookout construction for wide overhang.

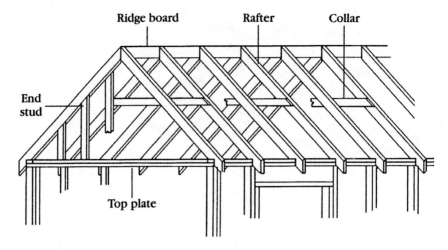

14-6 A simple gable roof.

The rafters of this roof are all cut the same length and pattern. Each pair is nailed at the top to a ridge board, a 1 × 8 or 2 × 6 member for 2 × 6 rafters. The ridge board is a key component in stick framing, providing support and a nailing surface for the rafters at the peak of the roof. The ridge board will be perfectly straight when the walls are straight and the rafters are uniformly cut. See Fig. 14-7.

14-7 Properly fitted rafters ensure a straight ridge.

A slightly more complicated roof is shown in Fig. 14-8. This is a basic gable roof with a shed dormer and gable dormers. It's the familiar Cape-Cod style and is a one-story structure since the majority of the rafters rest directly on the first-floor top plate. The attic space obtainable with this style can be significant, and sufficient light and ventilation is available through the dormer windows. Use a 9/12 to 12/12 roof slope for this roof in order to have the required headroom. As you can see, the house design makes excellent use of materials to provide valuable space.

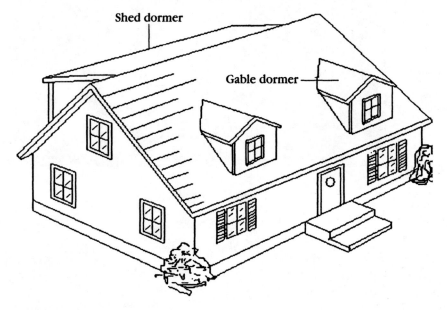

14-8 A Cape-Cod gable roof.

BELT RAIL

Houses with steep-pitched roofs and overhang might require a belt rail to ensure sufficient space between the soffit and window (see Fig. 14-9). Note that the belt rail lifts the rafter ends above and away from the window opening and allows space above the window for finish materials such as brick veneer.

Figure 14-10 shows a belt rail that's a 2 × 10 capped with a 2 × 4. The rail rests directly on the top plate. The rafter's birdsmouth fits on the belt rail. The belt rail also provides additional headroom in the attic. More floor space is provided in the attic space in Fig. 14-11 because the belt rail allows the knee walls to be positioned closer to the eaves.

The roof system at the gable end must be extended to allow for brick veneer or stone. Figure 14-12 shows how this is accomplished. The top member of the side-wall double-member top plate is extended beyond the end wall the distance required for the exterior finish, which, in this case, is five inches for sheathing and standard brick. The belt rail fits flush with the end of the top-plate members. A joist-sized member is installed at the end between the belt rails as a "bulkhead" to support the gable-end studs. Brick are laid up to the bulkhead. See Fig. 14-12.

Belt rail

Top plate

Window
header

14-9 Belt rail in place.

Belt rail

Top plate

14-10 A 2 × 10 belt rail capped with a 2 × 4.

RIDGE-BEAM CONSTRUCTION

You might need a glue-laminated ridge beam to span open areas in a low-pitch roof. The beam is usually supported by a post, interior partition, or exterior wall, and it must be adequate for the span and roof load. Figure 14-13 illustrates how to secure spaced rafters to the beam.

14-11 Gaining more attic headroom and floor area with belt rail.

Belt rail

Top plate

Bulkhead

14-12 A gable-end bulkhead extends five inches for brick veneer.

In this type of construction, thick plank decking can serve as roof support and sheathing. The planks extend from the ridge beam to the top plate and beyond to form the required overhang at the eaves.

Structural fiberboard can be used as decking instead of wood in the system shown in Fig. 14-13. Also, the rafters can rest on top of the beam rather than butting to the beam.

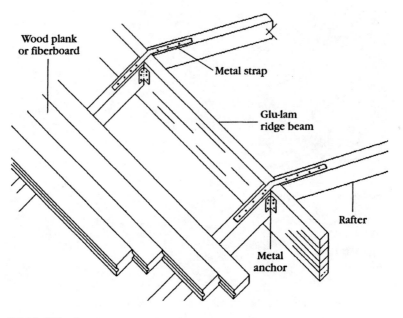

Wood plank
or fiberboard

Metal strap

Glu-lam
ridge beam

Rafter

Metal
anchor

14-13 Ridge beam.

DORMER CONSTRUCTION

Figure 14-14 shows two dormers being framed in the roof. Note also that the second-story floor joists extend beyond the first-floor wall to cantilever over a porch area.

The dormer in Fig. 14-15 has a double rafter at each sidewall. The short-side studs and short valley rest on the double rafter. The side-wall studs can also extend to a sole plate nailed to the subflooring, as shown in Fig. 14-14. The side walls of a

14-14 Framing the dormers, photo.

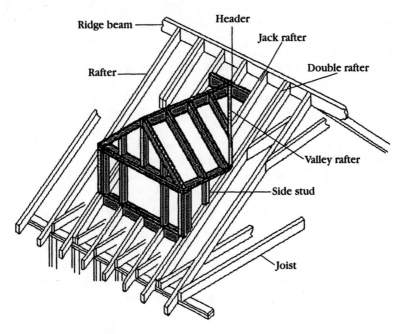

14-15 Framing the dormers, diagram.

shed dormer (Fig. 14-16) are framed in the same manner. Framing anchors provide a strong fastener for dormer framing members.

The ridge of the dormer can be at the same level or below the main roof ridge. The house plan should indicate the ridge placement as well as the location of the

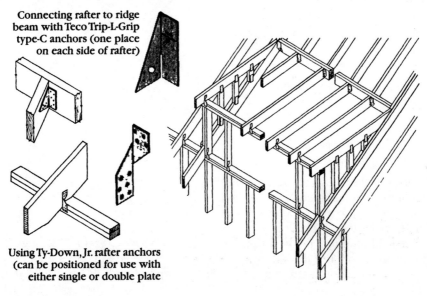

Connecting rafter to ridge beam with Teco Trip-L-Grip type-C anchors (one place on each side of rafter)

Using Ty-Down, Jr. rafter anchors (can be positioned for use with either single or double plate

14-16 Shed dormer. Teco

dormer from the wall. The studs, plates, and window openings are framed the same as a wall of the main structure.

With the front wall raised, install the side walls, extending the studs from the floor, as shown in Fig. 14-14, or from a double common rafter, as shown in Fig. 14-15. The top plates of the front and side walls must, of course, be the same height. Extend the side top plate to the main roof rafter. If the side-wall studs are supported by the main roof rafters (see Fig. 14-15), the wall plate will rest directly on the main rafters. If the studs extend to the floor (see Fig. 14-14), the wall plate will extend to the side of the main rafter.

The dormer rafters are measured, cut, and erected in the same manner as the main rafters of the roof, which is explained in detail in chapter 15.

FRAMING THE GABLE OVERHANG

The roof overhang at the gable end can be framed in different ways. The outrigger method, shown in Fig. 14-17, works well. The outrigger member is nailed to the rafter beyond the end-wall rafter, supported in a notch in the end-wall rafter, and extended to support the fascia or "fly" rafter. The fascia rafter is secured to the extended ridge board and the extended-eave fascia board.

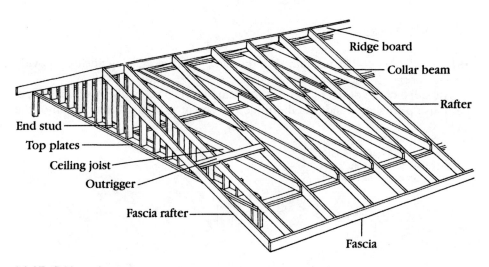

14-17 Gable-end outrigger. American Plywood Assoc

Face-nail the rafters to the 2 × 6 outrigger with three 16d nails. Face-nail the outrigger at the notched member with three 10d nails. Use three 10d nails to fasten the fascia rafter at the ridge board and at the eave fascia board. Another outrigger method, which uses lookout rafters, is shown in Fig. 14-18.

The gable-framing method I prefer is illustrated in Fig. 14-19. The ridge board and bottom member of the side-wall top plate is extended beyond the end wall by the overhang distance. The extended plate is capped with a 2 × 4 to match the double top plate. A common rafter is then fastened to the ridge board and extended plate as a fascia or "fly" rafter. No outrigging is required, except that, in

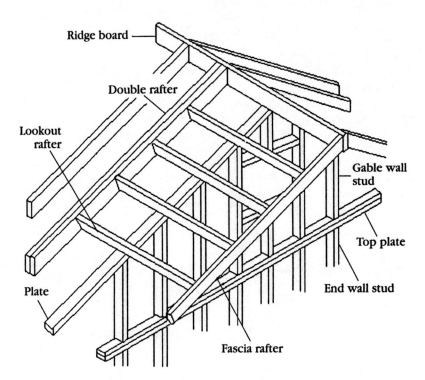

14-18 Outrigger with lookout rafters.

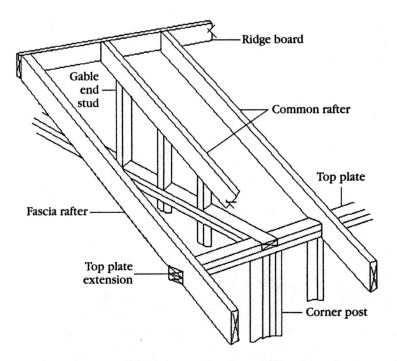

14-19 A simple and economic technique.

long rafter spans, a single outrigger in the middle of the span will add structural strength to the rafter.

Gable-end studs

The studs for the gable-end walls are cut to fit and nailed to the end rafters (not fascia rafters) and top plate, or to the bulkhead where the gable end is projected for brick or stone. The stud is notched to fit flush with the end rafter. See Figs. 14-20 and 14-21.

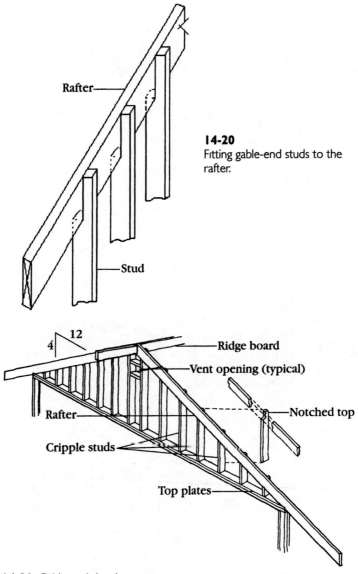

Rafter

14-20
Fitting gable-end studs to the rafter.

Stud

12
4

Ridge board

Vent opening (typical)

Rafter

Notched top

Cripple studs

Top plates

14-21 Gable-end details. American Plywood Assoc

FRAMING A VALLEY

The roof valley is the internal angle formed where two sloping roof surfaces meet. The valley rafter forms the valley base, or bottom. A double valley rafter is often used when two equal-sized roof sections join. Also, a valley member two inches wider than the common rafters provide a full-contact surface for the jack rafters. Jack rafters are nailed to the ridge and toe-nailed to the valley rafter with three 10d nails (see Fig. 14-22).

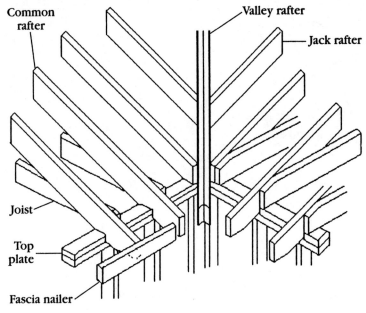

14-22 Roof-valley framing.

HIP ROOFS

Hip roofs have no gables. The roof is framed the same as gable roofs at the structure's center section, as illustrated in Fig. 14-23. Figure 14-24 shows a top view of this roof, with the two roofs intersecting. The hip rafters extend from each outside corner of the wall to the ridge board at a 45-degree angle. A hip-roof corner detail is illustrated in Fig. 14-25. The end of the hip rafter is cut in a V to provide a surface for the cornice board. The roof valley, discussed previously, also applies to hip roofs.

Figure 14-26 shows how to find the intersection of the hip rafters with the ridge board at point B. The distance AB is equal to BC, making the two squares equal in size. The distance BD is the diagonal of the square ABCD, and shows the run of the hip rafter.

In a conventional hip roof, the length of the ridge board is the building length minus the building width. For example, a 48-foot-long house has a standard hip roof. The house is 26 feet wide. What's the length of the ridge? The ridge equals the house length minus the house width, so:

$$48 - 26 = 22 \text{ feet}$$

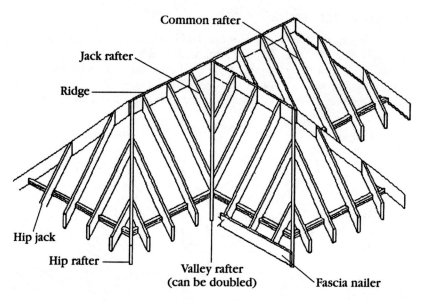

14-23 Hip-roof framing.

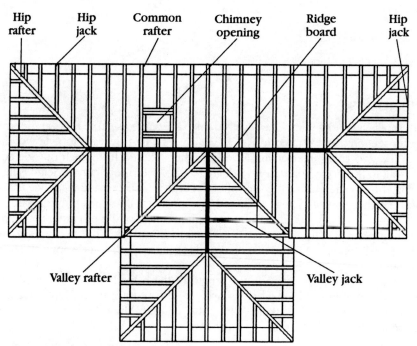

14-24 Plan of the intersecting hip roofs.

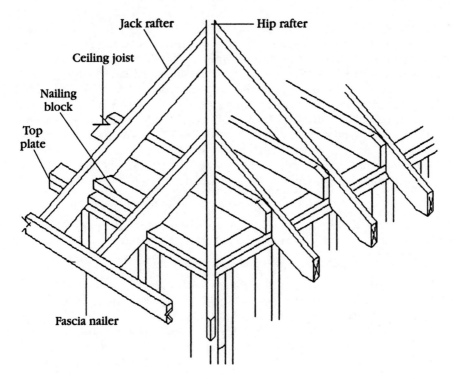

14-25 Hip-roof corner detail.

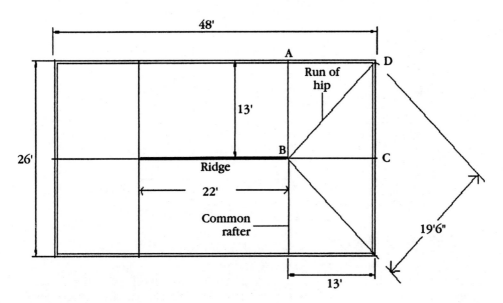

14-26 Hip-roof layout.

From this you can determine the length of the hip rafter. The hip rafter (line BD in Fig. 14-26) runs at a 45-degree angle to the corner and is, therefore, longer than common rafters. While there are several ways to find the length of the hip rafter, a simple way is to use the rafter table on your framing square.

If you know the rise (consult the house plan), you can determine the length of the hip rafter. Assume your plan calls for a 6/12 pitch, which is a six-inch rise for every 12 inches of run. Below the six-inch mark on the body of the square, the "Length Common Rafter Per Foot Run" should be 13.42. The next line, "Length of Hip or Valley Rafter Per Foot of Run" should be 18.

The run of the common rafter in line AB of Fig. 14-26 is 13 feet. To determine the common rafter length, multiply the per foot run (13.42") by 13, the run:

$$13.42 \times 13 = 174.46 \text{ inches} = 14.53 \text{ feet}$$

You can find the length of the hip rafter the same way. The per foot run of the hip rafter is 18 inches, which you multiply by 13 feet, the run of the *common* rafter:

$$18 \times 13 = 234 \text{ inches} = 19.5 \text{ feet } (19'6")$$

These lengths for the hip and common rafters are the mathematical lengths, which is the rafter length from the outside edge of the wall plate to the center of the ridge board. Subtract half the thickness of the ridge board to arrive at the true length of the rafters along the measuring line. See Fig. 14-27. The measuring line is from the depth of the inner angle of the birdsmouth, running parallel to the top surface of the rafter to the ridge board. It's the line from which the step-off measuring system is used, which is covered in detail in chapter 15.

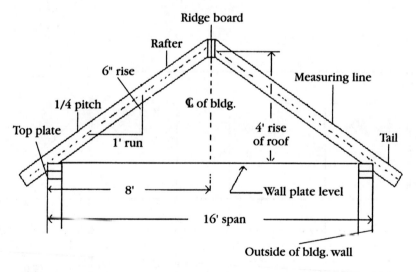

14-27 Key roof definitions.

You can find the solution to most roof-framing questions with the framing square, although using a calculator to perform similar calculations is sometimes quicker.

THE RAFTER RUN

Rafters are the structural components of a roof. They support the sheathing and roofing. Common rafters are those that extend in a straight run from the ridge to the eave.

Figure 14-27 gives the details of roof dimensions. The run of a rafter is the horizontal distance from the outside surface of the wall plate to a point directly under the ridge, which is exactly half the span of the roof.

THE RAFTER RISE

The rafter rise is the vertical distance from the top of the wall plate to the rafter measuring-line at the ridge. To determine the rise, calculate the distance from the top of the top plate line to the point where the measuring line meets the ridge board, as illustrated in Fig. 14-27. You must, of course, consider the overhang dimensions when determining the overall length. See Fig. 14-28.

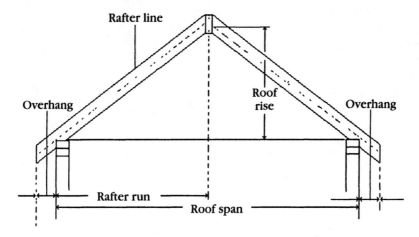

14-28 Determining the overall length of rafter.

THE ROOF SPAN

The roof span is the distance between the outer surface of the wall top plates supporting the rafters. The span is twice the run of a rafter in a gable roof with a centered ridge.

In a gable roof, the span, run, and rise are shown in Fig. 14-28. Figure 14-29 illustrates those same points in a shed-type roof. The gambrel roof has a set of rafters to consider when determining the span, run, and rise. See Fig. 14-30.

THE ROOF PITCH

The terms *slope*, *slant*, and *pitch* mean the same thing: the degree of incline a roof has from the top plate to the ridge. Since the slope of a roof changes if the rise or span changes, it's expressed in the ratio of the rise to the span. Thus, a 1/3 pitch

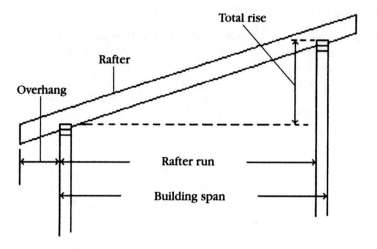

14-29 Rafter configuration in a shed roof.

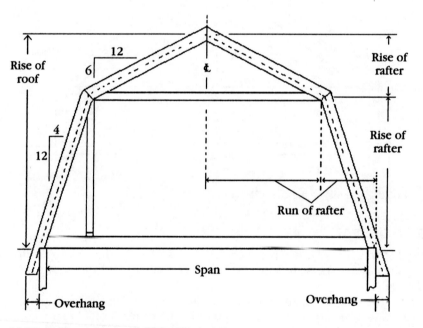

14-30 Rafter configuration in a gambrel roof.

means the rise is ⅓ of the span (Fig. 14-31), and a 1/4 pitch reveals that the rise is ¼ of the span (Fig. 14-32).

You can also say that the pitch of a roof is the increase in the rise for each foot of run. A six-inch-per-foot slope means that the rafters rise six inches for every foot of run.

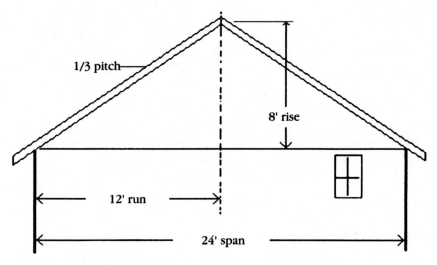

14-31 One-third pitch roof.

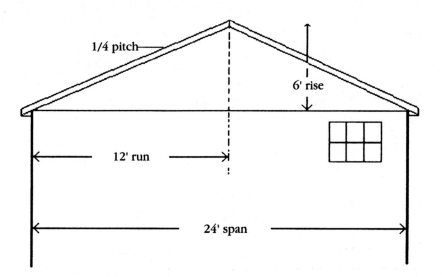

14-32 One-quarter pitch roof.

A third method for giving the pitch of a roof is shown in Fig. 14-30. A 6/12 triangle means the rafters are pitched to rise six inches for every 12 inches of run, and a 12/4 triangle means the rafters will rise 12 inches for every four inches of run.

For a 1/3 pitch, then, you could express the rise of the rafter as:

- One foot for three feet of span
- Eight inches for one foot of run
- One foot for every 1½ feet of run

A simple way to find the rise of a roof when the pitch is known is to multiply the pitch by the span. Thus, a house 24 feet wide having a roof pitch of 1/3 (24 × ⅓) would have an eight-foot rise. Then you can find the pitch of a roof by dividing the rise by the span. Thus, a house having a 24-foot span with a rise of six feet (6 ÷ 24) would have a 1/4 pitch (0.25).

A simple method to find the number of inches of rise per foot of run is to multiply the rise in feet by 12 to find the total number of inches in the rise. Then divide the total number of inches in the rise by the length of the run in feet. Let's say you want to find the rise per foot of run of a roof when the span is 30 feet and the rise is 10 feet. If the span is 30 feet, the run is half of 30, or 15. And:

$$10 \times 12 = 120" \div 15 = 8$$

Thus, the rise is eight inches per foot.

COMMON RAFTER PITCHES

The eight common roof pitches are illustrated in Fig. 14-33 with the use of a framing square. The body of the square is vertical and the tongue is horizontal on a level surface. Numbers on the body represent the inches of rise. The 12 on the tongue represents one foot of run. A roof, as you've seen, rises x number of inches for each foot of run, which establishes the pitch. For example, 24' on the body and 12" on the tongue represent 1 pitch; 6" on the body would be 6/24 of 1 pitch, or 1/4 pitch; 12" on the body would be 12/24 of 1 pitch, or 1/2 pitch, and so on.

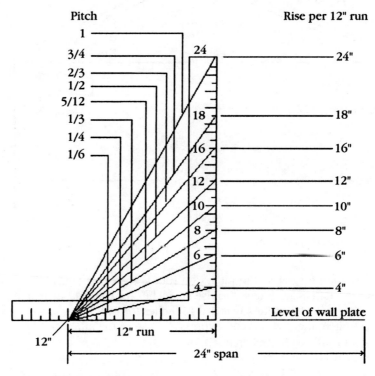

14-33 Common roof pitches.

Collar beams

Collar beams (Fig. 14-17) are generally 1 × 6 members and are installed on every other pair of rafters. Face-nail each end to the rafter with four 8d nails. Locate the collar beams in the upper third section of the attic. Collar beams greatly assist in the structural strength of the roof by preventing rafter spread and resisting wind forces.

Rafter overhang

The part of a roof that extends beyond the side wall is the overhang. The rafter tail extends past the building line, creating the eave. The rafter tail is always added to the calculated length of the rafter. You can cut the rafter end in different ways to accommodate a particular eave finish. This is covered in detail in chapter 15.

RAFTER TYPES

There are several different kinds of rafters. Common rafters extend from the plate to the ridge, at right angles to both. The name *common* applies because the rafter is common to all roof types. Hip rafters extend diagonally from the plate to the ridge to form a hip on the roof. Valley rafters run diagonally from the plate to the ridge, forming a valley at an inside corner plane in a roof. Jack rafters are short members that run from hip to ridge, hip to plate, ridge to valley, or plate to valley. You'll find jack rafters on any roof that's broken up in some way. Cripple jack rafters run between hip and valley rafters, as shown in Fig. 14-34.

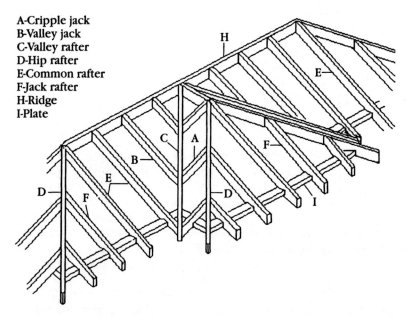

A-Cripple jack
B-Valley jack
C-Valley rafter
D-Hip rafter
E-Common rafter
F-Jack rafter
H-Ridge
I-Plate

14-34 Cripple jack rafters.

THE GAMBREL ROOF

The gambrel roof, shown in Fig. 14-35, is a popular design because the steep-slope portion of the roof serves as both roof and wall. The gambrel is basically a gable roof with two sloped surfaces on each side, running from the ridge to the plate. The lower surface is high-pitch. The upper surface is low-pitch. This roof gives increased headroom without raising the height of the ridge.

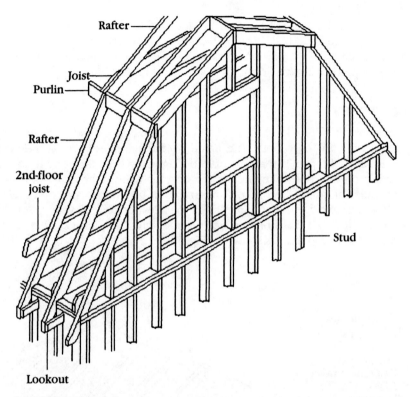

14-35 Gambrel roof.

RAFTER LAYOUT

Lay out the rafter location at the time the ceiling-joist layout is made. Keep in mind that the rafters must be nailed to the joists at the top plate. Flush the first rafter with the outside edge of the end wall or the outside edge of the bulkhead plate.

Conventional rafters are generally spaced the same as the ceiling joists in order to tie the two together at the plate. Position the second rafter 16 or 24 inches on center, depending on the joist spacing, from the end of the building or bulkhead. All other rafters will have the same spacing from center to center.

Ridge board installation

Begin by marking the rafter layout on the ridge board while the board is laying perpendicular across the ceiling joists in the approximate center of the building. Cut four rafters. Face-nail the ridge board to one rafter with three 16d nails. This rafter should be near the end of the ridge board. Face-nail the second rafter to the ridge board at the other end. The two rafters will fit on the same side of the roof.

Now, while someone else lifts the ridge board to the approximate rise height, tack the rafters at the plate. The next step is to butt the opposite two rafters against the ridge board and tack at the plate. Position the two rafters at the ridge board and face-nail through the ridge board with three 16d nails, as shown in Fig. 14-36.

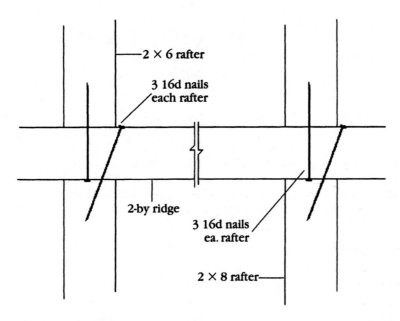

14-36 Nailing rafters at the ridge board.

Check the level of the ridge board and fit of the rafters at the plates and at the ridge board. Make any corrections required and complete nailing at the plates.

Brace the ridge board with upright and angle braces, as shown in Fig. 14-37. You're now ready to fill in the remaining rafters in this section, installing the rafters in pairs.

The house length might require several sections of ridge boards. The second ridge board can be spliced to the first one with a plywood splice and supported at the other end with an upright brace. It isn't necessary to nail rafters to the board before erecting, as was done with the first one. Toe-nail the rafters to the wall plate with two 10d nails, and face-nail them to the ceiling joists with four or more 10d nails, depending on the roof pitch.

Gable-end studs

A vent, centered under the ridge board, is commonly installed in the gable. Square a line across the end-wall plate or bulkhead directly below the ridge board. Measure half the vent's width on each side of the center mark for location of the first stud on

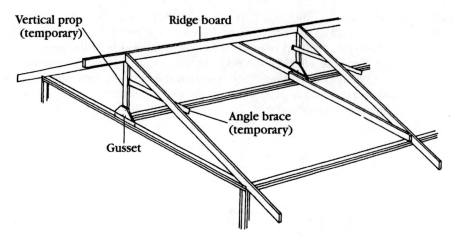

14-37 Bracing the ridge board. American Plywood Assoc

each side. Mark positions for the remaining studs on the same centers as the stud spacing on the wall below. Measure and cut each stud. Notch the top end of the stud to fit under the rafter so the stud bottom fits flush with the top plate or bulkhead. Cut cripple studs, headers, and sills to frame the vent opening. See Fig. 14-21.

Chimney framing

Figure 14-38 illustrates how to frame rafters for a chimney opening. You can use double rafters on each side of the opening, and also double the headers. Framing anchors provide structural strength to the opening. Building codes require a minimum two-inch clearance between the outside chimney surface and wood or other combustible materials.

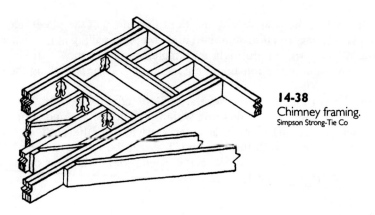

14-38
Chimney framing.
Simpson Strong-Tie Co

When a birdsmouth cut is not required

A metal anchor is available that fastens a rafter to the top plate without cutting the rafter to fit the contour of the top plate (see Fig. 14-39). Use the nails furnished with the anchor or those recommended by the anchor manufacturer.

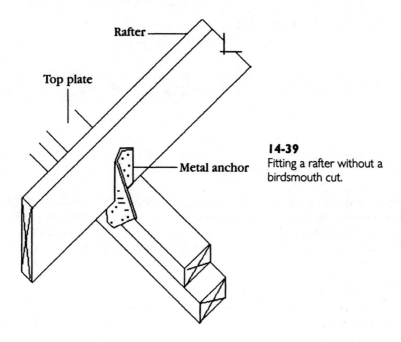

14-39
Fitting a rafter without a birdsmouth cut.

15
Cutting conventional rafters

It takes practice to properly cut rafters, whether the roof is a simple gable or a hip with several valleys. A good rafter cutter is a valuable asset to a builder or framing crew.

While several methods exist for finding the proper lengths and cuts of rafters, the basic principle behind all the procedures is geometric construction. There's the graphic method, which drafters might prefer because they can lay out the task with drafting instruments. I like the step-off approach, or the rafter table method, because I can lay out the work with a framing square. If you're good with a calculator you can probably come up with the answers more quickly, but the average carpenter generally prefers a framing square.

The step-off method is a tried-and-true approach, and is probably considered the most logical by experienced rafter cutters. The rafter tables on your framing square are also a sure bet. You can use the tables to check the accuracy of the step-off and vice versa. I'll confine my discussion of rafter cutting to these two methods.

A detailed discussion of rafter measuring and cutting, including all the methods and roof styles, would require an entire volume. This chapter contains only the basic principles for laying out the rafter type under consideration. While it's a good idea to learn different methods of rafter erection, it's probably best to stick with one method until you know it thoroughly.

If you're a rafter cutter, you'll want to develop a system to follow when working; that is, the steps involved in getting the rafter lumber from the stack to the saw benches to the installation of the rafters should become second nature to you.

Always place the lumber in the same relative position on the bench. The crown edge should always be the top edge and should be toward you as you lay out the rafter. Hold the tongue (small arm) of the framing square in your left hand and the body (large arm) in the right. Thus, the tongue will form the vertical cut and the body will form the seat cut. See Fig. 15-1.

FINDING A COMMON RAFTER LENGTH

The framing square has many uses. With it you can find the approximate length of a common rafter. A common rafter, as you'll recall, runs from the ridge to the top plate without interruption.

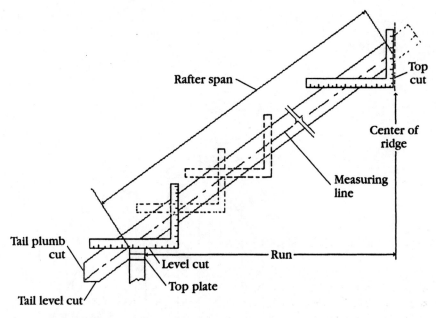

15-1 Using the square.

Let the tongue represent the rise in feet, and the body the run in feet. Using your tape measure, determine the length of the diagonal between the two points and add the length of the overhang. Assume that the total rise of a rafter is six feet and the run is 14 feet. Find 6 on the tongue and 14 on the body. Pull your tape measure between the two points, and the result will be 15¼" (which is read as feet), plus the length of the overhang. If the overhang is 1'6", an 18-foot-long rafter is required. See Fig. 15-2.

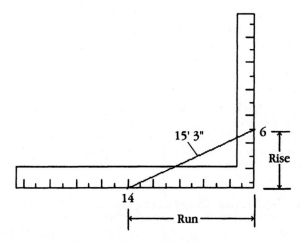

15-2 Finding the rough length of a rafter.

Figure 15-3 provides a quick guide for determining the rafter's horizontal span in feet, and it's often helpful to convert the roof pitch or slope into degrees, as shown in Fig. 15-4.

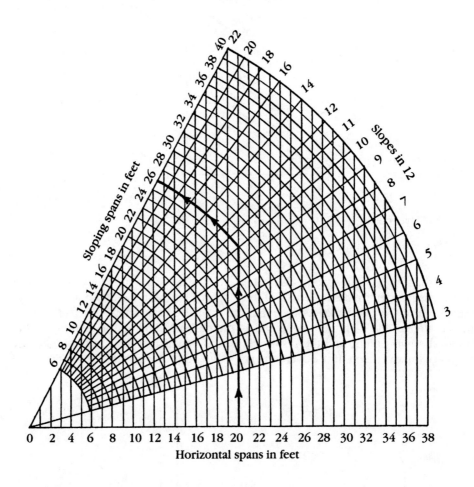

To find the rafter span when its horizontal span and slope are known, follow the vertical line from the horizontal span to its intersection with the radial line of the slope. From the intersection follow the curve line to the sloping span. The diagram can also be used to determine the horizontal span when the sloping span and slope are known, or to determine the slope when the sloping and horizontal spans are known.

Example: For a horizontal span of 20 feet and a slope of 10 in 12, the sloping span of the rafter is read directly from the diagram as 26 feet.

15-3 Horizontal spans in feet. US Dept HUD FHA

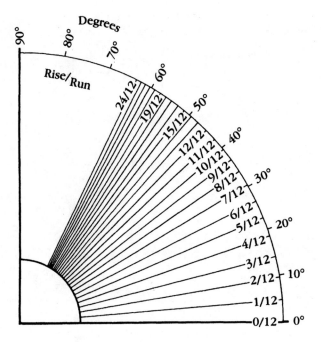

15-4 Roof-slope conversion chart. Simpson Strong-Tie Co

THE RAFTER MEASURING LINE

The key to accurate rafter layout is properly determining the measuring line. Neither a fairly simple roof (Fig. 15-5) nor a more complicated roof (Fig. 15-6) can be professionally framed if the measuring line hasn't been accurately established.

15-5 A good rafter layout begins with a measuring line.

15-6 The measuring line ensures that complex cuts will work.

The person who saws the lumber is a key individual in framing a house. With the aid of a framing square, he can make a complex angle and miter cut in one swift motion (see Fig. 15-7).

15-7 The rafter cutter must be a skilled craftsman.

Make sure the board selected for your first pattern rafter is straight. Lay the piece flat across two saw benches and place the square near the right end, as shown in Fig. 15-8.

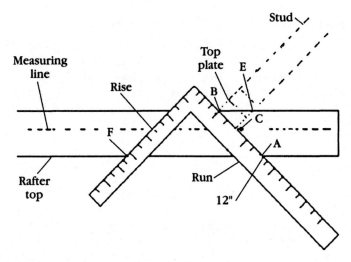

15-8 Establishing the rafter measuring line.

The 12-inch mark on the body of the framing square, in all cases, corresponds to the run of the rafter. An inch mark on the tongue corresponds to the rise of the rafter. Place the square on the rafter material so the run and rise marks intersect at the top of the rafter, as shown in points A and F of Fig. 15-9.

The next step is to draw line A-B on the rafter. This line represents the top of the wall plate. Measure 3⅝ inches along this line, from B to C, to locate the outside top corner of the top plate. Be sure this line is far enough from the right-hand end

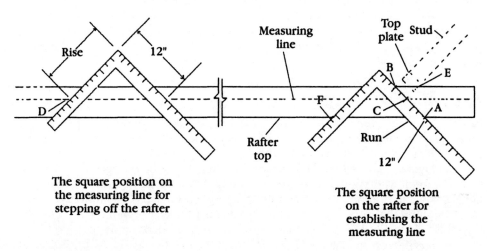

The square position on the measuring line for stepping off the rafter

The square position on the rafter for establishing the measuring line

15-9 The measuring line.

of the rafter to allow for the overhang (tail). Then run the measuring line (C-D) parallel to the edge of the rafter to the ridge end. Subsequent rafter layout work is based on this crucial line.

STEP-OFF METHOD FOR COMMON RAFTERS

Let's say you're framing a house 24 feet wide with a 5/12 rafter pitch (10 inches of rise on 12 inches of run), which might be expressed on the house plan as 10/12. To find the exact length of the rafter, place the square on the board so the 12-inch mark on the outside edge of the body of the square is at point C, as shown in Fig. 15-10, and the 10-inch mark on the outside edge of the tongue is on the measuring line at E. It's crucial that the square is exactly over this position.

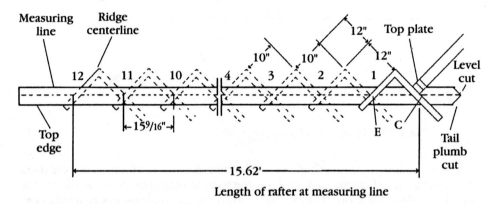

Length of rafter at measuring line

15-10 Stepping off a common rafter.

Mark along the outside edge of the body and tongue to locate point E on the measuring line. Slide the square to the left until the 12-inch mark is over E (position 2), and mark along the outside edge of the tongue and body. Continue stepping off as many times as there are feet of run in the rafter, which is 12 for a 24-foot-wide house.

When you reach the last position, draw a line along the tongue, across the rafter, to indicate the centerline of the ridge. If you carefully marked each step, the rafter will fit properly.

THE ODD-SPAN RAFTER

Not all rafters are even lengths. Some fall in the category of *odd-span rafters*. If the house used in the previous example is 25 feet wide instead of 24, the run will be half the width of the building, or 12'6".

The layout of the rafter is the same as the previous one except you'll need to take 12½ steps with your square. The additional half step is required for the additional six inches of run in the rafter. After marking the 12th step, as illustrated in Fig. 15-11, position the square on the rafter so 10 and 12 intersect with the top edge of the rafter, as shown. Move the square until the six-inch mark on the outside of the body is directly over the 12th step, plumb line A. Mark a line along the outside edge of the tongue to indicate the centerline of the ridge.

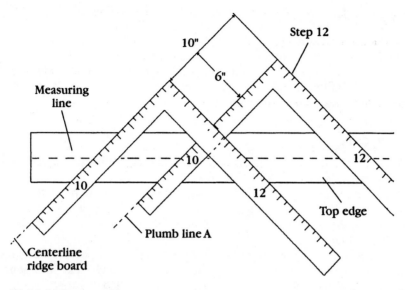

15-11 Half-step marking.

THE RIDGE BOARD ALLOWANCE

You'll have to shave half the ridge board thickness off the rafter you just stepped off. The last line you marked on the rafter is where the rafter would be cut off if there was no ridge board, leaving the rafters to butt at the ridge.

To lay out this line, slide the square back from the last line, position 12 in Fig. 15-10, to half the thickness of the ridge board. Mark the plumb cut along the edge of the tongue, and take measurements from the original line and at right angles to the line. Figure 15-12 explains.

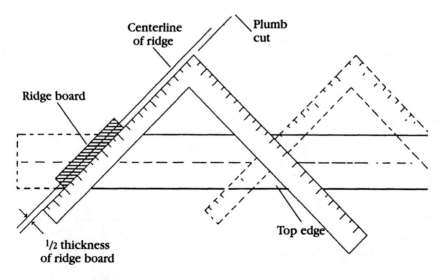

15-12 Ridge board allowance.

THE SEAT CUT

The seat cut is the bottom cut for the fit at the top plate, the *birdsmouth*. It's a combination of the level and plumb cuts. The level cut (B-C in Fig. 15-9) rests on the top surface of the wall top plate. The plumb cut (C-E) fits against the outside edge of the wall plate. You can find the plumb cut by squaring a line from line A-B in Fig. 15-9 through point C. The plumb cut is line C-E.

THE TAIL CUT

Depending on the overhang finish, you can leave the rafter tail square or cut it plumb or level at the bottom for soffit finish.

If the rafter tail is to be a plumb cut, as shown in Fig. 15-10, make the cut along the line, as shown. You can find the level cut at the end of the tail (illustrated in Fig. 15-1) by sliding the square toward the tail until the body intersects with the plumb and measuring line.

If you're a beginner, you might be a bit confused at this point. Be assured that those of us who earn our living building houses were somewhat skeptical when first confronted with the framing square and cutting rafters. Don't expect to digest the how-tos at first reading. In due time, you'll be able to cut rafters to an exact fit by studying the house plans.

The tail of the rafter must be cut differently for a box cornice, as illustrated in Fig. 15-13. The level and plumb cuts are laid out as before, but you want to allow for the thickness of the wall sheathing.

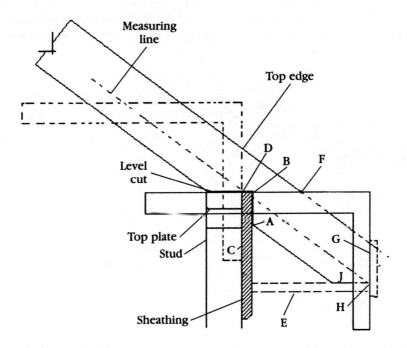

15-13 Rafter tail cuts.

Lay out line A-B parallel to line C-D, and the sheathing thickness away from line C-D. The line of the level cut at D is then extended to meet line A-B. The rafter cut along these lines will fit over the plate and sheathing. Assume that a 12-inch-wide soffit member is to be used at E. Continue the line of the level cut through B to F on top of the rafter. Place the body of the square along this line with the 12-inch mark at the outside edge directly over point B. Mark a line, G-H, along the outer edge of the tongue across the rafter. The point H where this line meets the measuring line represents the tip of the rafter. Square the line H-J across the rafter from line G-H to find J.

The J line is omitted in a different kind of cornice framing. Some framers prefer to delay cutting off the end of the rafter (line G-H) until after all the rafters are nailed into place. Before making this cut, pull a taut line from the outside rafter at each end to establish the tail end of all the rafters. Mark line G-H on each rafter with a bevel square using the string as a guide. Using a power saw, cut each rafter on the same side of the line. This method ensures a straight and uniform cut of the rafter tails even if the wall is slightly uneven. Use protective goggles when making the cuts.

THE RAFTER TABLE

Your framing or steel square has rafter tables stamped on it, and an instruction booklet explaining how to use the square is usually available. Also, the book *Rafter Length Manual*, gives the exact rafter lengths for every roof span and rise. It's published by:

Craftsman Book Company
Box 6500
Carlsbad, CA 92008

How do you use the rafter length table? Pick up your square. The inch marks on the outside edge of the body indicate the rise per foot of run. For example, the 12-inch mark means 12 inches of rise per foot of run. Directly below each of the inch marks is the length of the common rafters per foot of run. Under the 12-inch mark, 16.97 is listed, which means that, for a 12/12 roof, the rafter length is 16.97 inches for each foot of run. If the run of the rafter is 12 feet, 12 × 16.97 = 203.64 inches or 16.97 feet. If the run of the rafter is 10 feet, 10 × 16.97 = 169.7 inches or 14.14 feet as the rafter length.

RAFTER BRACING

Brace the rafter ridge with diagonal bracing at each end. Run the brace at about a 45-degree angle (Fig. 14-37) and nail to a center catwalk or a 2-by installed over several rafters.

A common bracing method is shown in Fig. 15-14. Nail a 2-by flat to each ceiling joist with two 16d nails, then install another 2-by edgewise directly alongside the first 2-by. Face-nail it to the flat 2-by with 16d nails spaced 16 inches apart, and toe-nail to each joist with one 8d nail. This forms a "trough" that extends from end joist to end joist and is installed at the centerline of the rafter span. The trough stabilizes the ceiling joists and provides a base for the rafter bracing.

Locate a 2 × 4 rafter purlin at the bottomside of the rafters, extending from end rafter to end rafter. Face-nail the purlin to the rafter underside with two 16d nails.

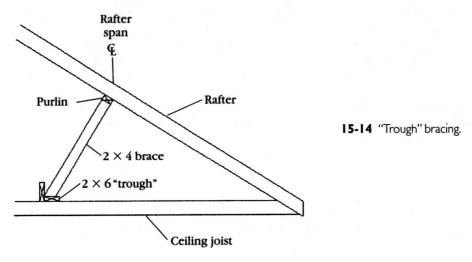

Install a 2 × 4 brace perpendicular to the rafter slope at every other rafter. Toe-nail the brace to the trough with two 8d nails, and face-nail the brace at the purlin with two 16d nails.

JACK RAFTERS

Jack rafters are spaced the same as common rafters, 16 or 24 inches on center. The jack rafter, as you've seen, fits directly against the valley or hip rafter. The first jack is x inches long, the second jack is two times x, and the third jack is three times x. Stated another way, the second jack rafter is twice as long as the first jack, the third jack rafter is three times as long as the first one, and so on.

You can find the length of the jack rafters in the rafter tables of a framing square. The third and fourth lines list the following information:

> Difference in length of jacks: 16-inch centers
> Difference in lengths of jacks: 2-foot centers

The figures in the tables give the length of the first or shortest jack, which is also the difference in length between the first and second rafters, second and third, third and fourth, etc., as explained previously. You also have to deduct half the diagonal (45-degree) thickness of the valley or hip rafter.

The rule is: To find the length of a jack rafter, multiply the value given in the framing square table by the number indicating the position (second, third, etc.) of the jack. From the sum, subtract half the diagonal (45-degree) thickness of the valley or hip rafter. This explanation, however, can confuse the best of minds.

A simple example should do the trick: All you have to do is find the length of the first jack and the rest is easy. Assume the roof has a 6/12 pitch, which, as you know, is six inches of rise for each 12 inches of run. The rafter spacing is 16 inches on center. Pick up your square. On the outer edge of the body find 6, which corresponds to the rise of the roof. On the third line of the rafter table under 6 find 17⅞. This means that the first jack rafter will be 17⅞ inches long. The second jack rafter will be 2 × 17⅞ inches, the third jack 3 × 17⅞ inches, the fourth jack 4 × 17⅞, and so on. Next, deduct half the diagonal (45-degree) thickness of the valley or hip rafter. Figure 15-15 shows how to do this.

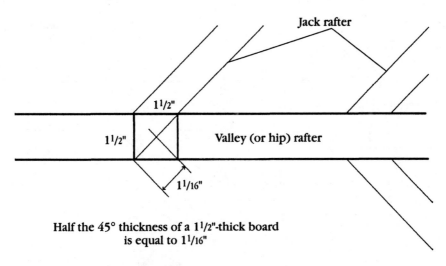

Jack rafter

1½"

1½"

Valley (or hip) rafter

1¹/₁₆"

Half the 45° thickness of a 1½"-thick board
is equal to 1¹/₁₆"

15-15 Deducting for the jack rafters.

Since jack rafters have the same rise as common rafters, the method of obtaining the top and bottom cuts are the same as for common rafters.

At the top of the jack rafter in a hip and at the bottom of the jack in a valley, a cheek or side cut is required to fit the jack to the hip or valley. The side cuts for jacks are found on the fifth line of the rafter table, printed on the framing square as "Side cuts of jacks use." The rule is: To obtain the side cut for a jack rafter, take the figure shown in the table on the body of the square and 12 inches on the tongue. Mark along the tongue for the side cut.

Let's do an example and find the side cut for a jack rafter for a 6/12 roof pitch. Under the figure 6 in the fifth line of the table, find 10¾. This figure, taken on the outside edge of the body and 12 inches on the tongue, will give the side cut (see Fig. 15-16).

HIP AND VALLEY RAFTERS

You measure and cut hip and valley rafters in much the same way as common rafters. The important factor is that hip and valley rafters fit the wall plate at 45 degrees rather than 90 degrees as is the case with common rafters.

Let's assume that the roof pitch is 6/12 and the common rafters run is 14 feet, giving a rafter span of 15.65 feet. You marked the common rafters for cuts using the six-inch mark on the tongue and 12-inch mark on the body. For a hip or a valley rafter with the same 6/12 pitch, the cut is marked with the body at the 17-inch mark and the tongue again at the six-inch mark. The square is set at 17 on the body because hip and valley rafters are longer than common rafters on the same roof. The actual pitch of a hip or valley rafter is less, so the inch measurement used on the body of the square will *always* be 17 regardless of the roof slope. Figure 15-17 illustrates the square position for the vertical cut on the ridge of a hip or valley rafter. Figure 15-18 shows how to place the square for the vertical cut of a hip or valley seat. The horizontal (level) seat cut is shown in Fig. 15-19.

Remember, regardless of the roof slope, that a hip rafter runs 17 inches horizontally for every 12 inches that a common rafter travels horizontally.

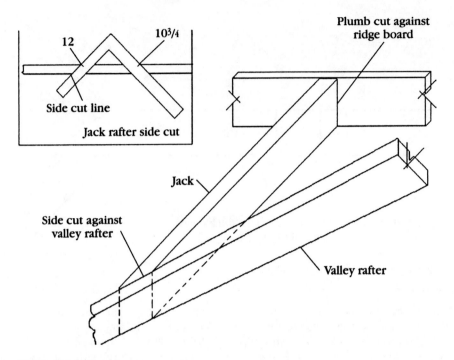

15-16 Jack rafter side cut.

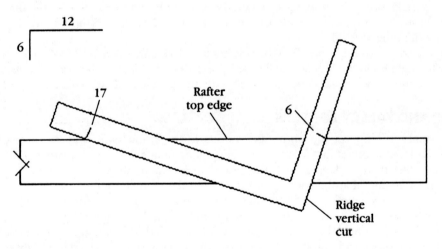

15-17 Marking the hip and valley rafter vertical cuts.

Dropping the hip

The perfect roof plane is even, and the rafters merge with the hip without any distortion of the plane. However, rafters of a hip roof line up with the centerline of the hip rafter, which is lower than the top outside edges. In roofs with a nominal two-inch-thick hip rafter, this problem is generally ignored since the crest of the distor-

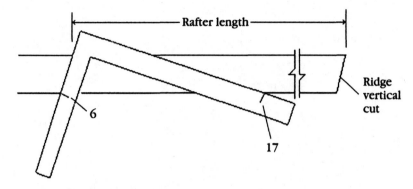

15-18 The hip/valley vertical seat cut.

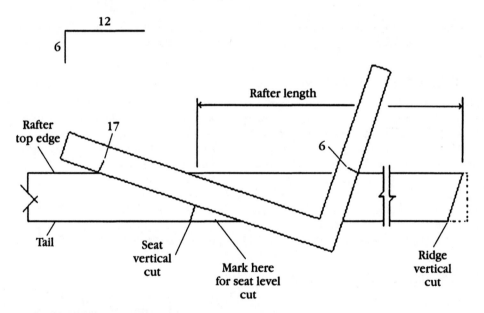

15-19 The hip/valley level seat cut.

tion is minor and goes unnoticed when roofing is applied. If the ridge rafter is a doubled 2-by or larger, then the distortion becomes too pronounced to ignore.

One solution is to rip off the edges of the hip, which is called a *backing chamfer* (Fig. 15-20). A better method is to drop the hip. Valley rafters offer no such problem.

When marking the seat cut on the hip, make the cut ¼ inch deeper than the original seat in order to drop the hip. Or, on a steep-pitch roof where an uneven plane

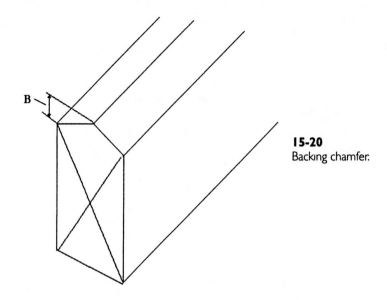

15-20
Backing chamfer.

would be more noticeable, make the seat cut the distance of B in Fig. 15-20, which makes the backing-off (chamfer) of the hip rafter unnecessary.

ESTIMATING MATERIALS

Determine the number and length of the common rafters first. The house plan should indicate the roof pitch and show the roof type. Go to Table 13-1 in chapter 13 to estimate lengths by using the ratio factors for common, hip, and valley rafters. Simply multiply the rise ratio by the amount of run to get the rafter length. Add the overhang length and round off to the next standard lumber length.

You might want to refer to Fig. 15-21 when estimating rafters to avoid having to figure each length separately. Rafters A and H can both be cut from a piece 16 feet long. Rafters B and G can be cut from one piece, and so can rafters C and F. Estimate one 16-footer for each two jack rafters. For the total board feet of material and nails required for all types of rafters per square foot of surface, see Table 15-1.

Ridge boards

The ridge board of a main gable roof is the length of the roof. For a gable roof ell or tee, the ridge is half the width of the house plus the length of the ell or tee. In a hip roof, the ridge board is the house length minus the house width.

Collar beams

Collar beams are horizontal framing members used to tie rafters together at the upper third part of the attic space below the ridge. Collar beams help control the roof thrust. Collar beams are generally installed on every second or third rafter pair. In no case are they installed on spacing greater than 48 inches. A 1 × 6 makes a good collar beam member. Divide the building length by the collar beam's spacing to determine the number of pieces required.

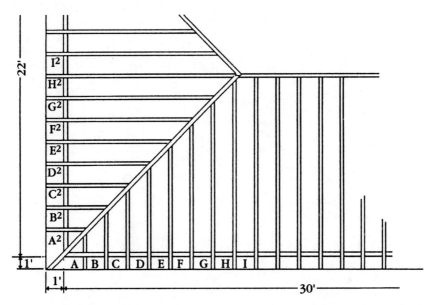

15-21 Hip-roof rafter material.

Table 15-1
Rafter framing BF required for 100 sq. ft. of
surface area, including all rafters (valley, hip,
and common) and ridge boards

Lumber size	12" oc	16" oc	24" oc	Nails per 1,000 BF (lbs.)
2 × 6	129	102	75	12
2 × 8	171	134	112	9
2 × 10	212	167	121	7
2 × 12	252	197	143	6

Roof bracing materials

Roof bracing materials are required for the trough, purlins, diagonal ridge board braces, and perpendicular rafter to trough braces. 2 × 6s are generally used for the trough, and all other bracing is commonly of 2 × 4s. For troughs, multiply the building length by four to determine the linear feet required. The building length multiplied by two gives the linear feet of purlin needed. The amount of 2 × 4 diagonal and perpendicular bracing depends on the roof pitch and rise.

Lookouts

Lookouts are short 2 × 4s nailed to the tail of rafters and to a nailer installed on the wall. Lookouts provide the framework for the soffit finish at the roof overhang (see Fig. 15-22).

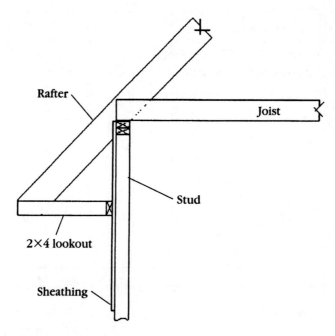

15-22 Lookout members.

Each rafter requires a lookout. The length of the lookout is generally shown on the wall section of the house plans, and 2 × 4s are commonly used. Multiply the number of lookouts by the length to determine the linear feet of material required. The amount of nailer needed will be the building length times two.

ESTIMATING LABOR

Estimate rafter labor as follows:

Common rafters	35 BF per hour
Hip and valley rafters	35 BF per hour
Jack rafters	35 BF per hour
Ridge board	40 BF per hour
Collar beams	40 BF per hour
Trough	30 BF per hour
Bracing	25 BF per hour
Lookouts	25 BF per hour

In a building 26 feet wide by 40 feet long with a 6/12 roof pitch and plain gable roof, the rafter horizon span is 13 feet and the sloping span is 14.54 feet. Assuming there's a 12-inch overhang, a 16-foot-long rafter would be required.

A building 40 feet long having a 12-inch extension at each gable would result in a 42-foot-long roof. The rafter spacing is 16 inches on center. Calculate 42 × 0.75 = 31.5, plus 1 rafter for the end, for a total of 32 rafters on each side. A grand total of 64 rafters are required.

A 16-foot-long 2 × 6 has 16 board feet. In 64 rafters there are 1,024 board feet. At a labor rate of 35 BF per hour, 29.26 hours are required to install the 64 rafters.

A rule of thumb for estimating the number of hours for 2 × 6 rafter framing, 16 inches on center, is to multiply the square feet of the roof area by 1.5 minutes to determine the hours, two-thirds of which is skilled.

16

Roof sheathing

The roof sheathing, also called *decking*, is applied directly to the rafters or trusses. Half-inch plywood and ⅞₆-inch OSB panels are used in the majority of homes constructed today. Board sheathing is used occasionally, particularly when wood shingles or shakes are installed as the roof covering.

The greater the roof slope, the more time it takes to install the sheathing and, needless to say, the more hazardous it is. On steep roofs, nail down 2 × 4 cleats for footing support. Use scrap pieces two feet or longer. Install the cleats as you work up the roof.

Some framers hand the sheathing material up, one piece at a time, as it's nailed down. Some prefer to build a rack against the structure and stack the material at or about roof level so the sheathing can be pulled off the rack onto the roof. Another procedure is to stack the material on the roof, but beware—you can overload the rafter or trusses at that point with too much weight. Such a concentrated load could cause the roof framing to give way.

BOARD ROOF SHEATHING

Pine, fir, spruce, and hemlock are some of the woods used in board sheathing. Board sheathing, while used very little in today's construction, works well with wood shingles or shakes in damp climates. Also, spaced boards can be used for metal roofing. Space the boards as illustrated in Fig. 16-1. This permits air to freely circulate under the shingles. Underlayment such as roofing felt isn't required under wood shingles, except for possible ice dams along the eaves. Air circulation under the shingles is essential for proper drying. Use 1 × 4s spaced the same distance on center as the shingles are laid to the weather. If the shingles are laid five inches to the weather and nominal 1 × 4 boards are used, there will be about a 1½-inch space between each board.

PLYWOOD ROOF SHEATHING

Plywood makes a strong, smooth, and solid deck that works well with nearly any roofing material. APA-rated sheathing is marked with a span rating, which tells you the recommended rafter spacing for the panel thickness. On rafters spaced 24 inches on center, panels with a 24/0 marking are adequate. Sheathing panels with this span rating are available in ⅜", ⅞₆", ¹⁵⁄₃₂", and ½" thicknesses.

The roof overhang can be open or closed. The house plan will show either open soffits or closed (boxed) soffits (Fig. 16-2). If the soffit is closed, all the roof

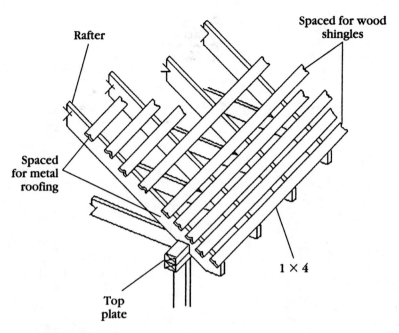

Rafter

Spaced for wood shingles

Spaced for metal roofing

Top plate

1 × 4

16-1 Roof sheathing boards.

sheathing can be APA-rated exposure 1 sheathing. In open soffits, use panels marked exterior or exterior 1 of the appropriate grade to permit painting or staining to blend with the rest of the house. Many of the texture-finished plywoods of ½-inch and ⅝-inch thickness can be used with the textured side down to provide an attractive open soffit.

The house plan might specify that the open soffit be of board material. In this case, the roof sheathing at the overhang will consist of dressed boards (or rough-sawn if so specified) laid from the fascia to the frieze block, as shown in Fig. 16-3. These *starter boards* are usually 1 × 8s cut so the joint forms a V groove instead of a plain butt joint, which is seldom a satisfactory finish except in a barn. Install the boards in the sequence shown in Fig. 16-3. Face-nail the boards to each rafter with three 8d nails. Shim the plywood panel at each rafter to flush the panel with the top surface of the boards.

With either an open or boxed soffit, you should have a sheathing layout, whether a rough or mental sketch (a mental sketch will suffice if you're experienced in sheathing work). Draw the layout relatively close to scale. For a plain gable roof, the easiest method is to draw a simple rectangle to represent half the roof. The long side represents the length of the ridge board and the short side represents the length of the rafter, including the overhang. If the soffit is open, draw a second line, dotted if you prefer, inside the ends and bottom to show the area that must be covered by exterior or exposure 1 panels (or starter boards).

Since this is only half of the roof, you can plan any panel cutting on this side so the cut-off portions are useful on the other side. If the eave overhang is less than two feet and the soffit is open, you might start with a panel half the normal width.

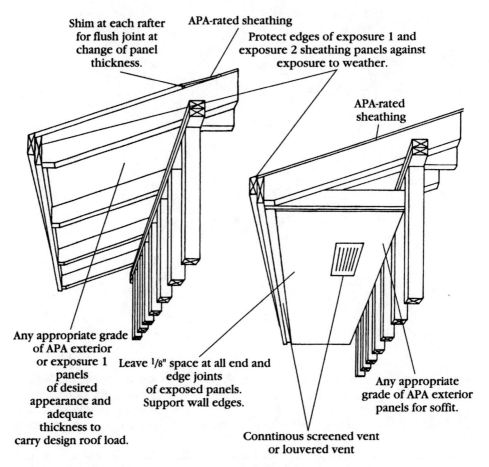

Shim at each rafter for flush joint at change of panel thickness.

APA-rated sheathing

Protect edges of exposure 1 and exposure 2 sheathing panels against exposure to weather.

APA-rated sheathing

Any appropriate grade of APA exterior or exposure 1 panels of desired appearance and adequate thickness to carry design roof load.

Leave 1/8" space at all end and edge joints of exposed panels. Support wall edges.

Any appropriate grade of APA exterior panels for soffit.

Conntinous screened vent or louvered vent

16-2 Open soffit (left) and closed or boxed soffit (right). American Plywood Assoc

Otherwise, you'll probably start with a full 4 × 8 section of sheathing at the bottom of the roof and work upward toward the ridge, where you might have to cut the last row of panels. Be sure to stagger the panels in succeeding rows so the ends fall on different framing members.

The completed layout for the entire roof will show panel size and placement as well as sheathing panels needed (see Fig. 16-4). The sketch reveals that nearly half the panels are soffit panels. Rather than shimming to level the surfaces of soffit and interior sheathing panels, as shown in Fig. 16-2, consider using interior sheathing panels of the same thickness as the soffit panels even if they're a little thicker than the minimum required.

Begin panel installation at the bottom corner of the roof. Remember to place soffit panels with the best or textured side down. Fasten each panel in the first course (row) to the rafters using 8d common, ring shank, or spiral-threaded nails. Space the nails six inches apart along panel ends and 12 inches apart at intermediate supports. Leave ⅛-inch space at panel end and edge joints.

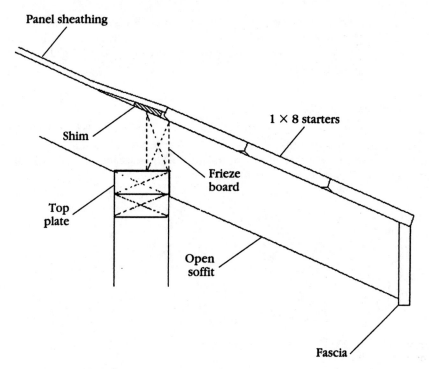

16-3 Board open soffit.

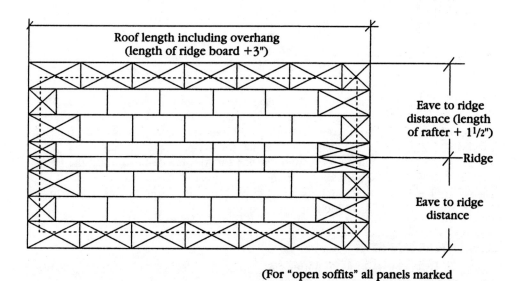

Roof length including overhang
(length of ridge board +3")

Eave to ridge
distance (length
of rafter + 1½")

Ridge

Eave to ridge
distance

(For "open soffits" all panels marked
with Xs must be exterior or exposure 1.)

16-4 Roof sheathing layout. American Plywood Assoc

Install the second course using a soffit half panel in the first (overhang) position at the gable end. If the main sheathing panels are thinner than the soffit sheathing, install small shims to smooth the joint surfaces. Continue installing the remaining courses in the same manner.

General notes

Place plywood roof sheathing with the face grain perpendicular to the rafters, as shown in Fig. 16-5. Make the end joints over the center of the rafters, and stagger them by at least one rafter. Panel clips are useful in a situation where roof framing is spaced 24 inches on center and ⅜-inch-thick panels are used.

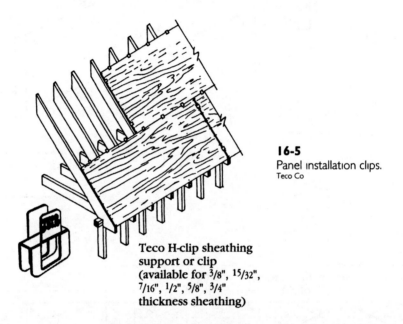

16-5
Panel installation clips.
Teco Co

Teco H-clip sheathing
support or clip
(available for 3/8", 15/32",
7/16", 1/2", 5/8", 3/4"
thickness sheathing)

APA-rated panel sheathing makes a good base under built-up roofing, asphalt and fiberglass or asphalt and asbestos shingles, tile roofing, and wood shingles (shakes), except in damp areas. Also, ¾-inch, 48/24-rated panels over framing spaced 48 inches on center are a good choice for flat or sloped roofs.

Table 16-1 gives nailing recommendations for APA-rated sheathing. When support spacing exceeds the maximum length of an unsupported edge, provide blocking or other edge support, such as panel clips. Use one clip for spans less than 48 inches and two clips for 48-inch or longer spans.

APA PANEL SOFFITS

The recommended spans for open and closed soffits (Fig. 16-2) are given in Tables 16-2 and 16-3. Panels are assumed to be continuous over two or more spans, with the long dimension across the supports. Provide blocking for spans of 32 and 48

Table 16-1 APA panel nailing recommendation

Panel span rating	Panel thickness (inches)	*Maximum span (inches)* With edge support*	*Maximum span (inches)* Without edge support	Nail size and type	*Nail spacing (inches)* Panel edges	*Nail spacing (inches)* Intermediate
12/0	$5/16$	12	12			
16/0	$5/16, 3/8$	16	16			
20/0	$5/16, 3/8$	20	20	8d common		
24/0	$3/8, 7/16, 1/2$	24	20***			
24/16	$7/16, 1/2$	24	24			
32/16	$1/2$	32	28		6	12
32/16	$5/8$	32	28			
42/20**	$5/8, 3/4, 7/8$	42	32	8d common		
48/24**	$3/4, 7/8$	48	36		6	6

Note All panels will support at least 30 psf live load plus 10 psf dead load at maximum span, except as noted

* Tongue-and-groove edges, panel edge clips (one between each support, except two between supports 48 inches oc, lumber blocking, or other

** PS 1 plywood panels with span ratings of 42/20 and 48/24 will support 35 psf live load plus 5 psf dead load at maximum span For 40 psf live load, specify structural I

*** 24 inches for ½-inch panels

Courtesy American Plywood Assoc

Table 16-2 APA open soffit panels

Maximum span (inches)	Panel description (all exterior, exposure 1, or interior panels with exterior glue)	Species group for plywood
16	$15/32$" APA 303 siding	1,2,3,4
	½" APA sanded plywood	1,2,3,4
	APA-rated Sturd-I-Floor, 16 oc	—
24	$15/32$" APA 303 siding	1
	½" APA sanded plywood	1,2,3,4
	$19/32$" APA 303 siding	1,2,3,4
	⅝" APA sanded plywood	1,2,3,4
	APA-rated Sturd-I-Floor, 20 oc	—
32*	⅝" APA sanded plywood	1
	$23/32$" APA 303 siding	1,2,3,4
	¾" APA sanded plywood	1,2,3,4
	APA-rated Sturd-I-Floor, 24 oc	—
48*	1⅛" APA textured plywood**	1,2,3,4
	APA-rated Sturd-I-Floor, 48 oc	

Note: All panels will support at least 30 psf live load plus 10 psf dead load at maximum span, except as noted.

* Provide adequate blocking, tongue-and-groove edges, or other suitable edge supports, such as panel clips

** 1⅛" panels of group 2, 3, or 4 species will support 35 psf live load plus 5 psf dead load

Courtesy American Plywood Assoc

Table 16-3 APA closed soffit panels

Maximum span (inches), all edges supported	Nominal panel thickness	Species group	Nail size and type*
24	$^{11}\!/_{32}$" APA**		6d nonstaining box or casing
32	$^{15}\!/_{32}$" APA**	All species groups	
48	$^{19}\!/_{32}$" APA**		8d nonstaining box or casing

* Space nails 6 inches at panel edges and 12 inches at intermediate supports for spans less than 48 inches; 6 inches at all supports for 48-inch spans

** Any suitable grade of exterior panel that meets appearance requirements

Courtesy: American Plywood Assoc

inches in open soffits. In lieu of blocking, you can use tongue-and-groove edges or panel clips. Minimum loads are at least a 40-psf live load and a 5-psf dead load, with the exception of the 1⅛-inch panels of group 2, 3, or 4 species, which support a 35-psf live load.

TIPS FOR INSTALLING APA-RATED SHEATHING

Figure 16-6 gives the sequence for the proper installation of sheathing panels. Like all construction materials, plywood sheathing panels must be installed correctly to ensure quality performance. If you do the following, you'll increase the service life of the roof and eliminate call-backs to correct a problem:

- Always check for a level nail surface, with a 10-foot-long, straight 2 × 4 and a carpenter's level. Shim trusses or rafters as necessary to provide a level nailing surface. An unlevel surface will be highlighted by the roofing material.
- Install blocking to straighten a warped or lowered rafter or trusses.
- Provide roof ventilators as specified by the building codes. You want a minimum net free-ventilation area of 960 square inches for each 1,000 square feet of ceiling area. When vents are located at eaves or soffits, near the peak of the roof, or along ridge for maximum air flow, the free-ventilation area can be reduced to a minimum of 480 square inches per 1,000 square feet.
- Be sure that insulation doesn't block the air space required for ventilation paths from the eaves to the peak. For vaulted or cathedral roof construction, provide a free-ventilation path from eaves to the ridge between all rafters.
- Avoid cutting sheathing panels on sloping roofs until all the full panels are installed. The sawdust underfoot can send you into a tail-dive toward the ground.
- Cover sheathing with roof felt as soon as possible to minimize exposing the sheathing to the weather.

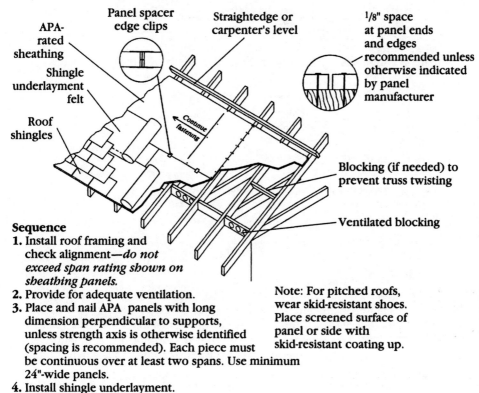

APA-
rated
sheathing

Panel spacer
edge clips

Straightedge or
carpenter's level

¹/₈" space
at panel ends
and edges
recommended unless
otherwise indicated
by panel
manufacturer

Shingle
underlayment
felt

Roof
shingles

Continue
fastening

Blocking (if needed) to
prevent truss twisting

Ventilated blocking

Sequence
1. Install roof framing and
   check alignment—*do not
   exceed span rating shown on
   sheathing panels.*
2. Provide for adequate ventilation.
3. Place and nail APA panels with long
   dimension perpendicular to supports,
   unless strength axis is otherwise identified
   (spacing is recommended). Each piece must
   be continuous over at least two spans. Use minimum
   24"-wide panels.
4. Install shingle underlayment.
5. Install roof covering.

Note: For pitched roofs,
wear skid-resistant shoes.
Place screened surface of
panel or side with
skid-resistant coating up.

16-6 Installing APA-rated sheathing. American Plywood Assoc

OSB PANELS

Oriented strand board carries an APA sheathing rating. OSB sheathing is available in thicknesses from ⅜ inch through 1⅛ inches. Table 16-4 gives the APA span rating for various thicknesses. APA-rated OSB sheathing panels carry the exposure 1 or structural 1 marking.

For standard sheathing requirements, use APA-rated exposure 1 sheathing. Structural 1 panels are engineered for use where high winds or earthquake conditions exist.

The ⁷/₁₆-inch panel can be used on roof framing spaced 24 inches on center. The ¹⁵/₃₂-inch and ½-inch panels are approved for 32-inch-spaced framing members. For rafters or trusses spaced 40 inches on center, use ¹⁹/₃₂-inch panels.

OSB panels generally have a smooth and a rough side. Install the smooth side down. The rough, or textured, side provides a safer walking surface on pitched roofs.

OSB panels are widely used for floor, wall, and roof sheathing in residential and commercial construction. OSB is an engineered product that makes good use of natural resources while providing an excellent building material. Install OSB sheathing in the same manner as described for plywood sheathing.

Table 16-4 APA OSB span ratings

Thickness	APA span rating	Maximum live load** for roof (lbs.)
⅜"*	24/0	30
⁷⁄₁₆"*	24/16	40
¹⁵⁄₃₂"*	32/16	70
½"*	32/16	70
¹⁹⁄₃₂"	40/20	130
²³⁄₃₂"	48/24	175
1⅛"	48/24	290

* Available with APA structural 1 rating

** Live load for 24" oc span conditions

Courtesy: American Plywood Assoc

PLANK DECKING

Plank decking is used mostly for roofs in post-and-beam construction, as I explained earlier, and is usually constructed of 2 × 6 T&G planks. Other common sizes are 3 × 6 and 4 × 6 V-grooved planks. These thicker pieces are suitable for longer spans, up to 10 and 12 feet. The maximum span for two-inch planking in most grades and species is eight feet when continuous over to support members. The span is limited to six feet over single spans.

Blind-nail the planks through the tongue and face-nail at supports. Predrill the 4 × 6 plank for edge nailing (see Fig. 11-19). A vapor barrier is generally required between the decking and the roof insulation, which can be fiberboard or other rigid insulation installed to reduce heat loss/gain through the planking.

USING BUILDING PAPER

One-ply, 15-pound, asphalt-saturated roofing felt is the building paper commonly used as an underlayment for many roofing materials. The term *15-pound* means the felt weighs 15 pounds per 100 square feet. Install the felt starting at the eave, overlapping each horizontal course a minimum two inches and vertical overlaps six inches.

The felt expands and contracts with temperature changes. If you're unable to apply the roofing right away, use roofing nails with thin plastic washers to secure the felt. Otherwise, the felt will work free of the regular roofing nails.

ESTIMATING MATERIALS

The first step in finding the quantity of materials required to deck a roof is finding the area of the roof. To obtain the area of a plain gable roof, multiply the length of the ridge by rafter length. The result is half of the roof. Double this figure for the total square feet of the roof surface.

To find the total area of a hip roof, treat it as if it were a gable roof of the same pitch, and multiply the longest side of the roof by the length of the common rafter.

Thus, a 62' × 28' house having a one-foot overhang on all sides and common rafters 18 feet long would have the same roof area, whether plain gable or hip. To find the hip-roof area, multiply 64 feet (long dimension of 62' plus 2' overhang) by 18 feet (length of common rafter). Thus, 64 × 18 = 1,152 square feet in half the roof, or 2,304 square feet for the entire roof.

A sheet of 4 × 8 plywood or OSB panel covers 32 square feet, so a 2,304-square-foot roof requires 72 panels (2,304 ÷ 32). Add 5 percent (3.6 panels, rounded off to 4), for waste, for a total of 76 panels.

Roofing felt

Roofing felt is 36 inches wide. A roll of 15-pound felt will cover about 500 square feet. To find how many rolls are needed to cover the above roof, divide 2,304 by 500 = 4.6 rolls, rounded to 5.

Nails

By spacing nails six inches on center along panel ends and 12 inches on center at intermediate supports, 38 nails are required to secure the panel on framing spaced 16 inches on center. For framing spaced 24 inches on center, you'd need 33 nails. For 16-inch spacing, 76 panels × 38 = 2,888 nails. For 24-inch spacing, 76 panels × 33 = 2,508 nails.

There are 106 8d common nails to a pound, thus 27.24 pounds are required to install 76 4' × 8' panels to framing spaced 16 inches on center. For 24-inch spacing, 23.66 pounds of 8d common nails are required.

Install roofing felt with roofing nails equipped with flat plastic washers, spaced 12 inches on center along the horizontal edges, six inches at vertical overlaps, and 36 inches in intermediate area. Estimate 175 to 200 nails per roll of 15-pound felt.

ESTIMATING LABOR

Estimate installing 4' × 8' sheathing panels at 10 to 12 labor hours per 1,000 square feet of panels. Obviously, the more cut up a roof is with hips and valleys, the longer the task will take. In the example roof requiring 76 panels, it will take 24.5 to 29 hours to do the job.

Keep in mind that my or anyone else's estimates are only that—estimates. Every job is different. Every framing crew is different, performing tasks at a different rate of time. The most accurate figures are those you compile from the jobs done by your crew in your own area. Use the estimates in this book only as guidelines.

Index

Illustration page numbers are in **boldface.**

I-beam rafters, 230-237, **230**, **233-235**
  allowable span, **232**
  plumb cut, **232**
  requirements, 231-237
in-line floor joists, 135, **136**
Inner-Seal flooring panels, 149-150
Inner-Seal Sturd-I-Floor fastening, **150**
inner-seal tongue-and-groove flooring, 146
interior wall T construction, 160
intersecting hip roofs, **252**
intersections, 72

J

jack rafters, 274, **275-276**
joints, 212
  caulking, 195-196
  ceiling, 199-212
  filler blocks, **202**
  floor, 109-143
  hanger, **122**
  hip-roof, 210
  I, 109-117, **110**
  layout, **210**
  ledger, 122
  length, **69**
  manufactured, 109-111
  off-center, 134-135
  rim, **111**
  second-floor, **53**
  solid-wood, 117-132
  spans, 211
  tie-in, 201
  trimmer, 138-139
  U hanger, **122**
joist/girder strength, 121-125
joist/rafter layout, **203**

K

kiln drying, lumber, 32
king post trusses, **215**, 218
knee walls, 22, **24-25**
knots, in lumber, 39

L

labor, estimating, 15-16
laminated beams, **200**

lateral bracing, 62
lath nailers, 204, **205**
ledger nailing, **123**
let-in bracing, 161-163, **165**
let-in ribbon, **177**
limited attic storage, 211
live load, 41, 102
lodgepole pine, 31
lookout members, **280**
lookout rafters, **249**
lookouts, 279
low-cost wall framing, 181-182
lumber, 18, 27-48
  allowable spans, 41-42
  checks and splits, 40
  crow, 139-140
  decay, 39
  density, 38
  drying, 32
  framing, **36**
  grade stamp, **35**
  grades, 37-40, **38**
  grading, 35-37
  green vs. dry, 33
  knots, 39
  lengths, 68
  measuring, 33
  nonstress-graded, 37
  pitch pockets, 40
  shake, 39
  shrinkage, 32
  size difference, **34**
  slope of grain, 39
  span tables, 42
  species, 28-28, **212**
  stress-graded, 37
  swelling, 32
  treated, 83-84
  visual grading, 38
  wane, 40

M

mansard trusses, **216**, **220-221**
measuring line, **254**, **268-269**
  establishing, **269**
  rafter, 267-270
metal anchors, **63**, **75**, **209**, **238**, 263
metal bridging, **141**
modern braced framing, **51**, 52

sill-plate anchor bolts, **12**
sill/pillar relation, 84-85
sills, 76-90
  balloon-frame, 78-79, **80**
  beam, **81**, **85**
  box, 77-79, **77**
  estimating labor, 89
  estimating materials, 86-89
  estimation sheet, **90**
  installing, **77**
  mud, 155
  plate, **79**, **82**, **100**
  rate, 155
  sealer, 13
  solid beam, 80-83
  wall, **76**
sitka spruce, 32
slant, 255
slope of grain, 39
slope, 255
soffit
  closed, **284**
  open, **284**, **285**, **287**
  panel, 286
  treatment, **236**
softwoods, 28-29
soil characteristics, 19
sole plate, 155
solid beam sill, 80-83
solid blocking, 143
solid bridging, **142,** 143
solid-wood joists, 117-132
southern yellow pine, **43-45**
spacer block details, **224**
spans,
  allowable, 231
  horizontal, **266**
  joist, 211
  rafter, **240**
speed-prong joist hanger, **122**
spliced joists, 134-135, **135**
springwood, 28
spruce, sitka, 32
spruce-pine fir, 42
square, **265**
stabilizing members, 227
starshake, **40**
steel anchors, **174**
steel girders, **104**
steel hangers, 75, **75**

steel-post girder support, 91-92
  installation, **92**
stepped footing, **7**
stone, 18
storm-resistant construction, 173
straps, twist, **224**
stress-graded lumber, 37
stud arrangements, **72**
stud spacing, 71-72
studs, gable-end, 250, 261-262
Sturd-I-Wall, 194-196, **195**
  installing panels, 194
subfloor, **52**, **148**
  completion, 147
  installing, 146-149
  lapped joists, 147
  nailing, 149
  panels, 132-134, 144
  staggering joists, 147
subfloor panel layout, 68, **70**, 147
sugar pine, 31
summerwood, 28

T

t-shaped foundation, **4**
tail cut, 272
tie-down anchors, **223**
ties
  hurricane, **224**
tilt-up framing, 160
tongue-and-groove flooring, 146
tongue-and-groove joint spacing, **152**
top plate alignment, 167-168
top-chord bearing, **221**
treated lumber, 83-84
tree trunk, parts, 28
trench excavation labor, **16**
trimmer joists, 138-139
Trip-L-Grip framing anchors, **176**
trough bracing, **274**
truss framing, techniques, 218-220
truss hangers, installing, **118**
trussed-rafter roof framing, **67**
trusses, **117**
  attic, **215**
  building, 227-228
  cantilever, **219**
  common, **217**
  flat, 217, **218**, **221**